SOUTH FROM EPHESUS

Brian Sewell took his degree in the History of Art at the Courtauld Institute, under Anthony Blunt, Johannes Wilde and Michael Kitson. He spent a year researching projects ranging from Rubens to Alma Tadema, and French Caravaggiesques to English Neo-Impressionists, before joining Christie's as an expert in old master paintings and drawings.

He is now the art critic of the *Evening Standard*, and of the *Tatler*, and is an occasional contributor to *The Times*, the *Sunday Times*, the *Spectator*, *Vanity Fair* and other journals. He is also the London-based adviser of museums in Germany, America and Africa.

He has been roaming Turkey since 1975, writing on travel, architecture, sculpture and the Greek and Roman cities of Asia Minor.

SOUTH FROM EPHESUS

Travels in Aegean Turkey

Brian Sewell

ARROW BOOKS

Arrow Books Limited
62–65 Chandos Place, London WC2N 4NW

An imprint of Century Hutchinson Limited

London Melbourne Sydney Auckland
Johannesburg and agencies throughout
the world

First published by Century 1988
Arrow edition 1989

© Brian Sewell 1988

Printed and bound in Great Britain by
Anchor Press Ltd, Tiptree, Essex

ISBN 0 09 958640 1

Contents

Acknowledgements

I am deeply grateful for the practical help of Mrs Susan Raven and Mark Ottaway of the *Sunday Times*, and to Lucretia Stewart, Editor of *Departures*, all of whom have commissioned from me articles on Turkey. To Steve Speck of British Airways I owe flights to Istanbul that could not otherwise have been made. Ian Bishop of the Natural History Museum has answered innumerable tiresome questions on goats, wild boar and the animal specimens sent back by Charles Fellows. In the British Museum, Terence Mitchell of the Department of Western Asiatic Antiquities, Brian Cook of the Department of Greek and Roman Antiquities, and Geoffrey House of the Department of Public Services have been more than patient with my enquiries – and the last has given me friendship and encouragement as well as scholarship. Roger Hudson and Anthony Lambert have made suggestions that rendered the text less imperfect, and Roger Schlesinger made others that rendered it less lubricious, giving me too the energy to complete it.

In Germany I owe a great debt to Dr Rüdiger Joppien, who has run errands without complaint, and supplied me with material not available here.

In Turkey Mrs Gülsen Kahraman has given me unstinting practical help, never asking a quid pro quo, and Mme Zehra

Sulupinar has worked small miracles. Without the hospitality and scholarship of Dr Kenan Erim, the chapter on Aphrodisias could not have been written. Without the advice of Ekrem Berik, and access to his research material, my comments on the sexual awareness of the Turks would have been less accurate. To Cafer Canli, of Türkiye Cumhuriyeti Turizm Bankasi, I owe gratitude for much hospitality. To Osman Delikkulak I owe friendship.

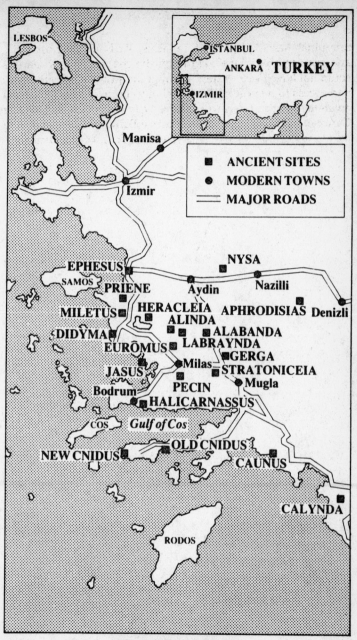

AEGEAN TURKEY

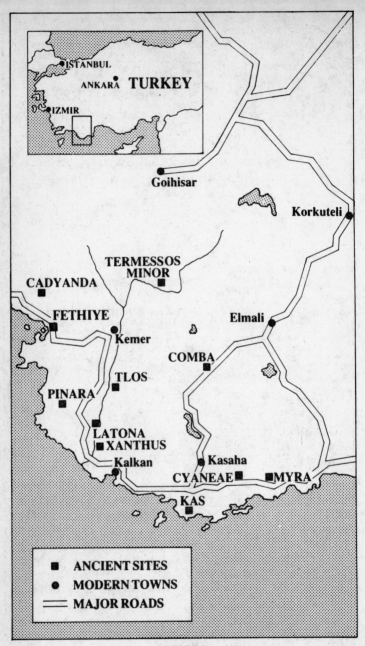

LYCIA

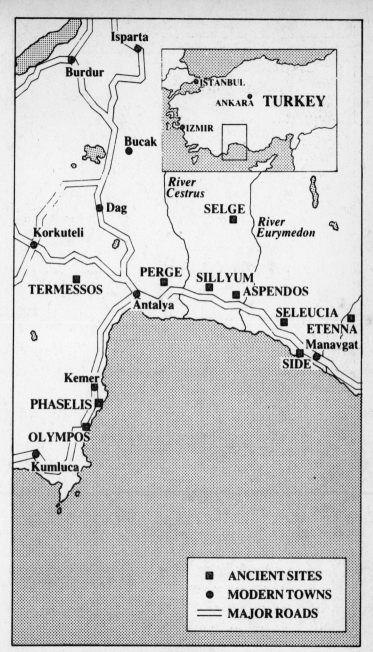

ANTALYA

Preface

This is a self-indulgent narrative. It reveals obsessions and prejudices that surprise even me. It is the record of a decade of
journeys, of the number of which I have lost count, overlaid as a
palimpsest, often with different companions to the same places.
It is the record of a love affair with a country that has opened my
eyes to the depth and breadth of a cultural heritage that as a boy I
thought resided only in the Church of England, that as a student
shifted to the Italy of the Renaissance, and as a young man
embraced the Catholic baroque and crept warily into the twentieth century. Until 1975 my notion of a holiday was to zigzag my
car across Europe looking at museums, galleries and churches;
I have lain in wait for the extremes of modern art even in
Eindhoven, caught by the Continental Monday closure, until the
doors opened at ten on Tuesday, to be rewarded only by some
obscene absurdity in bosomy and buttocky white plastic over-
flowing into the spectator's path, compelling me to squeeze past,
embarrassed by the sexy groans that my passing triggered from
some wretched machine hidden within the feminine forms; in
Malaga, impatient with the sun, I was delighted to find a museum
full of such awful pictures as could only be rivalled by Sotheby's
on a bad day; in Italy's instep it gave me wistful pleasure to pitch
my tent in the shadow of a Hohenstaufen tower, and in Capua

some mental aberration obliterated recall of the destruction of the great Hohenstaufen Arch in 1557, and I could not understand why it was not where I *knew* it to be.

It was to escape the tyranny of Western art that I fixed on Turkey; there, I thought, the opportunities for looking at things would be few, and the things when found would have no relevance to what I already knew of art and architecture, could be enjoyed for their own sake and forgotten – and if not forgotten, I would feel no compulsion to stitch them into the dense fabric of my art-historical memory. I was wholly mistaken, and I am still subject to a sense of rage that Renaissance studies were for me the start of art history and not the end, that I have spent so much of my life blinkered to Greece, Rome and Byzantium, oblivious of dangerous cross-currents from Armenia and the East – and I would now willingly swap David Hockney and all his works for one unmapped chapel on the summer snowline in the Pontic Alps, mutely speaking for a thousand years of the lively influence of ancient Rome long after we all thought it dead. I am enraged that I could have been so incurious at my Confirmation, not questioning the Nicene origin of the Creed or the Epistles of St Paul, thinking Christianity the child of Judaea and Rome, when in truth it is the child of Asia Minor. It seems to me now that there is no corner of Turkey that is not part of *European* history and culture, no site or monument that throws no light towards the West.

Turkey is the land of the Whirling Dervishes and the Seven Sleepers of Ephesus, of rich alluvial plains and desert plateaus, of sybaritic abundance and dry bread. Noah's Ark scraped to safety on its highest peak. The Argonauts sailed its northern coast to Colchis for the Golden Fleece, and the great Athenian expansion a millennium before Christ settled cities on its Aegean and southern shores. It was ancient Persia's gateway to Greece, and when Alexander slashed the knot at Gordium it was his to northern India. It was a dozen ancient kingdoms and cultures; the Hittites, amongst whom dwelt the Children of Israel, sold Abraham a tract of land, conquered Babylon, and came within an ace of providing a dynasty of Pharaohs; the Lycians were among the sea people who put a sudden and mysterious end to that empire, and, locked in their impregnable fortress of mountains and sea, were the last to be absorbed into the Roman Province of Asia Minor. Two of the Seven Wonders of the World were built here – the Temple of Artemis at Ephesus, and the tomb of Mausolus at Halicarnassus, still recalled in every Christian graveyard. It was here that Harpagus feasted on the flesh of his own boiled baby, and that Priapus was born, the dwarf demi-god whose monstrous and perpetually tumescent genitals live on in half a dozen English words. St John wrote his poetic Gospel and buried the Virgin Mary here; St Paul wrote most of his Epistles to its city states. Host to the Christian Creed, as Byzantium it spread from Tunis to the Caucasus, and with Constantinople at its centre became the Holy Roman Empire of the East. As William the Conqueror marshalled his forces for the invasion of England, the Seljuk Turks swept into Anatolia, bringing Islam and the exotic architecture of the East, the prelude to the abortive empire-building of the Crusades. With the fall of Byzantium, Constantine's great city became the centre of the Ottoman Empire, from Vienna to the Yemen, and Morocco to the Caspian Sea, sliding into the slow decadence that has for so long moulded our political attitude to Turkey.

To anyone to whom these broad historical concerns are of interest, travelling in Turkey is a brilliant reward, for bashed and battered though their remains may be, they are haunted by amiable ghosts, and their ancient grandeurs have mellowed into romantic ruins. Add long sandy beaches, rocky coves, deep fjord-like inlets, and the cleanest water in the Mediterranean. Add Turkish food, the best in what is left of the Levant – a sequence of largely vegetarian hors d'oeuvres, aubergines re-fined to a habit-forming sludge, white beans as crunchy as hazelnuts, tomatoes pulped with parsley and biting back with garlic, all subtly warmed with spices and cooled with yoghourt, followed by kebabs, or bass or crayfish. Add unpredictable wines and raki – the fierce drink that seems so friendly to boys brought up on aniseed balls. Add Matthew Arnold's ripe bursting figs, white mulberries, walnuts, almonds and all the gifts of harvest festival and hospital bed. Add the dried pips of sunflower and melon, and the charcoal-scorched corn cobs of the street vendors. Add music – not vox pop and the grinding of Japanese electric organs, but sad love laments in Ottoman Turkish and the eerie ululations of pre-pubertal boys to the accompaniment of medi-eval fiddle, fife and drum. Add the dance – not the sanitized belly-dancer of the tourist trap, but the real houri whose business is explicitly concerned with her loins and yours, and the men and boys who spontaneously drift into sexual ambivalence. And add the Turk, never Gladstone's unspeakable, but friendly, welcoming, curious and observant.

This cultural crucible of European civilization is not without blemish – nothing new in Turkey is worth tuppence, and most of it is concrete, in poor imitation of the worst rubbish of the West; when Atatürk tore up their Ottoman traditions, the Turks tore up their aesthetic roots, and our transplanted taste has done the rest. Some traditions remain; Western democracy is a concept beyond the comprehension of most Turkish voters – to the peasant scratching a living in the Taurus Mountains, the Anatolian plateau or the eastern highlands, universal suffrage means only that one man has as many votes as he has women in his household, for equality of gender is unthinkable and women still trudge behind their husbands' trotting donkeys, bear their burdens, work their fields, cook, clean and uncomplainingly satisfy their loins. Turkey may be an agnostic state, but its provincial manners and morals are conditioned by a harsh Mohammedanism that keeps its women in near slavery, arranges marriages, and tolerates the death feud for the infringement of the sexual code, preferring its young men to couple with a donkey than to commit adultery. By the same token, the poverty of Turks is accepted as the gift of God, they are without envy, and their charity and honesty towards strangers infinitely richer than themselves is humbling.

Democracy has been attempted, with limited success. In the later seventies Ankara constantly echoed the explosion of terrorist bombs, university education was riotously disrupted, and no street was safe; elsewhere, large areas of the country were manageable only as military zones, and few major cities were free of the risks of random terrorism. By 1982, under military rule, travel throughout the country was unrestricted, terrorism under control, and the promise of free elections capable of fulfilment. That the Army should restrict the number of parties was not unreasonable – fragmentation had been one of the major problems leading to the failure of elected government, and we do not tolerate it in our own House; that the Army should disband the old parties and prevent their leaders from standing was the only possible response to politicians who had led their country, albeit from the best of motives, into economic decline, political anarchy and democratic desuetude. The Army itself, with compulsory military service, is a considerable force for education and democracy, drawing many of its temporary subalterns from the working classes – though with cunning and a fat purse it is possible to escape the responsibility.

What the Turks now need are not the political shibboleths of the left and liberal West, but friends prepared to step back for a generation to allow the Turks themselves to reach a social and educational equilibrium that will foster democracy. Press comment would be better based on long and intimate experience of the whole country, taking as much account of the peasant living and working for less than we would give a dog, as of the vociferous intellectual. Turkey should be regarded less as an equal partner in NATO and the Council of Europe than as a fringe member of the Third World; it needs economic aid, the revision of the thousand-year-old prejudice engendered by the First Crusade, and the encouragement, not abuse, of its present tentative steps towards democracy.

Some of my journeys were made alone; they were not invariably calamitous, but all confronted me with difficulties that were joyless in solitude, and without the comfort of taped Schubert songs and Simon Raven's *Alms for Oblivion* might have been unbearable more often than they were. I was marooned at Afyon by a petrol shortage so acute that neither charm (not my strong point) nor bribery could get me out of a town that offered only a Turkish bath and an infinite variety of Turkish Delights to break the boredom of spending the day waiting in the petrol station, after nights broken by the constant baying of dogs. I coincided with a water shortage so acute that all hotel lavatories were blocked, their cisterns long empty, and in a restaurant I saw the water in which vegetables were boiled used again for washing dishes, and thanked the Lord that it was that way round; there was talk of cholera outbreaks, and the wilds of eastern Turkey seemed no place to be for an Englishman travelling alone for the suddenly frivolous purpose of looking at ruins, and I turned tail for northern Greece to follow the campaigns of the First World War in which Stanley Spencer had played so insignificant a part, but of which, in recollection, he painted some of the greatest pictures in the history of English art – alas, without preparation, it proved an idiotic whim. I coincided with bombs in Ankara, Kurdish insurrections in middle Turkey (far to the west of where I thought any Kurd might be), and the sudden imposition of unaccountable restrictions under military rule. I was duffed up by a soldier at a border post in the east; he was not to blame – the appearance of a solitary Englishman, knapsacked but obviously not a hippy, with a complexion the colour and texture of a dying nasturtium, bearing not the standard inadequate maps of eastern Turkey, but enormous aircraft navigation charts of the border country and neighbouring Russia, Persia and Iraq, could only be treated as suspicious, and he thought his rifle butt would speak a language that I might understand. In Istanbul, in the company of students, I was followed for several days by a man I took to be a secret policeman, for he wore the same kind of grey raincoat as is the uniform of Party Members in Albania, and appeared in such unlikely places as the Archaeological Museum (where nobody goes in midwinter, for it is bitterly cold and damp), and the dreary lobby of my hotel, the Akgün, which is always full of Polish housewives playing prostitute so that they may return to their husbands with stout leather jackets bought with the proceeds. And I witnessed an appalling accident between a horse-drawn cart and a Cadillac, in which a shaft was driven into the nag's belly and on up into the contents of its ribcage. The load was strewn about, the man and woman on the cart were flung into the road, unhurt but shocked, and the Cadillac was disabled with a punctured radiator; its driver was a bully – the fault was his, but he was determined to shed it.

My concern was for the horse; it was screaming, and thrashing its head hard against the stony, unmade road; it was bleeding from mouth and nostrils, as well as pumping blood from the point where the shaft entered its belly. I could think of nothing other than killing it – it was bound to die, but ex-sanguinating might have taken hours of agony. I had a knife in the car – the sort of thing that goes with Lederhosen and a funny hat, horn-handled, heavy, from Solingen, sharp, wickedly pointed, but the blade only four inches long. I thought to cut the horse's throat, but it would not be still, and I wondered how many bosh shots I would make before I got to anything vital, miserably recalling the mess that I had once made of despatching a myxomatosis-stricken rabbit in the grounds of Fonthill Abbey. I decided on the eye. Straight through the eye and into the brain. Four inches would be enough if I got the angle right. I knelt by its head waiting for the next thrash so that I could slip my knees under it –

it came down with a numbing thump and I struggled to hold it still, the eye wild but a clear target. It worked. The thrashing was replaced by tremors, fading, and the hideous noise was done. I think it was the sudden silence that broke the quarrel between the drivers, who now joined forces in an assault on me. How they could imagine that a horse with a shattered hind leg and a shaft of timber in its gut could ever draw a cart again, I do not know. I shouted back, at length, in English, in cold rage, and they made no attempt to prevent my driving away – yet I had meant to offer the driver of the cart what help I could, once the business of the horse was over. It occurred to me later that the reason for his anger might have been that I had killed the beast in such a way as made it inedible – had I known how to cut its throat in a clean sweep, it would have bled to death and been proper for the pot. It was not the only thing that occurred to me later, for night after night I woke with the smell and thickness of blood on my hands, a nightmare indeed, until I could stand the vision no longer and made for home – stopping by chance in Frankfurt for a night, only to be confronted in the Goethe Museum by Fuseli's *Nightmare*, in which a horse's head plays a devastating part; the shuddering laughter that was my response incurred the disapproval of the Hausfraus there (a man who laughs alone is mad), but it purged the worst of the recurring dream.

My companions have been many enough to merit a Dramatis Personae; in their various ways, lifting experience out of the commonplace and fixing it in my memory, these recollections are as much theirs as mine; visiting sites years later without them, or with different friends, their past companionship has often seemed present, and very much a part of re-experience.

Petter (1975, 1984–5, 1985–6) A Norwegian skiing companion, photographer, and a calm and stalwart friend. He climbs fearlessly, is practical in all things, has inexhaustible stamina, could charm the moustache off a Grand Vizier, and has only one disadvantage – a life of disciplined Scandinavian hygiene renders him vulnerable to any passing bug.

Colin (1975, 1984, 1986) Another skiing companion, expert on the oil industry and the inner workings of the Liberal Party, who shares my taste for Simon Raven and lubricious humour. He is given to flamboyant gestures with credit cards and wanders round ruins with touching wonder.

Michael (1975, 1982) A doctor, who drifted from skin diseases into venereology. A hypochondriac, ultra-sensitive to changes in temperature. A Roman Catholic by education, Jewish on his mother's side, and an expert casuist.

Jill (1976) A fellow art historian and friend dating back to student days at the Courtauld Institute. Her fields of expertise are Romanesque and High Victorian.

David (1976) Jill's husband, who has owned a Range-Rover for many years, and who is tolerant and forbearing to a saintly degree.

Ayhan (1984–5) A guide and driver generously supplied by the Turkish Government. He was the grit in the oyster, without which many of our days might have been dull – but never can a man have been more glad to see off his companions at the end of a journey, and return to the bosom of his unloved wife.

In 1983 Mrs Gülsen Kahraman of the Turkish Ministry of Culture and Tourism took me under her wing. I had by then written an article or two on Turkey, no holds barred in my comments on conditions there, but never once has she objected to my plain speaking; I continued to make independent journeys, but three longer and more ambitious explorations were made with her help, the cost and physical difficulties greatly eased by her Ministry – acts that seem to me the more generous in the light of my reputation for biting the hand that feeds.

This narrative is restricted to south-western Turkey, meandering from Ephesus to Side, and putting in that order recollections of things that occurred much more haphazardly. It is an impertinence for any journeyman scribbler to write about this area of Turkey, for it has been done before with scholarship, humour and wry hints of autobiography by George Bean, late professor of Classical Philology at Istanbul University. In four unbulky volumes he covers all the major and minor sites with only one misdirection, and renders professional guides and guide-books superfluous. To carry a Bean book, instantly recognizable in its vile orange wrapper, was in the seventies to carry a passport to immediate welcome by all the site guardians (most of whom had excavated with him) and the disclosure of recent unpublished finds; 'Ah Bin Bey', they invariably sighed, and would make the strange gesture of raising the hand, palm down, as far above the head as could be reached – Bean was very tall, and his gangling height amused the stocky Turks. No baggage is more essential for this journey than his books, for he brings as his companions Herodotus and Alexander, St Paul and Freya Stark, and with deft erudition raises the old stones that are the object of the trek.

Charles Fellows, in whose steps I have deliberately trodden, wrote in the preface to his journal of a journey made in 1838:

> It will be gathered from my journal that at the time of my arrival in the country I was strongly biassed in favour of the Greeks, and equally prejudiced against the Turks; and it will be seen in the course of the narrative how this unfavourable idea of the Turkish character was gradually removed by a personal intimacy with the people, generally in situations where they were remote from every restraint but those which their religion imposes.

I had no such prejudices, but like Fellows, my journeys established a respect and affection for Turkey and the Turks that is now unbreakable.

— I —

First Steps

Susie lay in Petter's lap, deeply asleep. The old bitch was a month past her sixteenth birthday, deaf and blind, but touch and smell kept her comforted and out of trouble, and she still enjoyed a gentle wrestling match with all the snarling and blunt biting that went with it. She had seemed slower than usual all day, not her wilful self, but a will relaxed as though overwhelmed by intense fatigue. Petter, watching television, made a sound – laughter, embarrassment, distaste; Susie, still sleeping, had emptied her bladder, and the urine was warm in his crutch and streaming down the flank of the chair. His gentleness with her then was gentleness with me.

During the night she barked, and I went down to the kitchen to quieten her. She barked again as soon as I returned to bed. My temper shortened; I slapped her rump and she scrabbled her way under the old day-bed. For a decade I have regretted that slap, and if I ever find myself outside St Peter's gate with Susie looking at me through the railing, it is the first thing for which I shall ask forgiveness. Of all my sins of commission it is the most oppressive. In the morning it was clear that she was ill, and I took her to the vet and left her.

We were leaving for Turkey the next day, and there were still things to be done – amongst them I had to buy a hat. My last sunhat, my school boater, had blown away on Dartmoor. The new hat had a tall crown and a broad brim, and I found it in a run-down shop in Soho where it may have lain for half a century, for the straw was yellow with age – it was not a gentleman's hat, nor yet a seaside hat, and no man would have worn it on a bowling-green, but Augustus John would have recognized its virtue, and John Singer Sargent might even have worn it, though his had a narrower brim. It was an artist's hat, and its wide shadow comforted me for a decade as its down-turned brim settled into an elegant asymmetry; a fierce gust of burning wind took it from me among the dunes that overwhelm the wide ruins of Side, and it was last seen blowing out to sea. On the day of its purchase I wore it home and jauntily raised it to my neighbours, trying it on the back of my head like the stitched linen hats of my childhood, and tilted forward over my nose like an officer cadet. At home there was a message from the vet. Susie had died. After sixteen years of sharing my bed she had died in an unfamiliar hygienic room, on a table, watched by strangers, with none of the consolations that the feel and smell of home and me might have brought her as she abandoned life. Of all my sins of omission, it is the most oppressive.

I collected her body, brown coat, brown eyes, brown nose, brown toenails, and drove to Winchelsea to bury it in the garden of a friend who had shared many a walk with her. Years later he sold the house to strangers and I dug up her bones and brought them home – a pathetically small remnant of something that was once so physical and loving; I can understand why the Crusaders boiled their dead and extracted the bones from the bottom of the pot to send home – so little is left in bulk and weight.

Driving to Turkey induces conflicting states of mind. There is the temptation to put the car through its paces, for there is sensual enjoyment in controlling the performance of a decent piece of machinery, and in a speed that enables the moving finger to trace the distance on a map. But that same map offers alternatives to the mad dash – Würzburg, for example, with its baroque architecture, frescoes by Tiepolo, and the engaging second-rate pictures of the early nineteenth century in its gloomy and neglected gallery; even Zagreb, in the steppes of Yugoslavia, whose outskirts promise worse than Slough and Harlow New Town, has, in a pretty palazzo in its old and engaging heart, a gallery full of respectable old masters and a peppering of master-pieces; and Ljubljana is still haunted by the ghosts of the Austro-Hungarian Empire, a Vienna in small. But Susie's death had put me into a mood for immediate change, and we drove fast from London to beyond Ulm on the first day, some seven hundred miles, and spent the night in an hotel where five extra marks were charged for possession of the turning part of the hot water tap. On the advice of the AA we then followed a slow zig-zag route through the Alps, and got no further than Udine on the second day; I was not too unhappy about this, for it was the road taken by Titian as an old man when he went from Venice to paint the Emperor Charles V, then holding court in Augsburg; what pleased me less was the traffic jam at what must be the most photographed town signs in Christendom – WANK it proclaims, and the village boys laugh every time a British car pauses, and many make appropriate gestures.

Udine resembles the set for almost any Italian opera, and is the only town in Italy that dies before dinner. We slept in a room with a large window that opened onto the passage leading to the hotel's only lavatory, and had an airless and rather smelly night. In the morning we sped into the mountains of Yugoslavia, where Colin mused aloud on the prehistoric upheavals that had brought about the Dolomites, and Petter snoozed. We spent the third night in a coastal village with so unpronounceable a name that we reduced it to 'Rusty Knickers'; it was pretty, and thinking to spend a few days there and swim, we found lodging in a private house where we were given two enormous double beds and no floor space. Petter found a girl and disappeared, or disappeared and found a girl – we next saw him at three in the morning climbing in through the window, soaking wet, for a drenching rainstorm had come down from the mountains. It rained all day, and there was nothing to do but sit on the huge beds, and then scuttle to lunch and dinner in the nearest restaurant; I remember nothing but the boredom of it, the steamed windows of the restaurant, and a pretty girl in a yellow sweatshirt embellished with a grinning black face and the legend 'Amin de Mood'. In the morning we made our apologies to the family that owned the beds and left in the unrelenting rain. Beyond Dubrovnik the road was clear of traffic, but not of rain, and not of single magpies. I am not superstitious, but I do not care for single magpies; there were too many to continue the prophylactic litany of greeting and good wishes that is supposed to avert the sorrow that they bring, but they were just too far apart to be counted in pairs, trios or quartets. Colin offered to count the total for the day and divide it, but at one stage he fell asleep, and at another I stopped the car to catch a cow, and we forgot the number. The cow had a rope round her neck, frayed, and she was running for all she was worth along a narrow mountain road from which she could not climb. But what can be done with a wild-eyed cow steaming in the rain, miles from anywhere, on the road to Titograd? With some misgiving we tied her to a telegraph pole that was just far enough from the edge of the road to prevent her from being thumped by passing traffic (of which there was very little), and drove on in the hope of seeing a farm, (and didn't).

It was still raining when we reached Titograd, a barren new town that is the bastard of Le Corbusier. The streets were so deep in water that Colin walked barefoot and rolled his trousers to his knees when we went in search of food and drink. The only remarkable thing about the town was the number of young people gathered in its cafés, and their extraordinary beauty – unselfconscious boys and girls infinitely more lively and attractive than the farrowings of King's Road and Carnaby Street, with a dark Mediterranean grace that redeemed their bleak surroundings. This was the birthplace of the Emperor Diocletian, and some nearby ruins are known as Dioclea. Diocletian virtually refounded the Roman Empire, making sense of the anarchy of the third century with reorganization of the structures of both military and civil government; he reformed taxation and coinage, and attempted to control inflation; he was the patron of much great architecture – Diocletian Antioch, a fine city in its day, now lies deep under the silt of the Orontes, but the ancient heart of the city of Split is still contained within the substantial remains of Diocletian's vast palace there. It is a pity that Titograd, rebuilt after devastating air raids and renamed in honour of the man who could well be described as Yugoslavia's Diocletian, should have been such a hasty and shoddy concrete job, an industrial city with aluminium, bauxite, tobacco, iron and plastics as its commercial base. The Yugoslavs were, I suppose, right to be proud of its recovery, and, quite liking tourists to pay obeisance, they gave the town one of the largest hotels in the country, the Crna Gora, Grand Hotel, in which gloomy monster we were compelled to stay.

It was still raining when we left Titograd; the dual-carriageway boulevard degenerated within a few hundred yards into a narrow road carrying as much water as a river through the chaos of mountains. Albania was to the south of us, black under the cloud and iron rods of rain; we were in the old Kingdom of Montenegro, whose dominating black mountain, Lovchen, visible from the sea, inspired the Venetian eponym for the country. But Montenegro seemed less black than Albania – Edward Lear described another part of Albania as 'shut out by iron walls of mountain, surrounded by the sternest features of savage scenery, rock and chasm, precipice and torrent, a more fearful prospect, and more chilling to the very blood, I never beheld – so gloomy and severe – so unredeemed by any beauty or cheerfulness.' He might well have been describing what we could see on our southern flank. For so distinguished a landscape painter to have seen nothing to redeem the view was harsh judgement, for even black mountains looming through the grey rain have the beauty at least of a steel engraving. The great Gibbon described Albania as 'a country within sight of Italy, which is less known than the interior of America', and James Bourchier, Balkan correspondent of *The Times* at the beginning of this century, wrote of it as wild and inaccessible, fierce and lawless, and complained that 'the inability of the Turkish authorities to afford a safe conduct in the remoter districts, renders Albania almost unknown to the foreign traveller, and many of its geographical problems remain unsolved'. Maps are a little better now (I presume that is what he means by 'geographical problems'), but little else has changed since independence from the Turks. Closed countries are a challenge, and by chance I was able to get into Albania twice in the later seventies; expecting things Turkish, I was disappointed to find that half a millennium of Ottoman occupation has been efficiently wiped from official memory.

Thessaloniki was full. We tried a dozen small hotels; we tried the university quarter; in desperation we discarded my habits of economy and tried the most expensive hotel in the city, but it was in mid-wedding and had no room for us. Then, out of the corner of my eye, up a narrow side street, I saw another hotel sign, braked with a force that dislodged all the clutter accumulated in the car, backed without thought of other traffic, swung in, and by a miracle parked immediately outside the hotel. Colin went in; a moment later he returned with the promise of a room with three beds, to be ready in fifteen minutes. It did not occur to any of us that for a room to be unprepared for guests late in the evening was a little odd. We unloaded our bags, presented our passports, and were puzzled by the dismay of the desk clerk. Colin's Greek was ancient and only worked one way – he could recall enough to make a simple request, but could never quite comprehend the answers. I thought that we were being thrown out and sat on the stairs in an attitude that I hoped would suggest determination to stay; Colin made hesitant declamations to the clerk. Petter smiled and rattled away in Norwegian – a trick useful in Turkey when not wanting to buy carpets from insistent vendors or roving touts. Three people came down the stairs, gave the clerk a key, and left; grudgingly the clerk gave Colin the same key, and at that moment an American sailor came in with bulging loins and a beautiful woman on his arm – the kind of long-limbed good looks that stop any man in his tracks. It was she who asked for a room, and then turned to her beau and said, 'You'll have to hold onto that thing until ten – these boys have just taken the only one.' At that point my slow wits recognized that we were in a whore-house, and I was mildly appalled at what the desk clerk and the American sailor might think we were up to – the Greek girl obviously took such things in her ancient Greek stride.

The room was a decent size and had seen better days. The mattresses were hollowed and the sheets spiked with pubic hair, so we turned them; unsheeted, the mattresses were stained like huge relief maps; there were no other bedclothes. The wash-basin drained into a bucket; the tap resisted Petter's effort to turn it on, and then twisted upside-down and spurted fiercely at the ceiling – the worst of having a nodding acquaintance with icon-ography is that one sees symbolism everywhere. Slightly hyster-ical I left the room and went in search of a bath; I found only a shower, of which the basin was so full of old French letters that the water would not drain away unless I removed them with my toe, and if I did not care to be ankle-deep in these sear and yellow leaves of passion, then I must balance on the narrow edges, legs astride – not the attitude in which to be found behind an unlocked door. With the sound of much coming in the neighbouring rooms, and much going in the corridor, we had a fitful night, and in the morning wondered about crabs.

There is something ludicrous about three men quietly contem-plating their genitals, carefully lifting them, stretching their scrotums, and murmuring reports on their search for lice. We none of us had any idea what we should do if we found them – I had had them once before, caught, I think, in a filthy French youth hostel that stank of urine, but identified in Zürich, where one of Zwingli's Godly Magistrates in the form of a malevolent pharmacist sold me a creamy white fluid to be generously applied; the fluid was Zwingli's Revenge – smooth as shaving soap at first, but after half a minute of calm deception it began to burn, shrivel and emasculate. I cringed at the searing recollection of it, but of Greek crabs there was no sign, and we tucked ourselves away and paid the bill.

Thessaloniki is a city without charm, and no-one in their senses should go there unless they must – bustling, dirty, windy, dusty, shoddily new, and with the nastiest outskirts of any town in Europe. My stepfather fought in the Macedonian campaign of the Great War, and had not a good word to say for it, before or after the devastating fire of 1917 – only that during that fire British soldiers saw more rats than in four years of trench warfare on the Western Front.

As soon as I could read I was given a substantial Bartholomew atlas with unbound maps that could be laid flat, published in the 1890s, and it fixed a Europe in my mind that I did not know was long lost; I came to terms with later, between-the-wars Bartholomews because I had to, but the post-1945 revision of borders with the loss of Latvia, Estonia, Lithuania and that medieval relic of Teutonic chivalry, East Prussia, I still find difficult to believe, just as I cannot look at a map of Yugoslavia without seeing the ghosts of Bosnia, Herzegovina, Serbia and all the other ancient names, as in a palimpsest. Map 34 of my Bartholomew is of the Balkan States, and the word TURKEY marches firmly across it from the Black Sea to the Adriatic; the Turkish border is within a hundred miles of Belgrade and twenty of Sofia (though it once reached the gates of Vienna); Eastern Roumelia is enclosed by both Turkish pink and Bulgarian green, running in parallel; and Greater Roumelia stretches from Albania to Constantinople, and is not the miserable remnant on the map that prefaces Patrick Leigh Fermor's *Roumeli*. It is the childhood conviction of this map that has conditioned my attitude to the Balkans – that Turkey is less the Asia Minor of the Romans than part of Europa Major, that when the Venetians took the Italian Renaissance to the coast of Illyria they did no more than build a screen for the toe-hold taken

with the profits gained from carrying the Crusaders who put
Constantinople to the sword, and that when the Turks took
over the fluctuating borders of the old Serbian Empire, Bosnia,
Wallachia and the unruly Principality of Albania, they replaced to
advantage a ragged confusion of rules. It might be argued that a
generally incompetent, but stable and permanent administration, tolerant of Christianity, making no demands for military
service from male Christians (who thus often had a commercial or
agricultural advantage over their Muslim neighbours), and not
unbearably harsh with its taxes, was indeed rather better than the
dominion of petty princes, Christian in title but not principle,
always warring with their neighbours. By this token we had
entered the Turkey of my childhood when we left Dubrovnik,
and the impression had been confirmed by the sight of an
occasional minaret before we reached the Greek border. By this
token Thessaloniki was our first major Turkish town.

The Turks took it in 1430. It had once been the second city of the
Byzantine Empire, but the Bulgarians invaded it at the end of the
ninth century, and Saracens from Cyrenaica stormed it in 904 and
sold 22,000 of its inhabitants into slavery. In 1185 Sicilian Normans took it with hideous and entertaining barbarity, of which
the then archbishop of the city, Eustathius, has left an account.
This wise old man was a pragmatist, prepared to accept the
notorious brutality and sexual excesses of the then Emperor of
Byzantium if he supported the poor against the rich, and the
Eastern Church against the Western. Andronikos 1 Comnenos
usurped the throne in 1183, strangled the boy emperor Alexios II
and threw his body into the Bosphorus, married and took to his
bed the boy's widow, the twelve-year old Agnes, daughter of
Louis VII of France (he was himself well into his sixties), murdered the former empress who as Alexios' mother had been his
regent, and embarked on an orgy of torture, burning, blinding
and decapitation. His political policies, beneficial for the Byzantine Empire, were in accord with the hopes of Eustathius but were
bitterly resented in the West; the Norman invasion of Albania
and Thessaloniki was the first step towards putting him down.
Neither city offered serious resistance; after nine days with its
harbour blocked by a Sicilian fleet and eighty thousand
mercenaries investing its walls, Thessaloniki gave way, and five
thousand of its citizens were slaughtered with the same public
relish as Andronikos had exhibited in Constantinople two years

before, exsanguinating from the loss of ears, noses, tongues, hands, feet and testicles, with eyes gouged out, never knowing what next was likely to be lopped from their anatomy, providing entertainment with their inarticulate gurgling shrieks and terminal tremors, the city's dogs ready thieves of the dismembered parts. Such horrors were justified in the Western mind as punishment for schism, and the fabric of the Orthodox churches of the city was the object of as much deliberate wrecking, spoliation and defilement as the worshippers within them.

In 1204, Baldwin of Flanders, elected Emperor of Byzantium by six Venetians and six Crusaders who had just sacked Constantinople and shown themselves worse by far than the Saracens they were supposed to be fighting in the Holy Land, saw to it that Boniface of Monferrat, his chief rival in the election, at least got second-best with the Kingdom of Thessalonika, which was made to reach as far as Athens. In 1222 Theodore, Despot of Epirus, took the city and was crowned its king. Few titles have undergone a greater change in meaning and popular appeal – 'Despot' is now only pejorative, but it once meant 'head of the household', and as such was applied to the Byzantine Emperor, and then to princes of the imperial house. It was an acceptable form of address to bishops – I can see a wry smile on the faces of those of that rank in the Church of England – and the Turks long continued to use it for compliant Christian rulers of subject territories. It was the French revolutionaries who, in exchanging one despotism for another, used the term in abuse, and so changed and restricted its meaning. Theodore was anxious to control what little was left of the Byzantine Empire – then roughly what is now Turkey in Europe, and as much again in Asia – but in 1230 he was defeated by another aspirant, Ivan Asen, Tsar of Bulgaria. Ivan died in 1241 with his hold hardly secure, and his successor was distracted by a Mongolian invasion to the north. In 1266 the Byzantine Emperor gave Thessaloniki to the Burgundians, and in 1320 they sold it to the Emperor of Rumania; it had been in Venetian hands for seven years, again by purchase, when Murad II of Turkey finally took it in 1430 and gave it peace for nearly five centuries.

If ever a city benefited from the stability of Turkish rule, it was Thessaloniki; the only invasion during their dominion was peaceful and wholly beneficial – when the Spaniards expelled their Jews in an excess of Catholic zeal, many of them settled in Thessaloniki, and their number multiplied to some 60,000 by the time the Germans occupied Greece in 1941. When the Germans withdrew, the Spanish Jews had been wiped out. In all those years only one event of real significance had taken place in the city, and that was the conspiracy of Turkish army officers who, in July 1908, compelled the Sultan, Abdul Hamid, to instal constitutional government in Turkey. A conservative counter-revolution in 1909 was unsuccessful, and in April the Sultan abdicated, leaving Mehmed V to preside over Turkey's defeat in the Great War, and the end of the Ottoman Empire and its long erratic line of Sultans. The Young Turks, as these officers were called, Kemal Atatürk among them, hoped to preserve the ancient territories of the Ottoman Empire against the nationalist movements that had grown up in the Balkans for the preceding thirty years or so, but they failed. That failure led directly to a Byzantine (in the pejorative sense) readjustment of Balkan borders, the intervention of the Great Powers for their own benefit, and to the assassination at Sarajevo and its appalling consequences.

In October 1912 King Nicholas of Montenegro declared war on Turkey; within ten days Greece, Serbia and Bulgaria had joined him, and when the First Balkan War came to an end with the Treaty of London in 1913, Turkey's European holding had been reduced to no more than a strip of land to the west of Istanbul; and then, with bloody and unmitigated violence, the little Balkan powers fell upon the corpse of Macedonia and began the Second Balkan War among themselves. In six weeks in the summer of 1913 the Balkan borders were again redrawn, Bulgaria was humiliated, Macedonia was divided roughly along its present borders between Greece and Yugoslavia (then Serbia), Turkey regained most of Thrace with Adrianople (now Edirne), and Thessaloniki became Greek.

Hanging in one of the darker passages of my parents' house, near the bottom of the back stairs where one could neither see it properly nor would one naturally pause, was the black and white original of an illustration from, perhaps, the *Illustrated London News*, showing the retreat of the Turks in the First Balkan War. The artist, Percy Jacomb-Hood, was certainly in Macedonia in 1912, but I suspect that this drawing was propaganda and not truth; his bleak panorama had the Turks and their baggage trains in the far distance, but what made the drawing fascinating and distasteful were the impaled Greeks in the foreground, writhing miserably on the sharpened stakes that with every movement thrust further into their bowels. There is a reference in *Edwin Drood* to stakes prepared by the Sultan for the punishment of Turkish brigands, but that must have been received mythology, for Dickens was no traveller in the Orient – it may nevertheless then have been a general truth; that the Turks would impale Europeans in the twentieth century seems unlikely, but anti-Turkish propaganda has always been so poisonous that it has often had, and still has, little or no connection with the truth. Lawrence of Arabia, whose interest in anal penetration was revealed by his description of the Deraa incident, would certainly have recorded instances of impalement had there been any during the course of his desert campaigns.

As an aside, the Deraa incident continues to puzzle commentators on *The Seven Pillars of Wisdom*. Lawrence, wearing a torn European jacket and not his full Arabian fig, was arrested by a Turkish sergeant and accused of being a deserter; he claimed exemption from military service as a Circassian (presumably Christian and therefore not subject to military service) – a fair-haired, blue-eyed race whose women had long provided the most desirable slaves for the Harem; in times of deprivation Turkish soldiers would find a fair-haired, blue-eyed boy as tempting as a woman. 'I cursed my littleness', Lawrence wrote, as he was first presented to the local Governor, whom he kneed in the crotch, and was then taken off to the guard-room to be beaten and sodomized by four soldiers and a corporal – 'the men . . . would squabble for the next turn, ease themselves, and play unspeakably with me'. The choice of the word 'play' is curious. 'I remember smiling idly at [the corporal], for a delicious warmth, probably sexual, was swelling through me . . .'; 'in Deraa that night the citadel of my integrity had been irrevocably lost'. The account should puzzle no-one, for it is perfectly clear that Lawrence experienced the masochist's sexual response to a sadistic sexual episode; as far as the randy Turks were concerned he was no more than a fair-haired boy who had made life difficult for himself. The matter only becomes a problem for those who seek to defend Lawrence from the implications of his own statements, and who find it impossible to accept that an imperishable champion of all that is noble, pure and true should self-indulgently expose himself as a homosexual masochist – there is also the point that none of the worthy international statesmen who carved up the world at the Paris Conference of 1919, nor

King George V (who gave him the Order of the Bath in the middle of it), would have relished the idea of their having consorted with a faggot (or whatever the common parlance was in those days). There can be only one reasonable interpretation of 'Pain of the slightest had been my obsession and secret terror, from a boy', and 'moaning in wonder that it was not a dream, and myself back five years ago, a timid recruit at Khalfati, where something, less staining, of the sort had happened'; and if the mysterious S.A. to whom the book is dedicated is Sheikh Ahmed, a young Arab whom he had known in Syria before the war, then 'Love, the way-weary, groped to your body, our brief wage ours for the moment/Before earth's soft hand explored your shape, and the blind worms grew fat upon your substance', is as clear a declaration of homosexual love as any, and beautiful to boot. A passage suppressed from the subscription edition states that the pain of the Deraa beating had induced in him since 'a fascination and morbid desire, lascivious and vicious . . .'. Lawrence at the time took the beating and the sodomy in his stride and fought on, his emotional and intellectual crisis following so many years later that it cannot have been the direct and simple consequence of it; his homosexuality is a biographical curiosity, though there can be no doubt that it formed the man and his attitudes – what is more important is that acting as a focus for anti-Turkish opinion and action, he formed the attitudes of the English press and the politicians who directed the war and the post-war settlement, and did more to revive hatred and mistrust of the Turks than any man since the Crusades, whipping it up with the fervour of a flagellant.

As for Thessaloniki, only in the northern quarter is there any remnant of the Turkish occupation – a few narrow streets with timber-frame houses, crowded by the instant slums of concrete redevelopment that surround them; among them in the house in which Atatürk was born in 1881.

The first stretch of the Via Appia south from Rome was planned by the Censor Appius Claudius Caecus in 312 BC. It was eventually extended to the Apulian coast at Egnatia, and then to Brindisi, the embarkation point for Greece; boats went to Apollonia, to the south of Durrës in Albania, and to Durrës itself, where the first Roman road built outside Italy was begun in 148 BC. The two initial stretches of the Via Egnatia meet in the Shkumbin Valley and unite to turn east across Albania following an ancient highway; travellers again took ship to cross the lake to Ochrid (where the enchanting Byzantine churches are covered with graffiti drawings of ships, as is the church of Santa Sophia at Trebizond), and then the road picked up an old Corinthian trade route through the mountains to Bitola, Edessa and Thessaloniki; thence it was later extended to follow, more or less, the coast of the Aegean eastwards to Byzantium. This stretch is a good road for walking, for the present highway follows its line but leaves most of it in peace, and, unlike many Roman roads, it is full of twists and turns; it dips down to the sea often enough, and it is peppered with not unfriendly villages and small towns; the only problem is that it is haunted. The ghosts are not the specific images of Pompey or Alexander the Great, nor even of common soldiers – indeed they are not ghosts in any conventional sense, for there is only a feeling of gentle restraint, as though my own time were moving faster than me, and leaving me behind. I am not alone in this – a perfectly rational friend remarked 'driving along here is like swimming in molasses', and then could not explain why he had said it; and Jill, tough and not given to nonsense, said, 'God. You can almost smell the Crusaders here.' She always prefaced her remarks with 'God', and it proved to be one of the most profoundly irritating things about that journey – but even she could sense some emanation from the past. Not only Alexander and the Romans and the Crusaders, but the British and French armies used it in the First World War, and the Germans in the Second. Once, quite late in the evening, I asked an old man sitting in a village street for a room; he had one eye and one hand, and his response was to ask if I were German; as I am not, I got my room.

The road to the Turkish border is littered with dead dogs. The dead dog sums up the difference between the Greek and the Turk. The Greek driver seeing a dog in the road a hundred yards ahead will accelerate and do his damnedest to run it down for sport; a Turk will maintain his speed and course, and if the dog happens to be in the way, will run over it – the one is vile, the other fatalistic, though I do not care for the indifference. I once scooped a kitten from the path of an Istanbul taxi with the speed and dexterity that I thought had left me when I stopped playing rugby – as the taxi shrieked to a halt the driver's scowl changed to laughter, but in Greece both I and the kitten would have been flattened. The dead dog is not a pretty sight; it swells tight as a drum and eventually explodes as did the entrails of Made-

moiselle, first cousin of Louis XIV, at her funeral service in the
Luxembourg, 'with a frightful noise and an intolerable stench' –
lords and ladies by the dozen jammed the doors with their wigs
and furbelows, fainted, had fits of the vapours and had to be
sprayed with perfume (traditionally the French answer to a bad
smell and body odour). There are more dead dogs by far to the
west of the border post at Ipsala than to the east of it.

Our first sight of Turkey was across the river at Evros, the
Hebron of antiquity; a Greek soldier, bayonet fixed, marched half
way across the bridge, turned smartly, and marched back again;
his Turkish counterpart, dowdy in fatigues, lounged against the
railing in the afternoon heat and watched him, expressionless.
The brisk show of the one and the lazy relaxation of the other
neatly characterized the races.

We spent the night in Tekirdağ, nine metres above the sea – the
Turks have the engaging habit of not only signposting their
towns, but of telling the entering visitor its height above sea-level
and the number of its population – sometimes, in the east, the
height in metres is the greater figure. A busy little white dog with
stumpy bow legs welcomed us after his fashion, which was to pee
on my luggage; from the balcony of our room I saw him a few
minutes later, dead in the road, bloody about the muzzle. I had,
thank God, laughed at his greeting and not scolded him. The
town climbs steeply away from the sea to considerably more than
nine metres, and has a fair number of traditional timber houses,
tall, silvered with age, seeming to lean outward with their full-
bosomed upper windows. From a distance a man sitting by the
gutter of a steep street appeared to be comforting a sheep in much
the same way as I might an old dog; close to, we saw that he had
cut its throat, and that he held it over his knees not in the spirit of
affection, but so that it could bleed to death downhill without
making a mess; its eyes were glazed and its limbs trembled with a
fluttering speed that I would not have thought possible from any
creature other than a bird. The town and its immediate environs
may have changed over the past two hundred years – I cannot
otherwise imagine why Voltaire chose it for an end to Candide's
wanderings, and put him to the cultivation of his garden. It is odd
that an English metaphor for retirement should have been conjured by a Frenchman from a Thracian town that he had never
seen; but he may have known something of the exile of Francis
Rákóczy II, Prince of Transylvania and leader of the Magyars
against the Austrians in an abortive alliance with Louis XIV – he

was forced to be Louis' pensioner from 1711 until 1717, when he committed the ultimate treachery of allying himself with the Turks; in Constantinople the Sultan gave him nothing to do, and he at last settled in self-imposed exile in Tekirdağ, in a small house that is now a museum – after fifteen years of cultivating its garden, he died there in 1735. He was a devout Catholic, and his remains were solemnly recovered by the Hungarians in 1907.

The road to Istanbul is a helter-skelter of dead ground and heavy traffic, worsening dramatically as the trans-European volume joins it from Bulgaria and Edirne; it is lined with recent concrete blocks masquerading as hotels, for it is almost always within sight of the sea; it is best driven with total concentration and as much speed as common sense allows. Near Istanbul airport it widens to motorway dimensions, but the speed and lunatic irresponsibility of drivers reduces the level of safety to that of the chariot race in *Ben-Hur*. It is a road that leads the unwitting directly to Asia, for the signposts name only the city's districts, which is as useful as naming Ponder's End to a man who wants the London Hilton; but in daylight, with foresight, and with driving skills that might have been forged in the Nürburgring, it is possible to find the way into Istanbul, and even to the Pera Palace.

The Pera Palace is an hotel that has fallen on hard times. It is the darling of the Victorian Society, and deservedly so, for it must once have combined the grandeurs of the Grand Tour with the splendours of the Sublime Porte. Now it does neither, and its wedding-cake architecture is the victim of package tourists and the desuetudinous plumbing that betokens hardened arteries. But it is a reliable meeting-place, and in the traditions of the last century allows ungrudging exploitation of its services as a poste restante. Here we found Michael, whose interest in St Paul and whose skills as a doctor had both seemed useful assets when planning the journey. Hence we embarked on so confused an excursion that when it ended a month later I immediately planned to return – we zig-zagged and back-tracked, were diverted by the false enthusiasms of other Europeans casually encountered, squabbled and were reconciled, and were seduced by the sun and the sea. Later journeys were better planned and covered less ground in greater detail, but it was not until this book was conceived that I set off with Petter again, in the winter of 1984–5 to check a mass of notes accumulated over ten years, and follow a route that, geographically at least, made better sense than all the others. Enter Ayhan.

— II —

Ephesus

M R SWELL. I have never cared for my surname, and cringe when I see it misspelt. The telephone lisps it to Fewell, and Italian waiters are flummoxed by the double this and double that; my peers at school cruelly converted it to 'Sewage'. At twenty-one I had the opportunity to change it, but then it seemed too savage a rejection of the stepfather whose name it was and of whom in young manhood I had at last become a little fond. Now it is too late. Kemal, the young man who was to ease our transfer at Istanbul airport, held a scrap of cardboard on which in large capitals he had printed MR SWELL; he was astonished when I approached him obliquely, like a rugby tackle on his blind side, snatched it from his fingers, tore it in pieces and stuffed it in my pocket. He was not to know that old miseries had swept back into my mind – including the wretched week at an art historians' congress in Paris, whose secretariat had labelled me as 'Miss Swell', so that I was constantly having to explain my disruption of formal *placements*, and why, unlike all others there, I was not wearing an identification badge. Kemal's dropped jaw was still open when I said, 'Call me Brian – it's easier', having forgotten that my Irish Christian name to a Turk is almost as confusing as my surname, and tends to be corrupted to *Ayran*, a drink of watered yoghourt, or to 'Brain'.

At Izmir I expected another MR SWELL notice, assuming that
Turkish officialdom would be consistent with the error, but there
was none. Among the group watching arrivals was a man who
looked like an English major in mufti, his tweeds immaculately
cut, his raincoat neatly folded over his arm, his eyes shaded by
the peak of one of those caps that were an almost compulsory
absurdity for shorn army cadets in my young day; the only
dissonances were struck by a brown leather handbag and a pipe
that was meerschaum when it should have been briar. I have to
confess to disappointment when he greeted us in perfect un-
accented English and announced that he was to be our guide and
guardian. Kinglake, at a like moment, describes his Tatar as 'sleek
and fresh from the bath . . . and carefully accoutred at every point
. . . a government courier sent with travellers to speed them on
their way and answer with his head for their safety'. Thus far the
same, but Kinglake's man was 'a glorious-looking fellow, with
that regular and handsome cast of countenance which is now
characteristic of the Ottoman race, hung about with weapons and
a great edifice of clothes'; ours looked as though he had just
stepped from Burberry's window. To give him his due, in sum-
ming up his charges he showed not the slightest misgiving at our
waterproof and booted appearance, and our general air of travel
weariness even before the travel had begun. He bustled about
and saw that our knapsacks were recovered promptly; it was
rather impressive – like having Moses for Tatar, so readily did the
crowd part for him.

He drove into Izmir, a city for which I do not care, with its
memories of lost luggage, pyjamaless nights, and the first per-
forming bear (I've seen many since) – a sad little creature dragged
through the traffic by two small gipsy children and prodded to
perform for us while we plodded miserably on with lunch, unable
to give it a titbit through its tight muzzle; God knows how it
perspired without being able to open its mouth. Ayhan seemed
disposed to show us the sights rather than the sites – I let him get
away with NATO Headquarters and then urged him on. He took
us to Selçuk and the ruined Cathedral of St John, tidy, ordered,
and, apart from its Byzantinisms, much like any neat English
ecclesiastical ruin – in the December sun, with so much greenery
about it, it could have been Fountains, or Rievaulx, or Bury St
Edmunds. In the museum we were compelled to admire Priapus
supporting a basket of fruit on his erection. Some years ago this

absurd little sculpture was not on open view, and European
visitors, asked if they would like to see the god Bes, invariably
assented, having not the slightest notion that they would then be
shown an ugly little monster sporting a proud member. It was an
awkward situation; should it be admired as a work or art and
antiquity, treated with awe for its prodigious instrument, or
greeted with laughter as a pornographic joke? I felt then that the
guardian was testing me, disapprovingly assuming most Europeans to be dirty-minded, and that a grave unsmiling grunt and
conventional thanks were the proper response. Postcards, now
in open racks, were then labelled 'Only for foregain (sic) tourists',
and no Turk might see them or the original terracotta. Across the
road was a public lavatory where a small boy lay in wait, imitating
the stance of Priapus but without the basket of fruit, and holding
out his hand for money; like the guardian he got a grunt, but
not unsmiling, for he cannot have been more than eight
and was showing great initiative. In front of the original, as
Ayhan expected amusement, I laughed, but it seemed to
me a poor grotesque thing compared with the phallic trophies
collected by Thorwaldsen, now displayed in Copenhagen as a
respectable precedent for the present prurience of the Danes.

The basket of fruit is not the sculptor's licence, but the other
symbol of Priapus. Most ancient authorities say that he was the
son of Dionysus and Aphrodite, and that jealous Hera, assisting
at his birth at Lampsakos on the Dardanelles, caused the gross
priapism that so appalled his mother that she deserted him; the
worthies of Lampsakos provided him with home and education,
but as he grew up he fell into 'vicious practices' (alas unspecified,
but the problems of adolescence for a boy endowed with a
permanent erection at least as long as his arm must have been
formidable) and had to be banished. But not for nothing was he
the son of gods, and he caused the Lampsakians an affliction of
the private parts so sore that on oracular advice (I wonder how
the question was put to the oracle) they begged him to return,
built temples to him, and made him protector of gardens and
vineyards – hence the basket of fruit. An alternative version
suggests that Aphrodite dumped him on the nearest hillside, and
that he was rescued from exposure by a shepherd, thus becoming
the protector of flocks; and his third duty was to protect sailors –
though whether this was the assumption of one of Aphrodite's
jobs, or a classical recognition of the randiness of mariners,

ancient authors do not vouchsafe. American readers will recognize the unconscious humour of the *Encyclopedia Britannica* when it was still Britannic, with 'the first fruits of gardens . . . and occasionally asses were offered to him'.

Priapus inevitably assumed the role of the god of sensuality, and his symbol, the phallus, began to lead a life of its own, independent of him, emblematic of fertility and a protection against the evil eye. Thorwaldsen had a terracotta monster the size of those earthenware 'chicken bricks' in which fowls are baked, with a phimotic foreskin tight as a budding violet at the business end and a mass of elegant curls at the other; in the same glass case are phallic whimsies with infibulated foreskins to be hung about the neck, and an upright walking penis with its own loins demurely clad. The museums of western Europe all have their share of these little jokes; a gryphon penis scratching under its wing was dug up in York in 1844, and its bronze twin was found in Pompeii; they appear as lamps, amulets, seals and bells, and in the Vatican there is the ultimate blasphemy of a cockerel's head beaked with an erect penis, wattled with testicles, and labelled ΚΟΣΜΟΥ ΣΩΤΗΡ, the Saviour of the world, which may reflect an eastern Gnostic heresy that Priapus was in business before the Creation – it is certainly in tune with the Gnostic dualism of the divine and material worlds, with a Redeemer in both, even if the statement may seem to us obscure and extreme.

As the god of gardens he took his place in them as a stone herm with an erection on which young women might hang a votive offering, or themselves, or a rough wooden carving stuck like a gnome among the bushes, his penis painted red; sometimes a phallic post was enough. His image was placed on tombs as a symbol of regeneration. His is never the idealized figure of most Greek and Roman gods – his features have an oriental cast, and most of his statues show him bearded, some wearing the Phrygian cap of his native north-western Turkey. Could the garden gnomes of today's suburbia with their red pointed hats be the distant descendants of his cult? If not, then all that we have left of him are words, of which the most telling is long obsolete – the verb 'to priape' which so perfectly describes the bathing habits of the rugby team; 'priapism' is an unfortunate condition to be wished on no enemy (one of my fellow students, now a distinguished museum director, was in his youth more often than not late for lectures because of it – he found it embarrassing to leave his bus in that condition, and would allow himself to be carried miles beyond his stop before it subsided; he eventually learned to affect the gait of Quasimodo), once believed to be brought on by potatoes as well as cantharides; the *Priapuloidea* are small marine creatures whose ringed and crusted forms could inspire the designers of French ticklers to new heights of fantasy (what can the marine biologist who invented the term have been thinking?); and I regret that 'priaprick' has not yet been invented.

I have forgotten how many breasts the Ephesian Artemis has and is supposed to have – my notebook records 'about forty-seven', but I suspect that to be an impatient exaggeration of the more probable twenty-six. They hang in sagging rows in the general area of armpit to navel. Rubens, arch-sensualist, in all his references to the huge statue as an allegory of plenty, gives them nipples, but they have none, and in any case are egg-shaped, graduated like eggs in a supermarket, and eggs they must be. But if they are eggs, then she must be flat-chested. Artemis Ephesia has little to do with the chaste huntress Artemis-Diana of the west, with her crescent diadem and those Lesbian shenanigans that enabled Jupiter, disguised as Diana, to rape her follower Callisto, and is an Anatolian divinity devoted to the reproductive forces of nature – though the poor priests who served her, were, according to Strabo, eunuchs. A tenth-century Christian source suggests that a portable replica of the statue was carried in procession with much frenzy, tumult and bloodshed, but Simeon Metaphrastes may not be a reliable witness, and may have confused the rites of Artemis with the rites of Cybele. Cybele was the great mother-goddess of Anatolia, concerned with fertility, wild nature, disease and protection; her spring rites included the (simulated?) castration and death of her young lover, Attis, and the *taurobolium*, in which a bull had its throat cut over a ditch where lay the dedicatee waiting to be swamped in blood – the bull's genitals were then cut off and carried in procession. There is some confusion over the castration of Attis – it was either inflicted by Cybele's father to prevent their marriage, or it was self-inflicted after Attis had broken a vow of celibacy taken as Cybele's first priest, or it was self-inflicted when a furiously jealous Cybele found that he wished to marry another woman and bewitched him with madness. Whichever the case, the mutilation occurred at the foot of a pine-tree, and death followed;

the pine-tree received his spirit, and from the blood at its roots sprang the wild violet. He was the son of a castrato; his father had been a man of such enormous strength that the gods in fear had castrated and killed him; from his blood grew the almond tree, and Attis was conceived when his mother ate its nuts – all very symbolic, for nuts to the ancients were as much a testicular reference as they are today, and the almond in particular became the 'mandorla', that enlarged halo that embraces the whole saint in early Renaissance art. Cybele's priests were invariably eunuchs, but the temple attendants and mendicants were not, and it was these that provided the high spectacle of self-castration during the festivals (which one commentator maintains appealed only to the lower classes); the priests, known in Anatolia as *Galli* and in Greece as *Corybantes*, mimicked the mad with shrieking and howling, beat swords on shields, danced to flutes, drums and cymbals, beat themselves with whips strung with knuckle-bones, and were notorious for the obscenity of things said and done. There is one odd Christian parallel – in the spring festival, more or less at the time of Easter, a pine-tree covered with violets was carried to the Galatian shrine of Cybele as a symbol of dead Attis; for three days he was mourned with extravagant grief, and then on the third, discovered alive again (presumably in the form of a young priest) and celebrated with a great beanfeast called the *Hilaria*.

I am tempted to see a precedent for the brutal emasculation of Peter Abelard in the tale of Cybele and Attis, but that is too remote from Ephesus and Artemis and the innumerable breasts. A close examination of these suggests that they are not a monstrous deformity, but part of the decoration of a full-length tunic falling in panels straight from the shoulders; the sculpture may well be an accurate record of the uncomfortable panoply worn by a priestess. She, and a smaller similar statue, were found in the ruins of the Prytaneum, a town hall of sorts near the eastern gate. The Artemis of the native Greek pantheon was born on Ortygia, the ancient name for Delos, but Tacitus records the Ephesian belief that she was a local girl, and there was indeed a grove near Ephesus called Ortygia in which she and her brother Apollo were supposed to have been born (Propertius calls the river Cayster at Ephesus the *Ortigius Cayster*). If she was a local girl, then it explains the great temple dedicated to her that so impressed Alexander the Great when he came to Ephesus in 334 BC (he

offered to pay for it, and was refused) and that became one of the
Seven Wonders of the World, three of which, if Rhodes is
included, are in Aegean Turkey. Little is left of it now – it was
burned by the Goths in AD 237, and plundered by the Christians
when Justinian, in the sixth century, founded the great church of
St John on the hill to the north-east that overlooks it; the vast
soggy pit that I saw in 1976 was so devastating to the imagination
of past grandeurs that I have not since returned.

Sogginess was a perpetual problem; the River Cayster, known
to the Turks as Küçük Menderes, or Little Maeander, brought silt
from a fertile valley to the north-east and made the coastal area
marshy. The earliest Ephesus was on the northern slope of
Mount Pion and overlooked an inlet of the sea that came inland as
far as modern Selçuk – it was founded by Androclus, one of the
younger sons of Codrus, the last King of Athens, after the
disputed succession a millennium before Christ, part of the Attic
colonization of Ionia. It lasted some four centuries, its prosperity
based on its harbour and the pilgrim cult of Artemis, skilfully
grafted by the invading Greeks on to the ancient native cult of
Cybele (so much for Artemis' local birthplace). In the sixth
century, Croesus, last king of nearby Lydia and the man of
legendary wealth, extended his borders westward from the
Cayster valley by invading Ephesus; he destroyed the city, and
constructed another on the level ground south of the Temple of
Artemis, unwalled and indefensible. After his death Lydia became a Persian satrapy, and Ephesus with it; the city survived this
change and many others, until after Alexander's death, when it
fell to his long-lived companion Lysimachus. This unpopular and
much denigrated tyrant observed that the Cayster was silting the
harbour, and it is probable that the water-table had risen too
(Herodotus, a hundred and fifty years earlier, had also seen the
consequences of the Cayster's silt), but when he decided to move
the city yet again, to its present site, he was baulked by its
citizens; he merely bricked up their drains and soaked them out.
The Cayster continued its work of extending Anatolia into the
Aegean – in Nero's time the harbour was dredged, and in
Hadrian's the river was diverted, but to no effect, and eventually
the harbours were landlocked and filled, and now the coastline is
a delta three miles from the city, and there is nothing to suggest
that Ephesus was ever the greatest maritime trading centre in
western Asia, with a population of a quarter of a million.

The British have a considerable stake in this Wonder of the World. Xenophon, writing of the earlier temple not long before its destruction on the night of Alexander's birth (at which Artemis was said to be in attendance, and thus not at home in her shrine, and unable to protect it – how limited were the powers of the ancient pantheon), noted that the River Selinus flowed nearby, rich in fish. Selinus is not to be confused with Cayster, though the presence of two rivers so close may seem unlikely; Strabo said that Selinus was a lake near the mouth of the Cayster; Pliny the Elder, writing after the birth of Christ, records in his *Natural History* two lakes formed by the stagnant waters of the Selinus, and describes two rivers passing the Artemision, which had been built on marshy ground specifically to reduce the effect of earthquakes. Neither gives any particular clue to the precise whereabouts of the temple, which eventually disappeared altogether; this was left to another Xenophon, the author of a feeble romantic novel called the *Ephesiaca*, with scant literary merit but the virtue of a topographical account of Ephesus in which he says that the temple was seven *stadia*, or some 1,400 metres, from the city. This Xenophon is undated, and experts put him down as anything from the second to the fourth century AD, but the likelihood is that his account dates from before the Gothic destruction of the Artemision in AD 263. In 1863 the British Museum gave funds and support to John Turtle Wood, an engineer, to work for a year at Ephesus and nearby Colophon (a city famous for its horses and its constantly victorious cavalry, and remarkable for using squadrons of dogs in battle – if they in any way resembled the Karabaş of the Anatolian shepherd, a black-headed, rough-coated mastiff capable of despatching a wolf, they must in any number have been terrifying ememies). He had an official permit from the Ottoman government both to excavate and to export his finds to London. He found nothing of the Artemision in the first twelve months and the British Museum dropped him. He then turned to the easier option of the theatre, and in 1868 a British warship carried off a rich haul of busts, reliefs and inscriptions, one of which contained a clue to the position of the Artemision and led to the discovery of the perimeter wall built round it by Augustus, with, miraculously, another inscription identifying it. Six years of hard work were at last rewarded in 1869, when Wood found the temple under twenty feet of alluvial depoist – and not only the Wonder, but its predecessor, built for King Croesus. Wood's excavations there continued until April 1874. In 1904 and 1905 the British Museum sent Professor D. G. Hogarth (sometime mentor to Lawrence of Arabia and Kim Philby's father) to work on the site, and he claimed to have found traces of at least three temples before that of Croesus – other scholars argue that there was only one. Hogarth unfortunately kept no record of the pottery he found, for this would have given a more precise clue to dating than any other artifacts, nor where it lay. What Wood sent back from the Artemision – Ionic capitals nine feet wide, and huge fragments of column drums and piers decorated with life-size sculpture in high relief – gives some inkling of the scale and grandeur of the building (though appallingly displayed in the drab subterranean galleries of the British Museum, deprived of daylight), and explains Alexander's reaction. There are no relics of this Wonder in any other museum, and most of it must still lie deep under the Cayster's soggy silt, amid the mass of charcoal and fleeces that were the preliminary foundations in the marsh.

The city itself is a dry, climbing site. We entered through the eastern, Magnesian Gate, the high point of the city, contained within two lines of low hills. We had descended from the House of the Virgin, high in the line to the south, which I had not wanted to see again; on my first visit, almost barefoot in the August heat, I had all but trodden in a nest of vipers, hundreds of them, it seemed, black and squirming (black? – then not vipers, but the image in this context is too powerful to lose), and I still have one of those strange external sights of myself, frozen in the forward fall of a footstep, and saved from death by some agency not quite my own. St John the Evangelist (of the Cathedral at Selçuk) is often portrayed holding a chalice with a viper in it, apparently in memory of an accepted challenge from an Ephesian priest of Diana, to drink a cup of poisoned wine. Pope Paul VI came to the Virgin's House in 1967, and the once deserted and unrewarding site of a building of the size and character of a cattle shed (in memory of Bethlehem, perhaps), and of no particular antiquity, is now fenced and gated, with a Jandarmerie, a tea-house, lavatories, innumerable papal ephemera, and the notice 'Defendu de PIQUE-NIQUER' – so great must be the summer crowds that no vipers could remain.

The Blessed Virgin Mary, according to apocryphal but canonical tradition, died in Jerusalem at the age of sixty-three and was briefly buried in Gethsemane – briefly, because she too was bodily resurrected, but in full view of the Apostles, to whom she just had time to throw her girdle as her upward flight began. She left in her tomb an 'exceeding sweet fragrance', which is the explanation of the flowers that so often spring from it in Renaissance paintings. Renaissance painters always treated her death as sleep, and the references are invariably to the Dormition of the Virgin; Caravaggio caused double offence as much by painting her well and truly dead and not sleeping as by using the body of a murdered prostitute dredged from the Tiber as his model. There is no scriptural evidence for any of this, or for the rival tale that Mary came to Ephesus with St John the Evangelist – but St Paul, when he began his peripatetics in Asia Minor, found Christian churches already established there, and it is more than possible that St John had preceded him, justifying the tag Evangelist always attached to his name when not Divine. It is only St John's Gospel, significantly, that records the touching moment of Christ's giving his mother into John's care – 'Woman, behold they son . . . behold thy mother.' If they stayed together, 'and from that hour the disciple took her into his own home', it may be reasonable to assume that Mary accompanied John on an unrecorded journey to Ephesus of which we know only from tradition – but then if that is true, the house of the Virgin must also have been John's house, and it seems pointless for an evangelist to have lived some six kilometres of long zigzags up and away in the hills to the south of the Magnesian Gate. But then there is Catherine Emmerich's vision to explain. This invalid German lady (1774–1824), confined to her bed for twelve years, who had never travelled beyond the bounds of her native Bavaria, had a vision of the Virgin's house on a mountain overshadowing Ephesus, and her tomb a mile or so away from it. In 1891, following her directions, the Superior of the Lazarists of Smyrna discovered that on 15 August every year the local Orthodox Greeks made a pilgrimage to the dilapidated foundations of what has now been restored as the House of the Virgin to commemorate her Dormition, apparently accompanied by the local Muslims, who also revered her as the mother of the Prophet Jesus. It would be rash to jettison the evidence of such a tradition, maintained through many generations and in spite of the decay and decline of Ephesus, and the absence of any nearby city to replace it. The fourth Ecumenical Council of Ephesus in 431 confirmed the Virgin's title as 'Mother of God', and quickened

her status as a subject of veneration – Ephesus' concern may have
been for a sometime local resident, or the commercial pressures to
find a reason for local pilgrimage may have played a part. The
Roman Church lagged in these matters, and did not concern itself
with the Virgin's Bodily Assumption until the end of the seventh
century, and did not proclaim it dogma until November 1950.

The other charming Ephesian tale is that of the Seven Sleepers,
young Christian men who left the city so as to avoid a compulsory
sacrifice in the temple of the Emperor Decius, who had come to
Ephesus in AD 250 or thereabouts to give Christians the choice of
that sacrifice or death. The seven had made one refusal and had
been given a second chance, to which their response was
the dispersal of their worldly goods among the poor, and flight
to a cave on nearby Mount Pion, about a kilometre from the
Magnesian Gate, from which the city derived its inexhaustible
store of marble. Decius found the cave and had its mouth closed
with masonry and stones so that the seven might die of starvation. Three hundred and sixty years later, when Theodosius
was Emperor, there developed a heresy denying the resurrection
of the dead; by chance, an Ephesian building a stable on the
mountain made use of the stones blocking the sleepers' cave, and
they awoke, as young and spirited as ever, and thinking that they
had slept only one night, one of them, Malchus, went down into
the city to buy bread. He was astonished to find a cross over the
Magnesian Gate, and over every other gate of the city. He then
attempted to buy bread, but his coins were three hundred and
seventy-seven years old (Jacobus de Voragine, the teller of this
tale, was, like all apocryphers, a stickler for detail) and he was
immediately arrested as the thief of buried treasure and dragged
through the streets to the Governor, who also happened to be the
local Bishop and a local saint, Martin (though I find him in no
hagiography, and he was certainly not the Martin who shared his
cloak with a beggar). There followed an utterly predictable inter-
rogation, with Martin at last recognizing some divine element in
the story and rushing with half the worthies of Ephesus to find
the other six sleepers 'with their faces fresh and blooming like
roses'. When the Emperor Theodosius went to have a look at
them, they told him that they had been resuscitated before the
day of general resurrection so that he might believe more firmly in
that dogma, and promptly died. Of the three emperors Theodosius, it was probably the first that they had to convince – the third,

who was Emperor for only a matter of months in 716–17, was no more than a paymaster to a rebellious Byzantine army; the second was amiable, inefficient, and died when he fell off his horse, though he did endow the university of Constantinople in 425, and hold the Council of Ephesus in 431. Theodosius I, the Great, was Emperor from 378 to 395, and a stout Christian who did much to tidy up the faith, particularly with the great Council of Constantinople in 383, and persecuted harshly those whose beliefs did not in every detail tally with his own – moreover, St Martin of Tours was his contemporary. Jacobus de Voragine had scant regard for chronology, and one commentator describes his tales as 'puerile' – if the characters he enlists have any historical foundation, then his dates are sadly wrong and the sleepers slept much less.

But it was an old tale. Muhammad adopted it for the Koran, with the endearing embellishment of the sleepers' dog, Kratim or Kratimer, endowed with the gift of prophecy, and admitted to the Muslim paradise, along with Jonah's whale, Solomon's ant, Ishmael's ram and the Queen of Sheba's ass. I find it comforting that there is a precedent for the bodily resurrection of dogs, and the recognition of the canine soul – I don't want to have to argue with St Peter after my lonely years in Purgatory. The sleepers are not alone in their long snooze; Endymion was perhaps the first – of whom more at Heracleia under Latmus – and Pliny told the story of Epimenides, who slept in a cave for 57 years and napped enough to last for 289; Siegfried, Charlemagne, Barbarossa, Brian Boru, William Tell, are all waiting in their mountain retreats for some call to arms; and St John the Divine, according to St Hippolitus, entombed himself at Ephesus, not dead but sleeping, having escaped unfried the martyrdom in a cauldron of boiling oil attempted by the Emperor Domitian. The most recent sleeper is the priest who celebrated mass in Santa Sophia as the Turks sacked Constantinople; as they burst into the great church he called on God to protect the Host from profanation, and the wall behind the altar opened and the priest with his chalice and paten were drawn into it, never to be seen again; thus the Sacrament is safely reserved in perpetuity in what became a cathedral of the Muslim faith, guarded by the sleeping priest. The Seven Sleepers have some slight connection with English history; they were supposed always to lie parallel on the same side, and to turn only when some great disaster was about to occur; Edward the

Confessor at his last Easter paid little attention to the feast of boiled baby or whatever delicacy they set before him, but mused and brooded in silence, and then broke into sudden laughter – he told Earl Harold that he had seen the Sleepers, boys of extraordinary beauty, turn in unison onto their left sides. Harold promptly sent a knight, a priest and a monk to Ephesus to see, and on entering the cave they found that the Sleepers were indeed on their left sides, and the local Bishop confirmed that for the past two hundred years they had been on their right. None of the authorities concerned mentions the prophetic dog, but by the time the knight, the priest and the monk returned to England, Harold was about to lose his new throne to William the Conqueror.

As for Ephesus on a late December afternoon, the light golden and the shadows soft, empty of people, it was not at all as I remembered it, but it still required from me a prodigious (and unsuccessful) effort to see it as a living city. Charles Fellows was downcast about it too in 1838 – 'one cannot but feel disappointed at not seeing realised all the ideas associated with it . . . memory of the past may perhaps have led [visitors] to indulge too freely their imagination whilst contemplating the few silent walls that remain'. Ayhan, not yet aware of our methods and the idiosyncracy of our tastes, assumed that we would only walk briskly down the main street, and decided to take the car to the further, Coressus, Gate, bidding us not to miss the antique public lavatory. Petter and I sat there, talking about St Paul; it is well preserved, a square room with pierced marble benches against the walls and comfortably large holes through which to drop one's waste into the channel of running water (running then, not now) well below; under foot there is what I take to be a drip drain. Privacy was presumably supplied by the amplitude of the toga, but it cannot have been easy to preserve dignity while suffering any of the conventional mishaps of the bowel, and it reminded me of embarrassing dawn conversations with senior army officers in the bucket-and-pole field latrines in the days of my National Service, and Charlemagne's complaint that riding-cloaks imported from England were too short to offer privacy when he was about this kind of business.

St Paul's first visit to Ephesus was short, and for yet another argument with the Jews in yet another synagogue (the notion of the wandering Jew spreading through the civilized world as a punishment for the Crucifixion of Christ is nonsense – they were hither and yon long before that, and must have been more easily convertible than any pagan). He was on his way to Jerusalem from Corinth where he had spent eighteen months in dispute with the local Jews, and had in the end so angered them that they dragged him before the local Roman Governor of Achaia in the hope of getting rid of him, but he, Pilate-like, found their dispute a matter of Jewish law and would give no judgement. After his departure from Ephesus the proselytizing was continued by Apollos, an Alexandrian Jew, who seems to have been altogether more tactful, so that when Paul eventually returned after a journey across Anatolia and along the Black Sea coast ('I am constantly astonished by the extent of his travels – see Acts 18.23 and 19.1), the mood of the Ephesian Jews was less hostile, and twelve Christian converts awaited baptism and the consequent gift of tongues. There followed three months of dispute in the synagogue, and two years of it in the Gymnasium of Tyrranus, with the usual miracles and cures, and even the burning of contrary books. The conversion of Greeks as well as Jews made inroads into the tourist traffic to the shrine of Diana, and the silversmiths of Ephesus, manufacturers of votive offerings and other knick-knacks, began to lose trade; they whipped up a riot against Paul, seized his companions Gaius and Aristarchus, and dragged them to the theatre for a protest meeting – but the crowd that gathered, though it was induced to spend two hours shouting 'Great is Diana of the Ephesians', had no idea why it was doing so, and eventually drifted away. Paul the while took the advice of friends and went nowhere near, but immediately slipped away to Greece. On yet another return journey to Jerusalem he deliberately bypassed Ephesus, protesting haste to be in the Holy Land for Pentecost, but he stopped nevertheless at Miletus, just down the coast, and sent messages to Ephesus that the elders should come to him there – much more time-consuming than disembarking at Ephesus himself; when they came, they were treated to a characteristic mixture of exhortation and sanctimonious self-adulation, a mode continued in his tedious epistle to them (abjuring fornication and jesting and wine, and recommending the submission of wives and servants that was part of law in this country well into this century), but nevertheless they wept when they put him back on his ship. It was on that journey that a young man was so bored by one of

Paul's open-air sermons that he fell fast asleep and tumbled to his death from a third-floor window; Paul, it has to be said, in a moment of uncharacteristic generosity restored poor Eutychus to life with an embrace.

Our notion of early Christian proselytizing is largely formed by the records of Paul in the Acts of the Apostles, but there is another book of Acts – those of St John the Evangelist. So much of this Greek apocryphal treatise, compiled towards the end of the second century, is connected with events in Ephesus that Ephesian authorship is almost certain. It paints a pretty picture of Christ's gentlest apostle in hell-fire mood, finding too slow the business of conversion with miracles of healing, and storming the great Temple of Artemis with the cry, 'Oh God . . . let the Demon that is here take flight in thy name' – at which the altar exploded in shards and half the temple collapsed. The watching Ephesians fell flat on their faces, tore their clothes in shreds (the traditional Greek gesture of grief and anguish), knelt in prayer, fled, or took up the cry, 'There is but one God, the God of John . . . now that we have seen thy marvellous works we are converted. Have mercy on us, Oh God, and save us from our great error.' It was in Ephesus that John and Paul usurped the classical tradition that worshippers should, if not convinced by reasonable faith, be threatened with the terrifying power of the divinity they preached, and, if necessary, be struck blind or dead by it. It was the stick and carrot of conversion, the kill or cure, that continued still in the nonconformist churches in my childhood, cruel in their contrast with the kinder tolerances of Catholicism.

There is no known trace of Paul's synagogue, nor of the Gymnasium of Tyrranus, and there is no reason to assume that he used the public lavatory – but it is an irreverent thought for those who, like H. V. Morton, seek to travel reverently in his footsteps. Perhaps not much of Pauline Ephesus remains – the three ident-ifiable gymnasiums date from the end of the first and second centuries; the theatre took seventy years to enlarge to a capacity of 24,000 and must have been chaotic throughout Paul's time; the baths were enlarged and restored in the fourth century (by Scholastica, a Christian lady who systematically despoiled the temple of Hestia Boulaea to supply the additional materials and columns, thus destroying the sanctuary of the city's eternal flame and its political centre; ironically, she left untouched or perhaps even sanctioned the inclusion of the brothel in her nexus, and incorporated in the façade the temple of Hadrian, an elegant and refined little building with pretty Corinthian columns – the complex was an odd combination of official religion encouraging loyalty to the State, with baths in which the discussion of philosophy was at least as important as bathing, and the machinery of that very random fornication forbidden by St Paul). The most remarkable building in Ephesus, the Library of Celsus, dates from the second century; there was a time when this resembled the work of a demented pastry-cook whose wedding-cake had been demolished by a misdirected bull, but work on the library is now almost finished, and the building makes sense as a Vitruvian design with a hint of Westbourne Grove about it. Austrian archaeologists have been working in Ephesus off and on since 1884, and the reconstruction is theirs – even the cranes bear Austrian names. I cannot quarrel with the general concept, but its bold statement of Vitruvian grandeur is more than slightly absurd with tilted horizontals and wayward verticals, and the whole façade has a heavily dog-chewed look about it, but then the site is full of starving dogs – five tiny bitch puppies at the Magnesian Gate, and a countless mixture of old dogs and puppies at the lower end of the city, all ribs and hunger; a gentle little black bitch near the library stood pleadingly by a waste bin, and I rummaged in it for a chocolate cake – nothing more substantial, and, thank Heaven, nothing foul.

The light faded fast and early, the hills to the south throwing a long shadow over the city. Ayhan, mystified that we could take so long to reach the car, blundered into the library forecourt, and hustled us, surprised to find us flat on our backs staring up at the façade. I have suffered so long the aches of that crooked condition dubbed 'fresco neck' that I now seize every chance to lie on my back when spending a long time examining a painted ceiling or a high building close to. It is a good position to be in when someone is mildly cross with you, for if you refuse to feel ridiculous and continue prone about your purposes, then the verbal assault fizzles out. It worked with Ayhan, whose measure was becoming apparent – he had in his leather handbag a schedule of dates, times, places, even the restaurants in which we should lunch, and he meant to keep to it; our wishes and purposes were irrelevant in the face of a bureaucratic missive that bore little resemblance to the list of sites that I had submitted to the Turkish authorities. None of these was particularly inaccessible, but I had

expected in midwinter that working sites might be closed, and
the company of an official amanuensis from the ministry might
open them; I had not expected to be guided or informed or
scheduled, but merely kept out of trouble caused by some innocence of language or some gentle trespass; I did not expect to be
the victim of a programme, and I would not be hurried. Haunted
by some erroneous recollection of the architectural styles invented by Osbert Lancaster, 'Late Wedding Cake' and 'Early
Water Closet' (the latter literally true of Ephesus), we eventually
left for Kuşadasi, the light almost gloaming. Richard Chandler in
1764 wrote lucidly of the theatre, odeum, and other buildings,
describing the Temple of Serapis as a 'prostrate heap', but he left
the city in an elegiac mood that I much prefer to my own – for him,
Ephesus:

> . . . was a ruinous place when the emperor Justinian filled
> Constantinople with its statues, and raised the church of St.
> Sophia on its columns [almost certainly not true]. Since then it
> has been almost quite exhausted. Its streets are obscured and
> overgrown. A herd of goats was driven to it for shelter from the
> sun at noon; and a noisy flight of crows from the quarries
> seemed to insult its silence. We heard the partridge call in the
> area of the theatre and of the stadium. The glorious pomp of its
> heathen worship is no longer remembered; and Christianity,
> which was there nursed by apostles, and fostered by general
> councils, until it increased to fulness of stature, barely lingers
> on in an existence hardly visible.

He conjures a Claudian mood, *et in Arcadia ego*, that I would
willingly exchange for the sanitized ruin of today with as much
mystery as Oxford Street and the Champs-Elysées, and the same
polyglot summer crowds.

— III —

Priene * Miletus * Didyma

Ayhan drove at speed into Kuşadasi and lodged us in an hotel that might have been a refugee from the Costa Brava. We walked in the dark in search of sights, sounds and smells, but found nothing native left in this deserted holiday town – apart that is from dogs and kittens in the usual half-starved state. Why dogs continue to give their loyalty and affection so unquestioningly to the human race is beyond my understanding. We found Ayhan distinctly mellow back in the hotel, smoking his pipe and halfway through his umpteenth raki (I made the mistake of paying for them) – the petulant bully of Ephesus had quite disappeared and I thought my judgement mistaken until he insisted on taking a table in the restaurant that was within arm's length of the 'Turkish music'. It was my turn to be petulant. The 'Turkish music' came from a Japanese electronic piano with switchgear that produced drums, cymbals, oboe and a host of unidentifiable sounds, amplified to the last painful and damaging decibel; I left Ayhan and made for the most distant corner, and was still deafened. I could see Petter explaining to him; and eventually, clutching his handbag to his belly like a hot-water bottle, he relented and came to sit with us and blow smoke at us. It was Saturday night and the few other diners were local Turks in Hammersmith Palais mood; a fat girl in a tight white sweater was almost belly-dancing, the rapid quiver of flesh hardly concealed by the fabric, but an irredeemably plain girl was almost made beautiful by the elegant waving gestures of her tiny hands and lateral neck movements – not to what I understand to be Turkish music, but to modern pop given an oriental gloss by this far-eastern monster.

Sunday was a grey day. A fierce wind had blown rain from the sea all night, there were deep puddles everywhere, and the sputter of drizzle on the screen as we drove past the holiday villages that lie between the road and the sea. Once one of the most beautiful stretches of coast road, with wide deserted bays of warm shallow water, it is now littered with holiday encampments, some of unspeakable meanness, others so discreetly hidden under spreading pine-trees that only close to can they be seen. There are still moments of romantic beauty – silhouetted cypresses, silver seas, the bamboo huts of fishermen an acceptable *japonaiserie* against the mountains across the bay, and the loneliness of a single fishing-boat in a vast expanse of water under a great dome of broken cloud and shafting sunset; I quite see why the German presence is so heavy here in summer, for it could well have been designed by Böcklin.

Priene, however, could have been designed by Metro-Goldwyn-Mayer, and the great tumble of its temples down the steep hillside would have given pleasure to any cinema buff in the age of the spectacular as the fluted column drums rolled like enormous liquorice allsorts, making mincemeat of the extras in their path. It is a small city, Greek rather than Roman, nestling under a towering rock that forms the acropolis; this was so inaccessible, even to the goat-footed ancients, that garrison commanders were, like lighthouse-keepers, forbidden to leave it during their terms of office of some four months at a stretch. There is now nothing much left of the garrison buildings, but the spectacular view over the plain towards the Latmus mountains makes the heady climb worthwhile. Chandler describes it accurately as 'steep, high, naked rock' which he descended 'avoiding as much as possible the frightful view of the abyss beneath us, and shrinking from the brink'. Laconic George Bean says only that 'the path is not exactly dangerous'. I felt like an unstoppered bottle upside down. The city below this rock is still high above the plain that now lies below it – this is mud from the Maeander that has banished the sea and covered all trace of the harbour, as well as of the earlier city that, like Ephesus, dated from the time of King Codrus, some thousand years before Christ. Alexander arrived in 334 BC on his way south from Ephesus and found the new temple of Athena unfinished – his offer to defray the building expenses was more successful here, and his dedication was made on the temple wall. Under the Romans the city fell into a decline, largely because its harbour became useless – Strabo, bridging from BC into AD, found the sea already forty stades away (a stade, according to the Latin dictionary I had at school, is precisely 606¾ English feet), and in the past two thousand years the Maeander, aided by the shifts in level caused by the great earthquake of AD 17, has stretched those eight kilometres to thirteen; even so, Priene survived into Byzantine times, and there is the messy ruin of an unremarkable church whose poky ground-plan abuts the proscenium of the theatre, and some defence earthworks thrown out to incorporate rocky outcrops.

It was a planned city, with streets on a regular grid pattern ignoring the steep slope of the site, occupying the whole of the available ground and with no room for expansion. Patrice Bonnet in 1911 made some remarkable reconstruction drawings of it, introducing the smoky romanticism of Piranesi to the logic of the street plan, with a swirl of light on the acropolis hill, and a swirl of currents in the water below. The theatre, I have to confess, seemed just another theatre, apart from the five handsome marble thrones of honour spaced at wide intervals in the front row of seats – lonely places from which to watch a performance, for they isolate the sitter from his neighbours, and lonelier still in some disputation – the slaughter of wild beasts and Christians can never have been on the agenda here. It has the reputation of being one of the best surviving examples of a Hellenistic theatre, with a *cavea* that is more than a semicircle, and only minor Roman interventions. In the western corner of the orchestra is a water-clock, of which only the base remains, and whose operation and function are obscure – theatrical performances were never limited in length, so the obvious conclusion is that speeches could be timed when the theatre was in use for disputations or as a court of law. Whatever the case, the object itself is of no aesthetic interest. The cushioned ashlar rustication of the walls supporting the temple of Athena, however, gave me great pleasure; why one should derive pleasure from a well-built wall I cannot explain, but these matching blocks, swelling amidships and trimmed smooth a ribbon width at the edges, are as neat and pleasing a piece of workmanship as I have ever seen. The temple itself was totally fallen in Chandler's day, but five of its Ionic columns have now been re-erected, and we caught them at one of those moments when nature plays at theatre, flooding them with brilliant sunshine when all about was leaden with cloud. Ayhan was anxious to move on and broke in with some rigmarole about 'narthex'. Now a narthex to someone like me is part of the western end of an early church, in some way set apart for women or penitents, but we were some distance from the ruins of the Byzantine church and Ayhan's sudden interest in it seemed misplaced and mistimed. But he had the advantage of me, for narthex is also the name of a plant, and this I did not know. He pointed to a desiccated spiky bush and told us that if he set fire to one of its twiglets, the spark would char its way inexorably down to the roots without ever bursting into flame. He tried with his lighter, and failed. Petter tried with matches, and failed. I was still in the mood to pay attention to Ayhan and sensed that his reputation was at stake in this matter – and we wasted many minutes looking for a more sympathetic narthex that would agree to char. We failed. But Ayhan had succeeded in his main object of breaking our concentration, and he began to chivvy us back to the car.

The ground was littered with wild lilies, asters, hyacinths, cyclamen, and carnations of such intense pink that only their minute size and the delicacy of their serrated petals prevented their having an Indian vulgarity, as well as those plump pink daisies that clump the borders of English cottage gardens; all were humming with bumble-bees, and seemed in mid-winter to be as mysterious and astonishing as any ruin. Even the huge hornets built like flying football socks that I remembered mobbing the fountain in midsummer were about their business, though without aggression. Below us the watery plain was laced with reflections, and it was not so difficult to imagine it as sea lapping at the harbour walls – indeed the orchard just below was under a foot of water or more, as we discovered when we tried to take photographs as though approaching the city by sea. In the far distance lay Lake Bafa, glistening, and the Latmus Mountains, flat and soft grey against the light.

On the long straight road across the marsh, drained by trenches and the many streams of the Maeander delta, we stopped to talk to a party of wild-fowlers – it was Sunday, the day when Turks, like Italians, take to the wilds and pot-shot at anything and everything. These dark-skinned moustachioed marksmen were as comprehensively equipped as any in the Essex marshes, even to the green wellies, but lacked a dog. Long-haired sheep drove past, their brilliant dye-marks streaming like pennants, with two amiable lumbering hounds that sat and panted near our feet – the right size for the Colophon canine legion, but not the temperament. A woman in flowered trousers disembarked from a small boat, carrying a newborn lamb comfortably against her ample breasts and a large white hen uncomfortably by its bound legs, and set off into the distance, though there was no sign of habitation; Turks seem always to appear from nowhere and to go nowhere, walking distances that would be unthinkable to Europeans.

Miletus lies in the centre of the plain, its great theatre rising like a moored liner in a calm sea. At first glance it seems to be the only ruin, its rows of seats open to the visitor as arms of welcome. William Pars, travelling with Chandler, painted a view of it from the same approach, with a river, wide as the Thames in London, in the foreground, and their party being loaded onto a platform ferry that could be hauled across on a rope pulley. Of this broad stream there is now no trace. The sun was at an angle that bathed the theatre's hidden passages in reflected light, and Petter disappeared inside them to take 'interesting' photographs, but as I clambered up the seats a perfect 'V' of nine pelicans rose from behind the retaining wall and lazed away on a thermal, and I cursed the dappled golden glow that lost a record of their astonishing size and proximity, large as Icarus in flight, and silent. Some minutes later they returned, now raggedly urgent, the 'V' broken, and only seven in number – Mrs Beeton is useful on seagull and rook (early editions only), but has nothing to say about pelican; if they had to die, then I hope it was for the pot and not for sport, but I damned the moustachioed marksmen and their green wellies.

The theatre is topped by the ruins of a Byzantine castle, from the broken ramparts of which the extensive site can be read as clearly as a ground-plan, but the only other standing building of note is the very handsome bath complex built by Faustina, the prodigal wife of Marcus Aurelius, that antique goody-goody of high stoic principle. She had a reputation for faithlessness and intrigue as well as extravagance, yet she died while accompanying her husband on the long trek to the East begun in AD 175, only in her late forties, and in the thirty years of their marriage she bore him at least thirteen children. Correspondence between Marcus Aurelius and his erstwhile tutor Fronto suggests that his domestic life was full of simple joys – certainly the Faustina whom he deeply loved and as deeply mourned had not impressed her husband as the prototype of Lucrezia Borgia. As for her baths, these are so large and splendid that I cannot believe that they could even have been designed, let alone built, in the time that she was in Miletus – Marcus Aurelius was, after all, on his way to a campaign in Syria and Egypt; perhaps the Emperor arrived just as they were completed, and the association of them with his wife's name was a politic politeness. In the cold plunge not only are there still in place sculptures of a recumbent river god (the Maeander, no doubt) and an amiable marble lion (onto which every tourist clambers to be photographed), but some of the original white marble cladding with prominent jazzy red and black veins that make the baths in which Alma-Tadema's languid heroines cavort seem plain and pallid. The entrance wall to the caldarium contains blocks of a soft rich red aggregate with chips and slivers of marble and a glinting ore of steel grey.

Miletus now lies low in the Maeander's sea of mud, but it was once a jutting promontory (easily discernible from the top of the theatre) with four harbours, one of which, Ayhan assured me, was known as Alexander's – this is marked by a monument on the edge of a muddy excavation that may soon be reconstructed in the style of the Vittorio-Emmanuele Monument in Rome; the inscription suggests Augustus rather than Alexander, perhaps celebrating the Battle of Actium in 31 BC, perhaps celebrating nothing, for all that can be seen is a stone circle three steps high, topped by two large fragments of relief sculpture, one with a Plain Jane nereid, and the other a joyful thing of wriggling fishes and the serpentine tails of sea-monsters. Alexander was certainly in the city, which was inclined to support the Persians against him; having ingeniously captured its four harbours and periphery, he settled down to besiege its centre by slow conventional means, but within three days a Persian fleet some four hundred vessels strong arrived from Egypt. Fearfully outnumbered, Alexander merely blocked the harbours, and the Persians, hungry and thirsty, made for Samos and provisions. They made a second attempt on Miletus, but that too failed for want of food and water, and Alexander was left convinced that he had no need of a navy if ships could be so easily defeated from dry land.

The island of Lade rising from the plain is a reminder of a naval battle that did take place. In 499 BC the cities of Ionia banded together to expel their pro-Persian tyrants – the idea was promoted by Aristagoras, himself the tyrant of Miletus, and who remained its tyrant when all the other cities became democracies. Five years later Darius arrived from Persia with a great naval force and defeated their combined fleet in the shallow waters near the island, set up siege engines and captured Miletus – it was the beginning of the Persian Wars that still make Darius and Xerxes household names for even the half-educated English, for Athens had played a supporting role in the Ionian revolt and Darius was bent on vengeance. The early Greek dramatist Phrynicus, none of whose work survives in more than fragments (but who was the first tragic poet to write a female role – played by a man behind a woman's mask), wrote a tragedy called *The Capture of Miletus*, moving so many of his Athenian audience to tears that he was fined for presenting too vivid a reminder of the dreadful fate of their ally.

Ayhan, who knew the site well, led us from market-place to market-place – all four, all flat. I knew the beautiful market gate in the drab light and living death of the museum in East Berlin, an almost baroque fantasy of *aediculae* centred on a massive broken pediment, far more exciting than the library of Celsus in Ephesus, taken to Prussia by Wiegand and Knackfuss in the early years of this century – to that I had responded with awe and anger, for without it the broad city of Miletus has nothing to rouse a response from the soul. There is a point with old paintings, ruined as a rule by restorers, when further work becomes pathology; the work of the modern archaeologist is never so damaging, and when they are first in the field with all their modern skills and diligence I feel a moral duty to be enthusiastic – but what can one say for earlier archaeologists who stole the picture and left the frame, who reduced Miletus to a mile of mud and not a single standing stone? Without the sea that made it important, Miletus, lacking the dramatic prominence of Priene, seems as a site rather boring, and the tourist who dismounts only for a quick clamber in the theatre or to conjure mischievous visions of luxury in the baths is to be forgiven. But he should make one more small effort.

In the south-western corner of the site is a marble mosque; this
was in use in Chandler's day and he describes it as 'a noble and
beautiful structure' – as indeed it is. When I first saw it in 1975 it
had recently been restored, and its condition was not far short of
its state in 1404, when it was built by Ilyas Bey, its heavily-veined
cladding of marble (never arranged in matching slabs as in Santa
Sophia) gleaming in the sun, but in 1985 weeds long-rooted
between the slabs were hanging in draggled tatters, their new
growth springing from the dead, and the pretty tiled dome was
all but lost under a ramshackle bonnet of creeper and birds' nests.
The lintel, merely out of true ten years ago, had slipped aslant, all
gloss had faded from the marble, in and out, water lay on the floor
and the pierced marble window lattices were broken; the mihrab,
and the squinches making the transition from the square chamber
to the circular dome were still undamaged. The dome has a
curious echo, devastating to the refinements of Oxford or
Edwardian speech, for while most sounds are reduced to mere
reverberance, sibilants are sharply accented, peppering conversation with a wren-like diminuendo 'ts, ts, ts' long after the
utterance of the offending original. The real wrens are among the
hatted gravestones outside, but for many minutes I was convinced that they infested the dome – they do not, and there are no
droppings.

At Didyma we paused for lunch – a mistake, for we were
already very late, and winter afternoons can be deceptively
brilliant with light at one moment and almost dark the next, so
rapidly does the sun sink. There were friendly dogs to greet,
almost starving, the kitchen welcome and the choice of bass so
small that they ought to have been thrown back into the sea. (I
said so, and found myself faced with polite incomprehension –
what indeed is the point of telling a simple waiter about the
conservation of fish stocks, and then eating the subject of your
rebuke?) Ayhan fussed over the state of the table; they brought a
clean cloth. He complained of the cutlery, and better was
brought. He told them that we were important journalists and
must be given special attention – they rightly looked sceptical
(Turkish journalists are immaculate and have an air of importance), and I immediately denied, as I always do, any connection
with the fourth estate, but the concept of art historian was beyond
Ayhan, and my argument with him undermined the status that
he was so busy establishing with the waiters. It was my first

glimpse of him as a bully; he was stiff with opinions (so perhaps am I) and demanded from us their whole-hearted acceptance. At first I had no objection to going through the motions of agreement, occasionally suggesting that there might be other views or interpretations of equal value, but in the end Petter and I would let him make his outrageous statements and just leave them hanging in the air unanswered, an invisible barrier with which he unknowingly excluded us, and behind which we could shelter and talk between ourselves until in puzzlement he would make a more temperate approach. What both of us found intolerable was his making every meal a misery with his constant bullying of waiters, until we found ourselves in alliance with them, winking and making faces behind his back.

We waited for our bass with a bottle of white wine the colour of jaundiced urine and, I imagine, much the same taste, labelled Doruk, which means either the peak of a mountain, or limpid; in achievement and appearance it was neither. An army jeep skidded to a halt outside and noisily disgorged a fat major. He came into the restaurant and was immediately given a great flurry of attention – all that Ayhan had achieved with complaint was achieved by him with silence – but after two minutes at his table he erupted with unaccountable rage and left, slamming the door. Our waiter immediately removed our dish of bread as though punishing us for it, and then stripped the major's table as though to remove all trace of his brief presence. When the bass at last arrived they were so shrunken and desiccated in the frying that they could be eaten as biscuits, bones and fins and all but the heads. A dish of Bulgarian fetta followed – why they should take such pride in its origin I cannot imagine, for it was indistinguishable from Greek fetta and the white cheese that is inevitable in Turkish breakfasts, but it clearly gave them pleasure – perhaps a small reminder of Ottoman days when Bulgaristan was by no means a far-flung province.

The Temple of Apollo was across the road. Petter and I went to it alone, for Ayhan had found some minor problem with the car that he thought required urgent cure, and it was a relief to wander in so strange and haunted a building without his intrusive presence. The architect is by some said to be the architect of the Artemision at Ephesus (improbable); be that as it may, in scale and grandeur it gives a clear impression of a Wonder of the World, for it is vast, and though all but three of its columns fell in the great earthquake of 1493, their tall stumps are still in position, and the walls of the cella still stand as they originally were, unroofed. One of the huge standing columns is unfinished in the sense that it is unfluted apart from a neat collar of fluting extending halfway down the topmost drum below the capital – evidence yet again that columns were sometimes fluted after the erection of buildings. The visitor must climb steps to the entrance, make his or her way through the remains of the thirty-two columns that supported the porch – a strange experience in itself for the stumps are not cleanly broken but like snapped tree-trunks, and their bases are set so close as to obstruct passage, exclusive rather than welcoming – and then he must descend arched passages into the deep interior, which even in high summer seems unaccountably cool; here there still is a sacred spring, and there was once a grove or avenue of small trees leading to the shrine of Apollo, a *tempietto* within the temple, with the enchanting appeal of an enclosed garden – perhaps the first *hortus conclusus* that medieval Northerners found so necessary in their imagery.

It was known as the fountain oracle of Apollo before the Ionians came, and the first temple (of which there is no trace) was approached by a sacred way from the nearby harbour of Panormus, flanked with enthroned portrait figures from the mid-sixth century BC, some of which stayed in position for 2,400 years before they were removed to the British Museum by Sir Charles Newton in 1858, who, having robbed the site, then abandoned it to confusion. One of these is inscribed 'Chares, son of Kleisis, Ruler of Teichioussa' (another dependency of Miletus, a few kilometres to the south-east); another, less appealing, is signed 'Eudemos made me'; all were presumably members of the Branchidae, a noble Carian family descended from Branchos, whose name is occasionally used for Didyma. 'Didyma' is a relic of ancient Anatolian and has nothing to do with the Greek for twins, *didymi*, and is not a reference to Apollo and Artemis; it is possible that it derives from one of the alternative names for Cybele, the great mother-goddess of Anatolia, 'Dindymene' (though that in turn derived from Mount Dindymus in Galatia, where were her oldest sanctuary and earliest effigy – a stone said to have fallen from Heaven resembling a sculpture by Henry Moore), and that her cult preceded that of Apollo, but without a temple. It was certainly dedicated to Apollo long before 600 BC, and Croesus consulted the oracle in the matter of an invasion of Persia. He consulted several after testing their competence with a trick question that Didyma failed to answer – 'What is King Croesus doing at this very moment?', to which the correct answer was 'Boiling a lamb and a tortoise together in a cauldron'. This improbable stew must have been kept on the hob for weeks if Apollo at distant Delphi was to give the right answer, which indeed he did – but then he followed it with an ambiguous response to the important question of the Persian invasion, which Croesus took to be assent; he crossed the river Halys and was utterly defeated. Looking back on the Delphic answer, 'Croesus by crossing the Halys will destroy a great empire', the last king of Lydia understood that it was his own destruction that Apollo had foreseen. At Didyma Apollo went on working well into the Christian era, merrily answering theological questions, until finally silenced by the Byzantine Emperor Theodosius the Great and first with his Edict of 385. Theodosius also put an end to the Olympic Games, that had been run every four years without a break since 776 BC, as part of his stern and unsentimental suppression of an obstinate pagan rearguard – it was perhaps easier for him to destroy the ancient world for he was no Greek, but a Spaniard, made emperor of the East at a time when the Visigoths seemed invincible to the Romans, and the Ostrogoths were being pushed westward to join them by the invasions of the Huns; by a wry twist of history, Alaric, who sacked Rome in 410, was an Ostrogoth who had been a Roman general under Theodosius, and was still technically Commander-in-Chief of the Balkans. It was the Goths who precipitated the decline of Didyma; in AD 262 the temple was converted into a fortress to beat them off – Christianity put in the boot.

Chandler in 1764 was poetic about the site – 'the memory of the pleasure which this spot afforded me will not be soon or easily erased . . . so vast and noble that it is impossible perhaps to conceive greater beauty and majesty of ruin' – yet he saw only the pair of columns still linked by a fragment of entablature and the single unfluted column, and a great heap of fallen masonry and column drums completely covering the sunken sanctuary full of spoil. As there was no town or village near-by, the site remained unplundered until the excavations of English, French and German archaeologists, who carried off to London whatever was portable. In 1875 enough had been excavated for Albert Thomas, a young French architect, to attempt a reconstruction, though the cella was then still full of earth and rubble, and a windmill had been built on top of the spoil that covered the porch, rising to much the same height as the three standing columns. The site now is in the sort of condition that gives no inkling of the extent of the work done in the last century – grass grows in the sanctuary, and the only hint that the fallen columns have been tidied a little is in the brick supports that here and there prevent their drums from slipping into less elegant recumbence. It is a moody ruin, and the mood changes abruptly between interior and exterior; outside it is possible to lie full length across the stump of a column and not feel irreverent, but inside all frivolity is oppressed – the Edict of Theodosius is ineffectual and the visitor is silenced by instinctive reverence for some ancient haunting presence.

On the south side of the temple is the stadium, for which the temple steps doubled as seats. There is some trace of a starting gate for foot races, but its stones have been disturbed. We were trying to work out how they should be (not easy, for the three largest have recently been removed) when Ayhan returned, assuming, it seemed, that we had seen and done nothing in his absence. He dredged Ekrem Akurgal's book from his handbag (worthy and indefatigable scholarship, but morphetic prose) and began to read it aloud with declamation and gesture. 'Dipteros' is the term for the two rows of columns that surround the cella, and it was a word for which Ayhan had great affection, for he used it again and again – 'peripteros' (one row) was another war cry. We tried to distract him, but failed to break the flow; I was tired, suffering dreadfully from coffee-deprivation, began to giggle and could not stop; Petter immediately caught the infection, and there we were, helpless, almost rolling, tearful, and still Ayhan read on. We crept away and left him to it, immaculate in his tweeds and cap, spouting to the column stumps.

The road from Didyma to Miletus runs very close to the sea; with Jill and David in midsummer it had been littered with ambling tortoises which we had often stopped to remove to safety – the ancients believed that no weight was too great to be borne on the back of a tortoise, which is why Florentine Renaissance sculptors more often than not stood their tombs on them, but we had our doubts about their tolerating the impact of a Range-Rover at speed. Besides, I knew from the murderous jealousy of one of my bitches that the shell of a tortoise bleeds when damaged – my mother had rescued it from the path of a number nine bus in Castelnau (that would have been a true test of the ancient belief) but it had a better chance of survival there than in my garden with Gamage, who simply held it on its side between her forepaws and gnawed it to death – not even the most sympathetic vet can do much for a half-eaten tortoise. In December they must have been sleeping, but the road is now so developed that I doubt if they survive in any quantity. What had survived was one of the worst hotels I ever slept in, now decrepit and turned into a house. It was circular, with a central light well round which were gathered all the loos and showers, and the rooms were shaped like fat wedges of cake with the ends bitten off; the most discreet emptying of bladders sounded throughout the hotel, and the petomanic mishaps that occasionally accompany occupation of the loo not only thundered in the well, but with egalitarian principle perfumed every room. But swimming in the warm shallow water of the bay below was recompense for any horrors.

— IV —

Heracleia * Milas

Lashing rain had again been blown in from the sea all night. Chandler and Fellows, living in tents, comment often enough on the weather and its hostility, and I began to understand their concern; in the summer there are the problems of heat and insects, but in the winter, though it is not cold, the boisterous noise of the weather breaks into sleep. Not that sleep had come easily, for Sunday night too was devoted to celebration in our hotel in Kuşadasi, and the Japanese–Turkish music had into the early hours beaten and drummed its way through the reverberating concrete. *Musique concrète* indeed. Outside the town the olive trees were washed to silver, their glaucous leaves pale and clean, and the bare poplars fanned a curiously warm pink and yellow screen of twigs against the dark ground of other trees, or against the darker sky. A bare poplar in a patch of pale sun can destroy all sense of aerial perspective, leaping forward in tone, and impossible to reproduce both correctly and believably in a painting. The road south crosses the Maeander and then follows the southern shore of Lake Bafa; the landscape changes abruptly from fertile plain to sub-Alpine, and the Latmian mountains are jagged and seem high. It is the end of Lydia and the beginning of Caria. The lake was once an inlet of the sea, the Gulf of Lade, but it is now another creature of the Maeander's silt,

closed, with a water level that is now much higher – and mark-
edly higher in winter than in summer. Chandler calls it Bafi,
and Fellows Baffy.

I asked Ayhan to slow the car and turn left down a path to the
lake that I knew we would reach almost at once; he replied that it
was not on the schedule and persisted at speed. 'Damn the
schedule, it's where I want to go.' And there it was. With an
explosion of rage on my part and an ill grace on his, he turned the
car and drove back to the path. 'It's too muddy.' 'No it's not.' We
sat there for a moment and then I got out with my knapsack and
strode down the path. Ayhan and the car followed. The object of
my interest was a tiny island just offshore that has the remains of
a group of Byzantine buildings on it. I had been there before, in
the heat of August, with Jill and David. Jill had been in her most
triumphantly St Trinian's mood, stomping all over the islands
with no regard for the lilies under her feet, checking the ruins
against a map published a hundred years before by some obscure
German – it was more checking stock against an inventory than
any aesthetic or visual enjoyment, and I had stripped off and
slipped into the water rather than be ill-humoured about it –
besides, at that stage, Byzantine art was no more than entertainment for me, and I could easily do without it (the passion came
later). I lazed on my back in the water among the moorhens, my
hat tilted over my nose (I always swim in a hat when the sun is
up), until Jill lumbered into view and shouted, 'There are eleven
Byzantine churches on this island, and I've seen them all' – it was
the signal to return to the Range-Rover and move on. The island
was then linked to the shore by a causeway; this time the
causeway was deep under water. Ayhan demurred. I threatened
to take off my trousers and wade – I was determined to see
for myself all eleven churches on this island the size of a tennis
court – but a fisherman appeared from a derelict tea-house
nearby, and offered his boat as a ferry. Ayhan agreed a price, and
the fisherman then did precisely what I had proposed to do, and
waded thigh deep to the island, for his boat was moored in its lee.
After much delay, Ayhan faffing over the damp seats and
concerned for his dapper raincoat, we all reached the island.

In winter, without the rich undergrowth that obscures them in
summer, the Byzantine traces are much easier to read, and I think
Jill and her worthy German were wrong; there is one very
beautiful apse-ended church, sans roof and dome, but with its

walls more or less intact, built of well-trimmed blocks of stone (presumably from a demolished classical building), with red-tile strips in the mortar, and the upper register, where the arches of the windows spring, in neat little red bricks; one or two of the other outlines may be the relics of hermit churches, and one large multi-aisled building in total disrepair is large enough to have served a community of considerable numbers. Perhaps the island housed just such a community – there is no other explanation of the large vaulted chamber that our ferryman called a cistern than that it was a dining-hall. He was concerned to show us three long stones set in a triangle in a low wall, for which I could offer no explanation other than that it might be a symbol of the Trinity (not an easy concept to explain to a Turkish peasant); Gian Domenico Tiepolo often gave triangular haloes to God the Father, but a connection between late-eighteenth-century Venetian painting and stones of unknown early date in wild Caria seems improbably tenuous. The island must always have been a holy place, for there are fragments of columns, both plain and fluted, and one that is both (perhaps once applied to a wall) with a long illegible Greek inscription inelegantly cut in its plain side; one large fragment of white marble, eroded and polished by water, appears to be drapery over a standing thigh. These are indications of a pagan shrine or temple before the Byzantines took over, and this may indeed be the island to which Chandler *waded*, noting it as walled (which it is), with a ruined church, and 'among the rubbish . . . a marble with a sepulchral inscription *Heraclides, son of Sotades, temple-sweeper to Hecate*'. Perhaps the temple was dedicated to this formidable minor deity, invoked in curses – there is a graffito in Ephesus, near the library of Celsus, that reads, 'He who urinates here shall suffer the wrath of Hecate' – and to whom young black bitches were sacrificed at night in graveyards and at crossroads. Medea, the witches in Macbeth, and all concerned with magic and enchantment are her servants. I paid her homage once by ordering a whippet in her name from Ian Lowe at the Ashmolean Museum – a blue bitch with blue eyes, blue nose and blue toenails, to be registered as Hecate; I had quite forgotten her when the telegram arrived – 'Hecate born last night. Delivery in eight weeks.' When she arrived she had only nine nipples, was no bigger than a rat, and for weeks I kept her like a ferret inside my jumper; she grew up to eat grapes and wire wool, and picked her own raspberries and blackberries without ever snagging a thorn. A very odd dog. As for Hecate's island, it all seemed sadly derelict and decaying, and the few standing walls unlikely to stand much longer – the damp rots the mortar, and now that the fishermen keep their stock of incestuous skewbald rabbits safe from predators there (grown plump on wild onions – no need for flavoured stuffing), the thrills of the chase mean much more wear and tear from their clambering than from the boots of the rare Byzantine tourist.

At the southern extremity of the lake a track leads to Heracleia under Latmus. All guide-books say it is fit only for a jeep, and Ayhan repeated the fiction. I replied that I had driven there ten years before, and that it was perfectly manageable in a car. He refused. I insisted. He refused again. 'Then we will walk.' It was beginning to dawn on me that the essential thing was to get Ayhan to stop the car, for I could then use my trump card of getting out. Ayhan begged and pleaded, saying that he was responsible for our safety, and then consulted a man walking towards us from the direction of Heracleia. This paragon gave the reply that I wanted and expected, and we all got back into the Renault, but after a hundred yards or so we came to a school, and Ayhan stopped again. 'I will go in and ask about the road.' He came out triumphant and said that it was deep in mud and impassable; before he could start the engine I leaped out and walked fast away. And in this stop-start progress (for he asked everyone we met on the way) we eventually got to Heracleia without the slightest hint of mortal danger. We were immediately surrounded by wild-fowlers with bundles of the sad corpses of moorhens, one of whom volunteered to be our guide – the others took off again in their boat, firing, it seemed to me, indiscriminately at any bird within range, with their dogs, mere mongrels, not professional brutes, barking furiously to be allowed to retrieve their successes – which they did, leaping hugely into the water with obvious enjoyment. There are moments when even I do not care for dogs.

I cannot explain the hold that Heracleia has; the cella of a small temple to Athena perched on a rock overlooking the lake, the grand Byzantine castle, the city ramparts running high into the wild hills behind, the Sir Walter Scottish air of the offshore island – all are fine romantic conventions for the traveller with an eye for ruins and landscape, but they do not make magic – that lies in the necropolis and the sanctuary of Endymion. The ancient

Heracleians hollowed coffin-size holes in the rocks by the water
and laid their dead in them under closing slabs. The slabs are not
so long gone, for many were still in place in Chandler's day when
it was noted that they were in the form of a low roof, gabled at
each end; then, as now, many of the tombs were under water,
and the smooth rocks have taken on the character of the old bones
that they once sheltered and look like giant jumbled skeletons
awash. Endymion's sanctuary is no more than a patch of grass
enclosed in a small and shallow apse of masonry bedded in and
linking three large rocks, behind three column stumps; when I
first stood in it I was held by some force or presence of such
unbearable sadness that I wept – I was alone, and not embarrassed to hunch on the grass and howl, but I was deeply concerned
by this brief possession, for possession it was – it was not my grief
that was purged, but my body had been used for the purging.
Nothing of this kind had ever happened to me before – though I
and my old dog Susie had felt oppressed in the stone circle of
Grey Weathers on Dartmoor (she shivered, then howled, then
ran, and I was glad to run after her), and I have felt a strange
constraint in places as far apart as Macedonia and Mentmore –
and when I got out of the sanctuary I looked back to see who had
used me, and in spite of seeing nothing made a small gesture of
farewell. One other thing puzzles me – in photographs taken
more than twenty years apart, the two small olive trees in the ruin
have grown not an inch.

There were two Endymions, both beautiful, of whom one, the
King of Elis in the Peloponnese, does not concern us; the Endymion of Latmus was a shepherd who, it is rumoured, slept naked
on the hillside and caught first the eye of Zeus (ever random in his
sexual interests) and then of Hera, his wife – odd to think of
Olympian divinities having *Bloody Sundays*. Zeus usually threw a
thunderbolt in such circumstances, but residual affection
tempered his rage, and he put the boy to perpetual sleep,
everlastingly beautiful. It was at this point that Selene, goddess of
the moon, caught sight of him, presumably still naked, and began
an affair that threw new moonlight on nocturnal emissions and
put her through the pangs of childbirth fifty times, bearing him
fifty daughters (there must have been something amiss with his
genes) without once waking him during the necessary coupling.
He should be remembered during the Olympic Games, as much
for this remarkable marathon as for his fifty daughters who came

to represent the fifty months between each set of Games –
certainly some active memorial of athletic congress might be more
widely amusing to spectators than many of the sports now
included. The tale is the earliest example of the ageless perpetual
sleeper (the Olympic Games were founded in 776 BC).

Chandler pitched his tent beside the market-place 'edged with
marble fragments', as it is still; the south side is supported by a
building divided into shops, in which the spacing of simple
regular blocks of stone and the intervals of windows and doors
provide rhythm and grandeur with remarkable economy, and a
suggestion of cornices and string-courses that is almost abstract.
On the further side is a new school; children, in their black and
white uniforms, were playing in the agora, and we trespassed in
search of their master. He maintained three classes in the one
large room, and had a tiny study for himself; the only visible
equipment was a very large map of the immediate locality
on which every village and track was clearly marked – more
useful than knowing the whereabouts of England and Norway.
Chandler's observation that the village was littered with marble
fragments of architecture and sculpture is still true, at least in part
– the sculpture has gone to museums and illicit traders, but
domestic hens still scratch among broken entablatures and the
drums of columns, and washing-lines run from column stumps
to olive trunks; new houses are perched on ruins, the earlier
foundations projecting here and there in backyards.

The promises of the old gods could not be kept under the new
contracts of Christianity; the Delphic oracle ironically uttered its
own epitaph in the reign of Julian the Apostate (AD 360–3) who
was trying to restore the ancient pantheon – 'Tell the king that the
splendid hall has fallen to the ground. Apollo no longer has his
dwelling, nor his prophetic laurel, nor his babbling spring; the
water of inspiration has ceased to flow.' With such a mood
abroad, it was time for ageless Endymion to die at last, but not
before dreary asexual Christian writers emasculated him by con-
verting him into a Carian mystic concerned to learn the true
name of God – and when he learned it from the moon, he died
and was entombed on Mount Latmus. Even then the Christians
would not leave him in peace, but annually opened his tomb and
disturbed his bones, for it was thought that one day the bones
would disclose the name – but all they ever did was to make a
strange humming sound, buzzing with anger no doubt (unless it

was the invention of Turkish music). But perhaps Keats was right – with a first line as famous as 'A thing of beauty is a joy for ever' who can recall the second – 'It will never pass into nothingness'?

Christians took over the mountain in much the same way as they took over Cappadocia, for it was ideal country for the hermit, the anchorite and small monastic communities, safe from Arab raiders from the coast tempted into the former gulf. Chandler puts it neatly, betraying Protestant prejudice – '. . . Heracleia became a holy retreat when monkery, spreading from Egypt towards the end of the fourth century, overran the Greek and Latin empires . . . a grand resort of fanciful devotees and secluded hermits, a nursery of saints, another Athos . . .'. Peasants had taken him into the mountains to see caves 'in one of the most wild and retired recesses imaginable', painted with episodes from the life of Christ, the heads of saints and bishops, the Virgin and a Christ Pantokrator; peasants now refused to take me (to Ayhan's great relief) – they claimed to know of these churches, but maintained that in the winter, the rocks wet, it was unsafe to climb to them, that indeed it was unsafe even to climb the remarkable city walls that rise to more than 1,500 feet up the mountain and run for more than six kilometres, broken by sixty-five towers, gates and posterns carefully socketed into the bedrock, with access stairs, windows and parapets. They were put there by Mausolus of Halicarnassus, who got the city in the fourth century BC and with Hellenistic zeal changed its name from Latmus (as it was known when it joined the Delian League in 478–477 BC to continue the naval war against Persia) to Heracleia, and thus one of perhaps as many as forty cities named after Hercules. *Lat* was the old Anatolian name for the goddess of the moon.

The Maeander cannot have closed the gulf completely until well into Imperial times, and how long it took to turn from salt to fresh water can only be guessed – but once fresh, the mosquito must have killed off the inhabitants who had survived its economic decline as a city cut off from the sea. It was the mosquito at least as much as earthquakes and war that put an end to all the cities within reach of the industrious Maeander.

We were offered more dead moorhens before our departure. They looked far more dead than most dead birds, their black plumage tattered with the blast of shot and their dying struggles with the mongrels, and most seem to have been retrieved alive and had their necks wrung. And they were wet. I have since found an English recipe for roasting them – perfectly conventional, for half an hour or so, basted frequently with butter. They are seasonable from October to March, and best, it seems, after the frosts have set in. The same book offers recipes for roast thrush (covered with buttered paper so as not to impair the delicate flavour), and for blackbird pie (halved, interspersed with hard-boiled eggs, seasonable in deep winter), and is, thank Heaven, long out of print.

Euromos is the perfect ruin for lazy guides. It is a single Corinthian temple standing in a wooded valley a mere hundred yards from the main road, and even in midwinter the track was dry. I had seen it many times, and had no wish to see it again; it is like one of Schubert's cooking songs, worth hearing once and then forgetting – but Ayhan would not let us forget. 'Perfection', he said, and drove to its foot. '*Peripteros, peripteros* – one row of columns', he cried. We pretended amazement, and clambered up the slope behind it to see if there were better camera angles, but the light was dim and the columns looked black. They look black in my old photographs too, and I cannot now understand why I once found it so beautiful, though Chandler describes it as 'noble'; in his day there were furnaces nearby for making lime and he neatly describes the melting away of the marble, but there were sixteen standing columns then, and there are sixteen now. A boy appeared from nowhere and pointed out inscriptions – Turks are convinced that all Europeans are interested in all inscriptions, and one must adopt a suitably reverential manner to great-aunt Jemima's gravestone if offence is to be avoided; but there is the chance that something of vital importance might be among them, though I have to admit that in ten years of attentive if jaundiced viewing I have found nothing and been shown nothing of any importance that was not already well-known; Chandler found no inscriptions at all, and even mistook the site for Labraynda. Some columns are not fluted, and we had the customary discussion as to whether columns were fluted before or after erection; all have a pronounced lean, and in my growing impatience with Ayhan I wished that I could give them a push – that would indeed have made a good photograph.

Milas was also on Ayhan's programme, but I urged him on,

content with recollection of the journey made with Jill and David. The diligent traveller will spend time in Milas, and with relaxation and some small effort may convince himself that the town is charming: it has old Turkish houses and winding streets, a handsome gate in a fragment of the city wall (Baltali Kapi) that once doubled as an aqueduct, only one standing Corinthian column from all the temples that once adorned the city, and a handsome free-standing Roman tomb called Gümüşkesen. This is a large *tempietto* of eight columns and four piers on a square podium, roofed by a low pyramid of blocks placed at angles to the blocks below, the interior ingeniously and elegantly coffered. The podium was a chamber for the ashes of the dead; in the open *tempietto* friends and relatives publicly celebrated anniversaries, and poured libations of wine and honey through a hole in the floor so that the departed might not feel excluded. But apart from these relics there is little to demonstrate the bustling town of Roman times, and it is what you see – a site continuously occupied since the days of King Mausolus that has constantly adapted and renewed itself, now burying its classical past under dual-carriageway boulevards and ugly concrete blocks. Chandler had hoped to find the temple dedicated to Augustus and the goddess Dea Roma, but it had only recently been demolished to provide marble for a new mosque; on the site itself a rich Turk had built a house incorporating six of the twenty-two columns that the temple was known to have had, but as the Turk also had a large harem, he would not give access to any member of Chandler's party – 'an obstacle not to be surmounted' as he glumly records.

To the south is a strange flat-topped hill, the Peçin citadel, some 700 feet high. Jill and David had driven up the dirt track to the top, while I had climbed on foot in search of walls, pursuing as vertical a line as possible through the brambles and vines, finding only an occasional block of trimmed masonry. It was August, and very hot, and I was torn and exhausted when I reached the top and found the others drinking tea with an ancient *hoca* and his very pretty young girl pupil in a cool Seljuk *medrese* dating from 1375. It is the sort of site that must have been occupied from the earliest times, for it is so easily defensible and has abundant water; Herodotus and Strabo record a great temple to Zeus on it, of which there is no trace – though when Chandler went to Paitchin, as he calls it, part of the fortress wall, then mounted with cannon, stood on a flight of marble steps that may have led to it. The re-use of Byzantine carved blocks by the Seljuks indicates early Christian occupation. If it was ever a city (and it could well have been like Sillyum, on a similar flat-topped hill near Antalya), desuetude came upon it when King Mausolus arrived with his grandiose plans for the redevelopment of all the cities under his wing, and the city of Milas was built in the plain below.

I have happier recollections of Jasus. Jill, David and I were in a mildly exhausted state when we reached Güllük and were lucky to choose an hotel that lay directly on the water's edge – indeed from my bedroom window it was possible to plop directly into the water. It was bleakly primitive, but the woman who owned it was a bustling motherly sort who cooked and cosseted with a grin, and her sons spent their time fishing and doling out raki. They had a liver and white pointer called Gümüs (Silver), that might have stepped from any hunting scene by Oudry, boisterous and busy with his snuffling, and to a dog-starved Englishman that was inducement enough to stay. When we were all stricken with a mild attack of Atatürk's Revenge, brought on, I suppose, by a stupid escapade in the blazing sun, we made it our base for a week or so.

Atatürk immobilized Jill and David on the day that we were to go to Jasus, but Dr Collis Browne's now forbidden Chlorodyne seemed to have defeated him for me. When the boatman arrived at the hotel, I was his only passenger, and we chugged off across the bay, the single-cylinder diesel engine reducing communication to grin and gesture. One of his large front teeth was gold, and, sitting against the light with his face dark mahogany in shadow, it had a lively glister that shattered the tonality – I spent most of the journey pondering how a painter might control this strange *contre-jour* effect, and, travelling backwards, all but missed the entrance to Jasus. It is now possible to drive there, but the sea approach is magically pretty, into a deep inlet past an island fort, with the city rising on a promontory on the right that is connected with the mainland by a narrow neck. We landed at a simple tea-house, and again I wondered at the financial viability of these establishments, often remote, and occupied by men of all ages who seem to have nothing to do and nowhere to go and to have come from nowhere, and who never seem to pay for their tea. I climbed away from it, up the steep rise, with growing

misgivings that quickly turned to misery – Atatürk had returned
to the attack, and Dr Collis Browne was in retreat. I had Bean's
book with me, mapped my path in it, and even had the temerity
to correct his plan of the city in some small particulars, but I have
no recollection of its theatre or agora, even though I have noted a
wide street connecting them. Nor have I any photographs, for my
Pentax had begun its long campaign of whimsical rebellion. One
thing is clear in my memory, and that is the discovery of a mosaic
pavement in a Christian basilica on the east side of the site;
stumps of porphyry columns drew me to it, and gentle kicking
aside of the earth and sand in one corner revealed intact mosaic. I
cannot have been the first to find it, and 'discovery' is a foolish
word to use – except that, as far as I know, it had not and has not
been published. It was small enough to clear in quarters and
photograph in detail (except that the camera's clicks were
meaningless), but the labour in the sun was exhausting, and
Atatürk's interventions added much to my misery. Finished in
more senses than one, I tottered down to the quay and was dosed
with sweet tea by the boatman.

It was Gerga that had undone us. Bean describes Gerga in such
a way as to make it irresistible to the ruin romantic – 'no place
more fascinating . . . a full day . . . mostly on foot . . . wild
mountain country'. We followed his instructions and set off from
the fine old bridge over the Çine river as an alternative to
'jumping from rock to rock across the stream at a point nearer to
Çine'. This was a fundamental error. There is indeed a path from
the bridge climbing gradually into hills that are grassy and openly
wooded with huge spreading pines – it fits comfortingly with
Bean's description of the approach, except that it is towards the
east instead of the north, and by some trick of geography, having
crossed the river you are on the wrong side of it. This we did not
realize until too late. After an hour and a half, with the trees
thinning and virtually no shade, Jill and David decided to return
to the car, but I obstinately plodded on, though had Bean's
directions been accurate we should have reached the site after an
hour or so. After more than two I found a small house and a
garden, with a woman who scuttled inside and shut the door. I
squatted in a patch of shade until she plucked up enough courage
and curiosity to come out again, but she had never heard of
Gerga, and after giving me water, told me how to find her
husband, who might know. On the hillside, he took some

finding, but he did know where Gerga was – on the other side of the river, and beyond the skyline hills.

Bean, skipping across the Çine from rock to rock, must have missed the confluence of two rivers downstream and found himself on the right bank of both. He compounds the confusion in his chapter on Alabanda by describing the river by its old name, the Marsyas, and the bridge as a fragment of the Alabanda aqueduct. But I was brave and foolish in those days, and the notion of wandering into the nearest village and finding a guide seemed lily-livered – and at that stage in my wanderings I had not recognized that in Turkey the word 'guide' does not mean something like the parrot-harridans who govern English country houses and the châteaux of the Loire, but simply a small boy who knows the way, or some ex-labourer for the last archaeologists on the site, or the local schoolmaster. The woman's husband did not offer to guide me – he had work to do in his little *bahçe* on the hillside – and I set off cross-country, taking a bead from a useful hill. The fall of the land grew steeper, and my useful hill disappeared; the river was wider, deeper and faster than I had expected, and the further bank was steep; the river bottom was eroded below the great boulders that seemed to offer assistance, and I could not use them for support without dropping suddenly chest-deep in the water; on the far side I could not get out, and I did not like the look of the climb ahead. I fell, and numbed my upper arm against a rock, and felt sick.

It was then that I decided to return to the others and take no more risks; already soaked, though somehow I had managed to keep my useless Pentax dry, I kept to the river, assuming that it would get me back to the bridge even if by a longer route, that I would not run out of drinking water, and that it would be cooler. It was cooler in the sense that I could stay wet, but there was no shade, the sun was unrelenting, and the rocks threw up as much heat as beat down. I had a vague misgiving that I had done too much and would be wise to find some shade and rest till evening, but that was countered by the thought of growing anxiety on the part of Jill and David. My notes are more telling than expanded prose – 'Hell of a day. Exhausted and ill with effort. River impossible to follow as an easy route – deep and rock-strewn, silted lumps looked temptingly like firm rocks, but sank underfoot. Black vulture, golden orioles, frogs, crabs and abundant fish.' Downstream, at the confluence of the two rivers, women were at their laundry and small boys were swimming, and it was then that I recognized Bean's misdirection.

Gerga was on my list of sites to see with Ayhan, but he refused, and my previous experience suggested that he was perhaps right to do so in midwinter, though for different reasons. But I am still torn by Bean's description of it, with great crude and archaic statues, inscribed rocks and pyramidal stelae, and I feel cheated by his final words – 'no-one who makes the effort to visit Gerga will feel that he has wasted his day'.

If Jasus and Gerga are for the romantic, then the other sites in this area, like Milas itself, are for the diligent. Alabanda, in its day a prosperous city with a reputation for luxury in its most decadent and interesting sense, is now a messy and dispiriting site in flat country, reached by driving through fields of scattered classical fragments to a small village; the children there horded round us, less than friendly, as we wandered round the handsome remains of the theatre, not at all well-preserved, and the Council House. Alinda is far more handsome on its steep hill overlooking the plain that lies to the north-east of the Latmus Mountains, well off the beaten track, with the charm that many ruins develop when long unexplored and unexploited; it has been the source of masonry for the neighbouring village, but no archaeologists have improved it, and its impressive fragments of major buildings – a theatre, market hall and aqueduct – are wooded and weedy. Labraynda, only ten miles away to the south of the Latmus Mountains, is another unspoilt site, approached by a long winding lane from Milas, easy enough for cars except for occasional gambolling cows; we found it occupied in a pastoral way by a resident guide and his family and farm animals – pleased but surprised to have visitors. Claiming friendship with George Bean by raising his hand high above his head and uttering 'Bin Bey' when he saw my copy of *Beyond the Maeander*, he insisted on tea before taking us round the site. He lived in a makeshift structure that was part ruin and part traditional black tent fabric, with privacy neither for himself nor his flock; his ten cows and two sheep grazed the steep ruin, and he grew a few beans and tomatoes nearby. He told us that he lived there all the year round, that the weather was invariably temperate, and that the mountains shouldered off the high winds and driving rain that plague Milas in midwinter; Labraynda is indeed sheltered on three sides by a ring of hills rising to perhaps 2,000 feet, and the fourth side is open and has splendid views of Milas and beyond. The guardian's quiet and sheltered life offered the obvious explanation for the siting of this sanctuary, which is best described by the amateur as a charming confusion of ruins, or a place to sit and sketch; more clearly than any temple I recall a huge, high, lemon-shaped rock with steps cut in one side, from which was to be seen a spectacular view – but a five foot standing jump was needed to reach the first step, or the most undignified scramble. It must have been an elegant place, terraced and ramped, with a network of stairs.

— V —

Bodrum

On New Year's Eve Ayhan drove us to Bodrum. I did not want to go, but coffee-deprivation had reduced my will-power to nothing, and I was content to drowse in the back of the car. He stopped outside the town at dusk and suggested that we take photographs of the spectacular sunset – we were to learn that panoramic views and vulgar sunsets were the only things to which he had a genuine visual response. All Turkey is full of sunsets, invariably of the ooh! and ah! kind, with vast domes of sky, or great tumbles of cloud, or dramatically picturesque silhouettes, and there comes a time when they seem commonplace and unremarkable unless they resemble some-thing – drive over the hills above Lausanne and catch sight of Lake Geneva just as the sun bloodies it, and you have a late Turner watercolour come to life – now that *is* a sunset; and so was the sunless evening near Kuşadasi that looked like a Böcklin waiting for a subject – but Bodrum gave us a wintry sunset that looked exactly what it was.

The town was busy with home-going traffic and Ayhan was impatient; I had the impression that he had not been before, was confused by the one-way system, and would not listen to direc-tions. He was determined to stay at the Pansyon Dinc (pro-nounced 'Dinge', more or less, which gave me an unhelpful fit of the giggles, and the momentary recollection of the Parisian hotel in which I stayed when a student – Sigmund Freud had stayed there too, and the lights in the lavatories would only go when you had locked yourself in their loathsome darkness), but when we found it, no rooms were to be had, for New Year's Eve is as much celebrated in Turkey as in Scotland, and Bodrum is a resort. With difficulty we found rooms in a run-down *pansyon* in a back street that was closed for the winter; the beds were damp, the water cold, there were no towels and not much privacy – sitting on the loo was only possible if the door was open to make room for my knees, and the walls were echo thin. Ayhan was greatly agitated about it, so we left him to his misery and went in search of things to photograph.

I had little confidence that we would find any. Ten years earlier I had spent a week here, swimming and lazing with Michael, and there had been little enough then – only the two beach boatyards, in one of which they made clumsy fishing-boats of chicken wire and cement (apparently very easy to repair after any accident – you simply add more cement), and in the other, elegant and high-buttocked sailing craft in timber that seemed not so distant from the Elizabethan pinnace. Both had gone, developed away under ugly new holiday houses. In the harbour there was nothing of charm, elegance or interest, and, thank God, no kittens – the last time I'd walked round it I had seen one drowning, and had only with the risk of drowning myself rescued it. And what do you do with a half-dead kitten in Turkey? When it was thoroughly dry I let it go with a prayer. Even the great Crusader Castle is now a litter of electric cables and advertisements on the harbour side. The restaurant where Michael had had his birthday party was closed. Michael always contrives to be abroad on his birthday, with friends who are in some way constrained to celebrate it at their own expense. I did my duty in Bodrum, and took him to what looked a suitably expensive restaurant, and found Klaus and Susannah there, whom we had met in Side. With four the party became a party, but with five it became a riot. The fifth was a sea-captain (his term for it) from Bodrum, a vast man who will need a cube for a coffin; he simply pulled up a chair, ordered raki by the bottle, and started competitive drinking that could not be refused. After repeated bouts of jaundice it was not the sport for me, and Michael, who has seen me through months of yellow misery and has a doctor's liver, inured to alcohol, covertly drank my share as well as his own. Conversation became more and more lubricious, until Susannah had a Lutheran huff and left, taking Klaus with her; I wanted to go too, but Michael was literally in the sea-captain's grip and could not move until the huge brute said, 'I know a place in town where fourteen-year-old girls do marvellous things for a man. We will go.' We went, and as far as I know, no-one paid the bill. I was gravely bothered by the idea of fourteen-year-old girls and their marvellous doings, and greatly relieved to find the place closed for the night – it was by then three in the morning, and I wanted to go to bed. But the captain wanted to go on drinking, and asked us to go back to his boat; I refused, and so I could, for he had no grip on me, but Michael was still in his embrace and very drunk – though not so drunk that he could not foresee one possible consequence, and as he was dragged off towards the harbour he called, 'What on earth shall I do if he wants me instead of the fourteen-year-old girl?'

It was in an appallingly hung-over state that Michael decided next day to go to Kos for a few hours and pay homage to Hippocrates, the father of his profession. I saw him onto the boat, and turned away, glad to have a quiet day alone, but had hardly left the harbour area when he caught up with me – he had discovered in the nick of time that because of the political situation then between Greece and Turkey, tourist traffic was one way only, and that he would not have been allowed to return. I have to confess that our relationship had so deteriorated that I would have relished being alone for the rest of the journey – and I recall with startling clarity the sense of freedom that overcame me when I at last saw him off after a glum lunch at Istanbul airport, opening all the car windows and playing Pavarotti at full blast against the buffeting of the wind, and driving very fast along the switchback road into Thrace. Holiday companionship is like marriage, except that everything likely to destroy it is concentrated and condensed to an intensity to which few marriages are exposed, and it is denied the gentling of sensuality and sexual exchange. On holiday, old adages about slurping soup and the decapitation of boiled eggs take on new urgency.

Petter took photographs of the floodlit castle from across the bay (they looked like cigarette advertisements when developed); it was fun, because rain was pelting down, and we had to 'improve' the foreground by removing junk and dragging a beached boat into the foreground. Drenched, we walked back past the Dinc and were hailed by Ayhan who was half cut with too much raki, and half cooked from sitting over an open log fire. Raki, he explained, was good for his digestion, and permitted for Muslims because it is not fermented – which seemed to me a Jesuitical argument, but he was too far gone to comprehend my notions of casuistry. Slightly fortified with segments of perfumed tangerine, we drank beer and steamed in the heat, feeling some slight compulsion to celebrate New Year's Eve in whatever might be the Turkish manner.

The promise of belly-dancers drew us into the night-club, but it was a chill cavern of a place, with water lying in the window embrasures and on the floor beneath them; the cushions were damp, the food cold, and the music intermittently unbearable when the live musicians were replaced by electronics. A young man played a violin, and simultaneously sang songs of cruel and selfish lovers, and conducted the small band in much the same way as might a Viennese violinist. A tall woman in her forties, coat-hanger bones jutting her silk dress in unlikely places, mimed and sang in silence until her amplifier was switched on – and then an eastern caterwaul belted out on the top line. Dancing with vaguely hip-thrusting movements, she worked herself into a frenzy of shrieks and dramatic attitudes, dragging back her long black hair to emphasize the noble nutcracker profile of a woman who with more flesh might have made a mistress for Edward VII. Ayhan, translating, I supposed, the Persian or Arabic of her old songs, shouted 'I need a lover. I need a lover' above the bedlam. He had earlier fallen into a maudlin state, and confessed at length and with appealing genuineness, some of the miseries of marriage; now he brightened suddenly to suggest with a wink that before the night was out we might all be committing adultery – I wondered if he too had heard of the wonderful fourteen-year-old girls. I could not follow his intellectual leap from random fornication to the comforts of freemasonry, but in so far as it was possible in that Saturnalian babel to be confidential, he told us sotto voce that after long investigation into his background he had been invited to join their number – an exclusive 4,000. 'It's a philosophy, you know, not a secret society.' 'Tell us more', we cried. 'I can't. I'm not allowed to.' He broke off, but saved face by making a fuss over the volume of the music.

An hour short of midnight, chilled through, my kidneys aching with cold from the damp wall and the sodden cushions against which I was resting, I would willingly have taken myself off to the not dissimilar conditions of our *pansyon* – at least before getting into the damp bed I could have donned as many layers of dry clothing as I possessed – but as that resolution was being formed into words that would not offend Ayhan, there swept onto the stage a middle-aged, double-chinned houri in a cloud of salmon pink as swathed and fluted as a fragment of classical architecture mysteriously in dissolution. I half expected the cry 'Dipteros' from Ayhan, for she was no belly-dancer; her clothes were braced about her hips with a girdle of black jet, a black sequined bra held her bosom in place, and her only naked parts were her right shoulder and her feet. After every dance this graceless Isadora rushed between the tables collecting bank-notes. There was a curious protocol about this, for the women present (and there were at least as many as men – though no children) drew the notes from their husbands, and either tucked them into her bra or stuck them to her brow with a pat of spittle; I saw no man touch her, though I had not realized this when I attempted to give her a note myself, and was confused and embarrassed to find that the bra was very tight and the breast within it very small, and that my big clumsy fingers could not easily get between them. The note immediately fell out, and the audience applauded my blushes. Her dancing degenerated to maenad frenzy, with the violinist steadily accelerating the pace – Ayhan and others in ecstatic response tore the heads off the miserable flowers on our tables and threw the petals in her hair as she passed. Her finale of at one moment kneeling on the stage, weaving about with her plump torso, seeming to tear her hair and rend her bosom, and the next leaping and prancing like an anchored Nureyev, dislodged her collection of bank-notes, and when the music ended she was left scrabbling about on the floor for her takings, while the master of ceremonies announced with the full effect of the amplifier's echo chamber that the final event of the evening had just flown in hot-foot from fame and fortune in Istanbul.

It was now more or less midnight. When asked the time for conversation's sake Ayhan replied 'Four minutes late', but he was far gone with raki; always a heavy smoker, he was in the state where if he rested a cigarette in the ash-tray he would immedi-ately light another, or his pipe, or both. If the moment of the New Year's birth was marked at all it was with champagne popping and spurting all over the massive young woman who was now singing, and by the waiters who scattered petals over their customers with random generosity – called to the kitchen before they'd finished, they simply emptied the remaining trays of petals over those nearest them, for whom the effect was like the first stage of the roses of Heliogabalus (he, you will recall, murdered a discarded boy-friend by having him smothered by a myriad roses). It was inconceivable that this singer could be the highlight of the evening, for she was fully clothed, had an overhanging belly, and danced with less grace than a Walt Disney hippopotamus. She was no more than an intermezzo – the spotlight abruptly left her for the dancer now on the edge of the stage, and the wretched girl fled in mid-song. What followed was an aggressive performance, and if it was real belly-dancing then I prefer the sanitized ladies in the tourist traps of Istanbul, for in those you pay your money to go in and that's an end to it – here more and more money was extracted from the men by means of embarrassment and torment. She was young, and there was an expanse of belly and a hint of buttock between her fringed bra and long loose skirt; her face was a harsh mask of cheekbones and the broad slash of lips; nothing about her was pretty or appealing, but the immediate sense of challenge was as adrenalin-raising as a slapped face. A few conventional dance movements done, she sank to her knees and made unmistakable gestures of masturbation, writhing, groaning and throwing back her head; I did not care to believe what my eyes were telling me, but when she turned to an imaginary partner and simulated masturbating him, there could be no mistake. The women in the audience applauded her with shrieks and claps, and rose to their feet as they stuffed their money into her bra – middle-aged women, respectable, wearing hats that might grace the Women's Institute, accompanying husbands, and for once they seemed infinitely more emancipated than their Western counterparts. Worse was to follow. The girl stepped from stage to table, and with the instincts of a cat performed in the debris of dinner, never once putting a bare foot on knife or plate; occasionally she would stand astride two tables, challenging their occupants to look up her raised skirt, or, having selected a victim, would lower herself into a crouch with knees apart and mons veneris thrusting rhythmically at his nose, and play castanets excruciatingly close to his ears, often with arms around his head so that he was enclosed in

flesh and clamour – and so it would go on until notes of suitable
value had been tucked into her skirt by the stupefied man. I
prepared to run.

Ayhan could barely walk; with Petter on one side and me on
the other we steered him through the rain to our *pansyon*,
listening to his drunken rant on masonic philosophy and good
works. The *pansyon* was in darkness and the door locked. Ayhan
sat on the step while we rang the bell and searched for open
windows, and then, suddenly sobered by the prospect of sleeping on the wet doorstep or in the car, roused himself to a frenzy of
ringing, banging, kicking and shouting. There were to be other
moments when he was to recall that we were the guests of the
Turkish Government, and in his charge, and that ancient laws of
hospitality were in force, but this was the first. I wandered off,
embarrassed and more than slightly giggly, to see if sleeping in
the car might be a practical solution; when I returned, it was to
find Ayhan organizing the wakened neighbours in a mass telephone reconnaissance, with hardly a closed and darkened window left in the small square. The boy who ran the *pansyon*
returned, grinning, and let us in – and then promptly invited us
to go out again and eat *işkèmbe* with him, a thin tripe soup that
though eaten all the year round is traditional fare for New Year,
with the additional benefit that it is believed to be an antidote to
alcohol. If that were true, then Ayhan needed it, and Petter
marched him off while I burrowed into the damp sheets and fell
into a fragmented and dream-filled sleep.

In the morning the floor was awash with condensation and,
feverish, my face resembled a scarlet raisin. It was too cold to
shave, and we dragged ourselves down to the Dinc in search of
breakfast – but they too had had a heavy night and all we got was
tea and tangerines. Ayhan ate an aspirin, denying that he had a
headache – 'This is to prevent it' – but this was after opening a film
case in mistake for an aspirin box. We drove the hundred yards or
so into the town centre, and parked while Ayhan went in search
of milk to settle the alcohol in his stomach and Petter returned to
the night-club to recover some mislaid part of his camera – both
were unsuccessful. I watched the village dogs and cats gathered
outside the butcher's shop, waiting, resigned, patient, and in
amity in the rain. In deference to my wishes my own dogs do not
chase cats, and have learned to tolerate a ragged stray or two, but
most English dogs throw all sense and discretion to the wind at

the first whiff of pussy; of all the things that I can recall of my first visit to Istanbul, it was the nocturnal rummaging in rubbish-dumps of dogs and cats about their business side by side, aggression subdued by hunger, that most surprised me. At the other end of the Mediterranean, in the backyard of the house once occupied by Paul Klee in Kairouan, I saw a heap of rubbish – bedsteads, boxes, timber, chairs – that might have made a *Merzbau* for Kurt Schwitters, in which young pullets, kittens and large brown rats were playing, as though it were a children's climbing-frame, under the benevolent eye of an old bitch resting her chin on the bloody ribcage of a cow. All it needed was a small child and a cockatrice to bring old Isaiah's prophecy to life.

Bodrum is Halicarnassus, a city that according to Vitruvius may have been a model of ancient town-planning, but is now a confused maze of narrow one-way streets. Its history is unremarkable, its famous sons few, and had not one of the Seven Wonders been constructed there, the great tomb of Mausolus, it would be forgotten. Herodotus, the great historian, traveller and observer was born there in 484 BC; by then some five centuries had passed since its foundation as a Greek city, and although for the previous sixty years it had been a Persian satrapy, the furthest outpost of the Persian empire, it was resolutely Greek in character. Mausolus, a Carian whose seat of government had been at Milas, observed that Halicarnassus had considerable advantages over that city of the plain, both in defence and maritime commerce, and made it his capital; he built its walls and imported enough citizens from neighbouring towns to multiply by five its population, but of his street-plan and his great palace of marble there is no trace. Nor is there much left of the Wonder of the World. Work on this tomb, so worthily fantastical that its memory survives in our word 'mausoleum', was begun by Mausolus' widow and sister, Artemisia (one and the same – the nasty habit of marriage between siblings was not exclusive to the Egyptians) between 353 BC, when Mausolus died, and her own death in 350 BC. It had a solid base supporting a colonnaded chamber, topped by a stepped pyramid, surmounted by a huge sculpture of four horses and a chariot with figures of Mausolus and his sister-wife, in all about as high as Nelson's Column. It stood for 1,500 years until felled by an earthquake, and in 1402 its ruins were plundered by the Christian Knights of St John for the castle that guards the harbour of Bodrum.

By chance, one of their number, the Commander de la Tourette, gave a brief account of their activities to d'Alechamps, a late-medieval editor of Pliny. It seems that a German knight called Schlegelholdt, having been given the work of building the castle, found a staircase of white marble standing in a field above the harbour and thought that the trimmed stones would be useful; as his men dismantled it they opened a way into the hidden space behind, and found there a vast square hall with marble columns that supported capitals, architraves, friezes and cornices carved in relief, which 'after having considered in their imagination the singularity of the work, at last they pulled down, cracked and broke up to use as they had done the rest'. They then found a door into another hall, in which lay a white marble tomb in the form of a vase, glistening and beautiful, which within a day was smashed and the ground about it strewn with fragments of the cloth of gold that had wrapped the corpse within. It is perhaps unreasonable to expect medieval warrior knights, particularly from Germany, with their record of blood lust and barbarity in the Baltic Crusades, to have been men of education and culture, but if none of them had heard of the Seven Wonders of the World, surely they must have known of the wonders of the Venusberg. I suspect that the tales of chivalrous good manners between Saladin and Coeur de Lion have given us an entirely false notion of Crusader courtesy, and that their truces, challenges, heralds, ransoms, jousts and picnics were no more than a veneer for a profession that licensed the knights to murder and rape the civilian population without pity, and to steal and destroy their property without remorse.

Had the Mausoleum survived a little longer, we might have had some better record of it, for the nearby Colossus of Rhodes was an object of much speculation in Renaissance times; as it is, only the de la Tourette report on the interior spans the gap between Pliny's description and the excavations of Sir Charles Newton in 1859. These were, alas, an appalling example of archaeological malpractice, and no excavation in any scientific sense; all that Newton did was to plunder every piece of sculpture he could find for the benefit of the British Museum, and leave it an inscrutable wreck – in his own words 'a desolate looking spot, of which the idea is finer than the reality'.

Most of his recoveries are battered and fragmentary, but even so, the realism of a running leopard is clear enough, and the rump of a gigantic and unmistakable stallion, and the gathered power of the life-size 'Persian Rider' and his horse at the gallop, are eloquent and talking testimonies to a great achievement. Of the two large fragments in high relief of the 'Battle between the Greeks and the Amazons', which ran in a continuous frieze round the whole building, one is in much better condition than the other – even so, it is not absurd to suggest that they are by different sculptors, and according to Vitruvius the greatest sculptors of the day, Leochares, Bryaxis, Skopas and Timotheos each worked on one side. These beauties are now in the basement of the British Museum, trapped under low ceilings when all originally stood high, in light that is flat and dull and deadening to the marble – brilliant Aegean sunlight bleaches marble white and makes its sugary crystals glister like ice in snow. The statue of Mausolus himself is slightly better off upstairs – a ten foot standing giant whose languorous contrapposto is swathed in heavy drapery, the sensuality reinforced by the massive face, the large eyes deep-socketed, the heavy lips in settled calm, the hair rising from the broad brow and falling in thick waves almost to the shoulders – it may be an heroic and idealized portrait, but it is of no classicized straight-nosed Greek.

The Mausoleum haunted the imaginations of nineteenth-century architects, and the reconstructions are ingenious and perhaps more fantastic than the original. The architect employed by Artemisia was Pytheos, the designer of the Temple of Athena at Priene, but that grand and plain building standing on a podium of cushioned ashlar is wholly different in style and treatment from the descriptions of the Mausoleum, and offers us no clues; but in Milas, the old capital of Mausolus, the free-standing tomb of Gümüşkesen may give some hint of its appearance – this dates from the second century AD, years too late, and far too small, but the proportions and feel of it are uncannily like Pliny's description of the Mausoleum. Vitruvius and Pliny kept its memory fresh, even though there were no visual records of it – the description of it as 'floating' may have depended on its having a green marble base that blended with the hill behind, or, low-toned, did not conflict with anything in its surroundings. Sir Christopher Wren borrowed its stepped pyramid for the bottom of the western dome of his Great Model design for St Paul's Cathedral, and in his youth had written a tract on the 'Tyrian Order' (which he supposed to be the earliest of architectural orders, but which does not exist) and mentions the Mausoleum in this context; we know that at a later stage he even made a reconstruction of it, but this, alas, has not survived. Charles Cockerell, architect of the National Monument in Edinburgh (1822–30) and the Ashmolean Museum in Oxford (1841–5), published a reconstruction in 1856 – he was then sixty-eight and the grand old man of British architecture, working on the Mausoleum without the benefit of Newton's depradations, which were to follow three years later. He gives it a low plain base with equestrian statues as outriders from the four corners, supporting very tall columns, topped by a very tall stepped pyramid with the steep rake of a mansard roof – rather elegant, if preposterous. In 1862 Newton himself published what he thought to be the authoritative view, with a huge rusticated podium more than half the height of the whole, topped by Ionic columns, the frieze of Greeks and Amazons (which would have been virtually invisible at that height), and a shallow stepped pyramid. James Fergusson, described in a Victorian valediction as a writer on architecture as important in the modern world as was Vitruvius in the ancient, and now quite forgotten, opposed Newton with the far more elegant but wholly insupportable solution of two orders of columns, of which the lower was somehow broken by a ledge at half its height to support a row of standing and equestrian figures. John James Stevenson, best known for imposing what he imagined to be the style of Queen Anne on vast areas of Kensington, tried his hand in 1896 with a reconstruction that resembles a palimpsest of garden follies, making the stepped pyramid seem as steep and narrow as Cleopatra's Needle. Danes, Germans and Americans joined in – Petersen, Oldfield, Six, Dinsmoor, Adler and Preedy – but the most elegant solution is perhaps that of the young Frenchman, Louis Bernier, who, though he took the trouble to go to Halicarnassus in 1877 as a student, found nothing there to constrain his imagination; he endowed the tomb with a handsome stair, each step of which supports a matching pair of recumbent lions, leading to a huge door in a porch topped by an equestrian Mausolus; his stepped pyramid is roughly of the proportions expected of a pyramid, neither squat nor lofty, and it is silhouetted against a sky of brilliant Kodak blue.

Authority has now come down more or less in favour of Newton, and the most recent reconstruction, by Kristian Jeppesen, is remarkably close to his heavy proportions and silhouette. But I wonder. The city of Thugga, in Tunisia, was established at a very early date, alas unknown, long before the Romans came to Carthage, a Numidian dependency. Its largely Roman ruins sit handsomely on a high sloping site, looking towards the great plains of the Numidian hinterland; down the hill, below the brothel with its phallic signpost, almost hidden in an olive grove in dead ground, stands a Libyo-Punic mausoleum that will stop short in his tracks any man concerned with the appearance of the Mausoleum at Halicarnassus. Built at the end of the third century BC, this tower tomb some 65 feet high consists of a square chamber standing on a podium of steps, topped by three more steps supporting another chamber decorated with applied half-columns, with equestrian sculptures standing above its corners, that seem to guard the next register, a tall narrow masonry support for the pyramid at its top. The British, who had colonial aspirations in Tunisia long before the French, overturned (the British Museum prefers the word 'dismantled') this monument in 1842, when Thomas Reed, the British Consul in Tunis, removed the inscription that identified it in both Libyan and Carthaginian as the tomb of a Numidian prince, Ateban, in the reign of Massinissa. This at the time dispossessed King of the eastern Numidians sided with Rome during the Second Punic War of 218–201 BC, and was rewarded by them with the whole of Numidia – the tomb cannot therefore be of an earlier date than circa 200 BC. All that the French archaeologist Poinssot found in place when he reconstructed it in 1910 were some two or three courses of masonry from the bottom register, standing secure on the five steps – the inscription had been inside the bottom chamber. He had a drawing to work from, made in 1765, which shows that the narrow tower and the pyramid had fallen, but at nearby Maktaris, an altogether meaner tomb of the same general pattern stands complete, if leaning like the tower of Pisa (and subject to some lavatorial abuse); this differs in having one register the less, and in that one wall of the upper chamber is opened by a great arch, a feature that appears again in the mausoleum at Cillium. These unrestored parallels suggest that Poinssot's reconstruction at Thugga is correct, and that he cannot be accused of incorporating ideas from Halicarnassus. It is, however, conceivable that young Louis Bernier in 1877 was not unaware of these Punic monuments when he was working at Bodrum. Whatever the case, it is clear that in the south-western

Mediterranean, over a wide area, and perhaps until as late as the fourth century AD, there existed a type of tomb that suggests some distant bastardized knowledge of the Mausoleum of Halicarnassus. There is some tacit recognition of this in the British Museum, for it keeps the Thugga inscription in the Department of Western Asiatic Antiquities, though Thugga is as far from westernmost Asia as London is from Istanbul.

I have a glass jar of marble fragments in my kitchen cupboard, gleaned from the Myndus headlands west of Bodrum, all green, but ranging from icy white to the mouldy black of ancient dinner jackets – they lend some small weight to the idea that the Mausoleum base was green, fading into the background of green hills, letting the white marble of the monument's upper registers seem to float above the city. Grassy hills hump their way down to the sea on the east side of the town, giving that deep seclusion that induces even the most staid and sane to doff the last shred of clothing and porpoise in the waves. Somewhere in the immediate area of Bodrum there was in antiquity a second harbour, but all trace of it is now lost – it may have been the shallow bay to the east, perfect for beaching boats, where ten years ago the boatyard was, now buried under new development.

— VI —

Cnidus * Caunus

Feverish and shivering I lay in the back of the car all the way to Marmaris, half-sleeping; my few half-waking moments invariably coincided with things no sane man cares to see – lovely countryside newly-murdered by open-cast coal-mining far into the distance, and a hideous power-station, cheaply built to Polish designs and specifications, its tubes and towers sprawling down a long slow hillside now naked even of weeds, serviced by peasants living in dreary modern blocks already decaying, bereft of anything that feeds the soul. I was asleep when we passed Stratoniceia, and Ayhan would never pause unasked for the yellow signs that denote an ancient city. It would have been a sentimental visit, for I have nothing but amused recollections of the village; Jill wedged the Range-Rover between the walls of a narrow street because she was in a foul temper with the grossly fat guardian of the little museum near the main road – he would not let us enter, and had then demanded, in German, a lift to the village – she summoned up 'Kein Platz, kein Platz' from her three-cornered store of German phrases, and roared off. In the village it would have been wiser to park in a patch of shade and explore on foot, but with the bit between her teeth Jill would not stop until she had found something worth stopping for. My notes simply say, 'Like the maze episode in *Three Men in a Boat* – only

Montmorency missing – nothing visible apart from classical fragments in high walls', and it was at this point that we jammed. We made almost as much noise un-jamming, for no-one could get out and help with directions, and the two small boys who climbed onto the back bumper and tried to direct us were worse than useless; once clear, and back at a junction, they demanded to be let in, and once again small boys proved their value as guides. They got us as near as possible to the theatre, and then led us on foot up the remains of a marble road with a clear stream running beside it. The theatre was small, much ruined, and unremarkable. I made Jehan and Abdullah sit a row or two, each moving on a space as I counted – something that they enjoyed and made a game, getting faster and faster; if ancient Carians had their slim hips, then fewer than 5,000 might fill the theatre, not more, and certainly not the 10,000 estimated by most writers. The upper rows were shaded by laden fig-trees growing in the seats; the boys climbed them and threw down the bursting fruit, sweet as honey and warm from the sun, but we were haunted by Atatürk's revenge, and dared not feast on them.

The village mosque is built over an ancient well or fountain connected with the stream that runs along the marble road; Jehan encouraged me to climb down into the channel and follow him under the building to another ancient fountain with a marble drain-slab still in place, where women were washing laundry. I cannot think why this gave me so much pleasure, for it was neither beautiful nor splendid – perhaps it was the simple thing of standing at the spot where two thousand years ago women filled their water jars, and recognizing the rarity of an ancient fountain still flowing, never interrupted by an earthquake.

A change in the pace of the car woke me; we were in a town, grey and smoggy with the smoke of countless chimneys held down by the drizzling rain. It was Muğla, which we could have bypassed, had Ayhan not still been in need of milk to settle the alcohol in his stomach – but the search was fruitless. Somewhere south of the town we stopped to admire a spectacular view high above a deep inlet of the sea that even in the wind and rain made its point about the beauty of the marriage of the Taurus Mountains with the Aegean Sea; and Ayhan made his point about the relentless intrusion of twentieth-century technology by announcing with some pride that a power-station was to be built at the head of the fjord, with the consequent devastation of heavily

wooded slopes, and polluted water. Turkey needs more trees,
not fewer, to remedy her semi-arid climate; in classical times the
great plains that surround Konya were forest, and in the early
nineteenth century the bare hills round Lake Van were wooded;
these and many other areas have been stripped by the charcoal
burners, followed by reduced rainfall and wind erosion. But
charcoal burning is an age-old folly. Time and again now the
visitor is struck by how little Turkey has learned from the mis-
takes of other nations, and how the erratic gallop of business and
government in their attempt to match European standards of
living has brought precisely the havoc and dereliction that
destroys existing but perhaps indefinable assets.

From a distance Marmaris looked like Bodrum without the
dramatic castle, and we bypassed it for the long peninsula of
Cnidus, pointing due west like an outstretched crab claw – not, of
course, without argument, for Ayhan was worried once more
about an hotel for the night, convinced that we should make
Marmaris our base for exploration. We drove to Datça, half way
along the peninsula, over so humped and switchbacked a road
that I had to ask to sit in the front of the car – Ayhan laughed at
me, relinquished the wheel to Petter, and took my place in the
back; within ten minutes he was so green that we had to change
places again. I knew that I would rather be on foot, and that with
time to waste the peninsula would provide a splendid walk –
given a dog for company, of course – but there was no time to
waste.

Bean, following Herodotus, points to a narrow isthmus at the
eastern end of the peninsula which the ancient Cnidians attempted to cut in 546 BC. They were under threat from the
invading Persian armies of Harpagus – he of the feast of his own
boiled baby, a fearful punishment inflicted by his former em-
ployer, Astyages, last king of the Medes, for not killing the
grandson who was to take his throne, the then infant Cyrus. (It
was my parish priest who always insisted that the baby was
boiled – such things make a lasting impression on the very young,
and I think he was implying a punishment for my consistent and
wilful failure to extinguish the altar candles cleanly, for he did not
share the ecstasy induced in me by the smell of a charring candle
wick. The baby would, I imagine, have tasted much better
roasted on a spit and served with an apple in its mouth.) Thinking
to make Cnidus an easily defensible island, they hacked away at

the half-mile neck of land, but so many workmen were injured and blinded by splinters from the hard rock that the city fathers consulted the Delphic Oracle, imagining that perhaps some divine dissuasion was at work; it was – the Oracle told them that if Zeus had wanted an island there, he would have made an island – so the Cnidians at once forbore with their digging and surrendered to Harpagus. It is a pretty tale, but there can be no substance to it – if Harpagus was hammering at the gates, as it were, there could have been little time to excavate a defensive channel of worthwhile size, and none to consult the Oracle in distant Delphi, and an invasion by sea in those sheltered waters would have been an easy alternative. But this does not mean that there was never an attempt to cut a channel; the eastern end of the peninsula is sheltered by another, pointing south-west, and by the island of Simi, but the waters at the western end are notoriously hostile to small boats, and the rocks are host to innumerable wrecks. Had it proved possible to cut through the isthmus, then the winter passage of small coast-hugging craft would have been shorter and safer, and the second city of Cnidus need never have been built at the peninsula's extremity. It is remembered that a hundred years ago small boats were manhandled over the land at this point, and if that happened in Ottoman times, there is no reason why the practice should not have started in antiquity – the isthmus is narrow enough to bear a Turkish name that can be translated as 'The place that fish can leap'.

Bean was there in 1950, and he records that he stopped the bus to Marmaris for half an hour while he searched for traces of the cut – the surprise is not the patient tolerance of the Turks for such eccentricity, but that as early as 1950 there was a road passable by bus and a bus to pass it. In 1841, responding to the published journals of Charles Fellows, the British Government despatched HMS *Beacon* and Lieutenant Thomas Abel Brimage Spratt to recover for the British Museum fragments and sculptures that Fellows had seen further along the coast at Xanthus. Spratt was accompanied by the naturalist Edward Forbes, and did not restrict his interests to archaeology or the ground broken by Fellows – for two years he was as much concerned with the bathymetrical distribution of marine life, natural history and geology as with the old stones of civilization, and indeed for the last ten years of his life was actively supporting early attempts at conservation in the River Mersey. He died, as do so many, in

Tunbridge Wells. Amongst many errands not in the footsteps of
Fellows, Spratt went to Cnidus and later claimed that he had seen
traces of the attempted cutting of the ancient channel. Bean found
nothing. Nor did we.

Datça was dead. It has a not inelegant hotel of the kind
associated with yachtsmen, fortunately closed, and we were
forced to look elsewhere. The village grocer showed us mercy and
offered rooms above his shop – no heat, no running water, no loo
paper, but clean and dry and overlooking the harbour at the back.
The landing at the top of the stairs was a tangle of firewood and
marmalade-and-tortoiseshell kittens that skidded and scuttled
spitting and hissing in all directions, like water dropped into a hot
frying-pan. A door opened and the grocer's shy wife and shyer
children inspected us – after a long hesitation she scurried to our
beds and snatched the small quilts that, apart from a bottom
sheet, were their only covering, and disappeared. This puzzling
behaviour was explained later, when we returned to find the
quilts back on our beds with small sheets tacked to them like
single-sided duvets – touched by this practical and ingenious
gesture, I wondered if it was a rare thing for our benefit, or simply
the custom of the house. We had a cold lunch in a bitterly cold
restaurant where the cooker had run out of gas; Ayhan had to be
consoled and reassured that we were perfectly content, and
during one of the endless displays of authority that he could not
resist whenever we were in a restaurant, Petter and I conspired.
We were staying in Datça because Ayhan thought it was Cnidus,
or as near as dammit. And so it had been, once, long before the
grandeur of new Cnidus appeared at the end of the peninsula
sometime before 355 BC, but little is left of it, and the peninsula's
real reward is the new city, thirty-two kilometres away. I had
tried to explain to Ayhan that we were on one site when my
interest lay with the other, but he had not believed my tale of two
cities and had quite obviously stopped listening to me – we had
noticed before that he had the trick of focussing on nothing and
that this always indicated that he was also hearing nothing, and
that he would then suddenly erupt into some irrelevant activity,
usually an intervention in the kitchen or a squabble with the
waiter – hence our conspiracy, which was to get Petter at the
wheel of the car and whizz off before Ayhan realized where we
were taking him, for he had a tendency to feel that the day ended
after lunch.

We were half way there before he understood that we had
kidnapped him, and he unwillingly agreed that we should go on.
The rain returned and the road deteriorated; the rain became
torrential and the road itself a torrent; water swept down hillsides
and across the road, taking the road water and the road surface
with it; in two villages built on steep slopes the way narrowed
between the houses, the car could not resist the increased force of
the water, and we slithered zigzag and helter-skelter into what
passed for village squares. Over an hour and a half passed before
we completed the thirty-two kilometres and saw the first of many
beautiful scraps of ancient wall nestling under briars at the
roadside, but by then the rain had eased and we had only a
scudding wind to contend with.

It is one of those sites so derelict that it requires a prodigious
effort to see it as a working city, though imagination is much
assisted by geography; it lies low at the very tip of the peninsula,
between the sea and a col to the north that provides an acropolis;
the island at the end has been joined to the mainland with a
narrow isthmus forming a small trireme harbour on the north and
the more conventional large shallow commercial harbour on the
south, overlooked by a small theatre with spacious marble seats
that may have held some 8,000 people – a much larger theatre,
very damaged, sets its shoulders into the scarp high above to the
north. When the hack Italian illustrator Luigi Mayer produced the
original drawings for his *Views of the Ottoman Empire, chiefly in
Caramania, a part of Asia Minor hitherto unexplored*, for Sir Robert
Ainslie, playing for him something of the same role as did Titta
Lusieri for Lord Elgin, much of the wall closing the smaller
harbour was still in place – the anonymous text observes, 'Now
barks enter it, to load themselves with stone from the ruins,
which the turks are continually breaking to pieces.' Not much is
known of Mayer – neither birth nor death dates even – but he
seems to have been attached to Ainslie as an itinerant draughtsman from 1776 until 1792, for the full duration of his appointment
as British ambassador to the Sublime Porte. Ainslie was said to
have been a boon companion to Abdul Hamid I, Sultan from 1773
when he was released after forty years in the Cage (the debilitat-
ing prison in which all possible claimants to the throne were kept)
on the death of his brother. Abdul Hamid made up for lost time
by fathering at least twenty-two children, and was enlightened
enough to have a French mistress, Aimée Dubucq de Rivery, the

notorious cousin of the Empress Josephine, to mother the only one of them to succeed to the throne; Ainslie, on the other hand, was more interested in antiquities, coins (of which he formed a vast and distinguished collection during his years as ambassador), natural history, and Ottoman daily life. Mayer's illustrations follow his travels from Carthage to Egypt, and from the Balkans to Palestine, recording archaeological sites, costumes and customs; they are for the most part so plodding and pedestrian that it is not unreasonable to suppose them accurate, seeming to betray an eye incapable of fantasy; when they were printed in 1803–4, eleven years after Mayer had disappeared into limbo, they were accompanied by an anonymous and equally pedestrian text, of which Ainslie himself was probably the modest author.

American archaeologists are slowly and diligently excavating the site, but almost nothing stands on it; one of their trenches has revealed the floor of a temple superimposed on another, a giant sandwich of marble and rubble, which may suggest that the city was more than once devastated by earthquakes. The island, which, according to Strabo, was the principal residential area of the city, is now occupied by a light-house and a military post full of gangling and curious National Servicemen who were pleased enough to have the tedium of their day broken by strangers, but who would not let us pass their barrier to look at the fine Roman tomb paved with pied mosaic described by Bean. The guardian of the site lived in a concrete block-house nearby, with a bright and busy cocker spaniel for company, and there were a number of well-fed and boisterous mongrels, except for one ribby little bitch too small for their rough and tumble ever to get her rations – I gave her all the biscuits from the car and she was clearly both ravenous and desperate with anxiety about the competition from the other dogs.

Cnidus, with the three cities of Rhodes, together with Kos and Halicarnassus, formed the Dorian Hexapolis, a miniature EEC. Every fourth year the Dorian Games were held there, the ceremonies probably carried out in the Doric temple of Apollo Karneios, and the Games themselves in the stadium outside the west city wall. There seems to have been no overall deity – Athena, Apollo and Demeter all had their temples – but if there was a cult following, it was yet again for Aphrodite. Her shrine housed a celebrated wholly nude statue by Praxiteles of which

there is now no relic, though a daunting Demeter has survived in
the British Museum; another Demeter also survives in the Izmir
Museum, and this may or may not have come from Cnidus. In
1953 Bean heard that fishermen had landed part of a bronze
statue near Bodrum; he found on the beach the draped and veiled
upper part of a more than life-size figure akin to but much more
touching than the British Museum marble, a huge hole in the
crown of the skull, and red paint newly applied to the lips as a
puerile joke. The fishermen were unhelpful when asked where
they had found it, but somewhere between Old and New Cnidus
seemed to be the answer. It may have been shipwrecked on its
way to the new city – certainly it seems to have been newly made
and never seen, for no copies or replicas have survived, and
Bean's hypothesis that it was intended for the new temple, lost,
and replaced by the less attractive marble now in the British
Museum, is appealing.

Our return was perhaps even worse than our outward journey,
for the rain began at once, and with it came darkness. Ayhan
developed an anxious fret about petrol, justified, for we were
rarely out of second gear, and there had been no garage other
than that in Datça, but the more he made the point, the more
determinedly unconcerned we became, and the atmosphere
deteriorated into recrimination on his part and silence on ours. At
times we could not distinguish the road from what flanked it –
and on the outward journey nothing but the empty air had
flanked it on one side or the other. We picked up a boy on foot,
partly out of sympathy, partly for reassurance that we were on
the road, but he was drenched to the skin and his steaming
clothes reduced our visibility to zero – but it is not possible to eject
a body into the rain simply because it is adding to one's inconvenience, even if that inconvenience may be lethal in its effect.
Ayhan complained bitterly every time the car scrabbled for its
footing, and I grew convinced that he did not know that the
Renault's driven wheels were at the front.

We found our grocer chopping wood for the stove, on which
stood a bucket of water, and the place full of stinging smoke; he
explained that the bucket could be emptied into a cistern in the
loo and the water dribbled from a small faucet beneath as a
makeshift shower. We stopped him. We knew that Ayhan, who
had disappeared, would not want a shower, and we could not
bear the thought of the grocer's exhausting his supply of kindling

and destroying the kittens' shelter for the sake of a couple of supposedly fussy Europeans. A ginger kitten allowed me to cuddle it briefly, but not take it to bed. The wind rattled the windows and drove such rain at them as made us seem at sea; unless curled in foetus position the makeshift duvets were too small for extremities, and it was an uneasy night.

I had a strange and uncomfortable dream in which I saw Anthony Blunt in Barcelona just as I was focussing my camera on some contorted decorative detail in an art nouveau restaurant – he was collecting letters from the bar, and through the lens I could quite clearly see his name on them. There followed a wretched scampering chase on foot through the Parc Güell, with his breathlessly explaining about dead-letter drops, while two hacks from the *Sunday Times* pursued us. I can occasionally explain the general sense of my vivid dreams, and this one was simple enough, but the circumstantial detail, seen with hallucinating clarity twenty years after I had last been in Barcelona and a year before the great Barcelona exhibition in London, was irrelevant, and the timing unaccountable.

Ayhan was up and about when I finally left my bed at seven, after an hour of such indecision as I remember from my days at school or in the army, when the warmed chill of my bed seemed infinitely preferable to the cold chill of the washroom, though even under the blankets I was shivering. He was again immaculate – I have never known any man show so little sign of the small distresses of travel. He produced sachets of Nescafé and parcels of butter providently pinched from the hotel in Ephesus, the grocer brought us tea and packets of fruit cake, cheese and salt sticks, and, with water boiled on a small gas cylinder, caffeine hauled me back into the land of the living.

My abiding recollections of Datça and the Cnidan peninsula are not only of the wildness of its wooded mountainous spine and the desolation of its ruins, but of a kindness and concern on the part of its inhabitants that outweighed the hostility of the weather, and of their physical beauty; I know nothing of the women of the village, apart from the dumpy bustle of the grocer's wife, but the men share a common fine-boned dark-eyed quality that suggests close kinship without the disaster of inbreeding that is evident in some remote American communities. Encountering a distinct physical type in so isolated a peninsula gives much the same pleasure as discovering a ruin – it is living archaeology.

Cnidus in its heyday provided not only safe anchorages on a major trade route, but a gathering-place for all the Dorian states, with games and festivals and the pilgrimage to the shrine of Praxiteles' Aphrodite. But all this was dying away even in Hellenistic times, and with drastic depopulation and desuetude came an isolation that perhaps preserved the looks of the native inhabitants.

We left Datça early, intending to spend a full day at Caunus. My recollections of exploring this watery site with Jill were of a smiling gold-toothed boatman who had marooned us we knew not where in relation to the city, of mosquitos that had within minutes turned every exposed inch of skin, even hairy knees, into flaming lunar landscapes, and, most important now, that morning light made an astonishing difference to photographs of the temple tombs in the rock face. We sped out of the sleeping village and up onto the road to Marmaris; within minutes Cnidus' humpy spine induced travel sickness, and Ayhan and I had constantly to change places.

We progressed in fits and starts, humps and bumps, blanched with nausea and sweating in spite of the cold, my hopes for morning photographs gradually diminishing as the supposed hour's journey to Marmaris stretched to two and more. Beyond Marmaris we stopped to buy tangerines from a roadside stall – not a simple transaction, but one requiring the maximum display from Ayhan as he explained that these were perfumed and without pith and pips; the perfume escaped me, and they proved to have both pith and pips in abundance, but they were easy and settling to our queasy stomachs, and the pause brought us the bonus of a faggot-gatherer. Now I have seen many an English painting of such subjects – Gainsborough began the genre, but no pictorial reminiscence matched the real thing; he was tall as Turks go, and his height was doubled by the burden that he carried, a great mass of twigs and boughs somehow secured to his shoulders and supported by a stout pole carried aslant – his head was hardly visible, and this great rook's nest seemed to have been built about it.

When we at last saw a signpost to Caunus, though aware that I was becoming increasingly fretful about the light, Ayhan overshot it; to my yelp of dismay he responded that it was faster to stay on the main road and take the next turning. The next turning was neither on my map nor on the ground, and it was some

fifteen kilometres before we left the road to helter-skelter through
the substantial town of Ortaca and eventually join the road that
we should have taken. By now even Ayhan was disconcerted,
and I was veering from rage to resignation, and then on to
incredulity when he ignored the harbour where I thought to find
another gold-toothed boatman, and took us to the dead end of the
road where there was no boat, nor any sign that there should be
one. A boy was messing about with a tarpaulin-covered craft on
the far side of the water, but he ignored Ayhan's shouts. I had a
tantrum, compounded by a need to urinate where there was no
cover; that embarrassment over (why are the English so timorous
about these unavoidable emergencies?), I decided to walk back to
the village; poor Petter, torn between soothing ruffled feathers
and coming with me, first argued against it, and we were but a
hundred yards down the road when Ayhan shouted that the boat
was coming.

Anger evaporates on a small boat; the chug of the engine at
heart-beat rate must recall the womb, and the breeze is enough to
comfortably ruffle the hair but not to tousle it; as the great ruddy
rock tombs came into sight above the reeds and clear reflecting
water, not even Ayhan's squawk of horror that he had left his
precious leather handbag on the bank where we had boarded
could disturb my new calm – Petter and I disembarked below the
tombs and sent him back to retrieve it. Tombs of one kind or
another are the prize in a journey of this kind; while the simple
Heracleians cut their plain coffin shapes in flat-topped rocks,
here, near the western edge of Lycia, the tourist finds his first
temple façades dating from the fourth century BC – twenty of
them cut in a near-vertical cliff that must once have dropped
straight into the water. There is now a broad skirt of flat silt below
them, with a few small damp houses and their muddy gardens,
barely above the level of the water; a woman winnowing a sack of
millet smiled as we clambered over her fence, and at the base of
the cliff a crumpled crone let loose a pair of goats that scrambled
ahead of us. It is the water and their accessibility that make the
tombs so attractive, but nothing is to be gained from climbing to
them, for theirs is the grandeur of the stage flat, and beyond the
tall columns and pilasters are only plain chambers ankle-deep in
goat droppings.

The city is downstream through the reeds – tall as young
poplars, luxuriant as ostrich feathers – grown out of the silt that

long ago killed the city. Strabo in his *Geographica* described
Caunus at more or less the time of Christ as unhealthy, blaming
the heat and the abundance of fruit – and it is still true that
bacteria from faeces-contaminated water can be carried in melons
and other members of the gourd family, though there is usually
some local immunity that makes only visitors its victims (the fig
can wreak disaster without the aid of microbes). At that time
Caunus was a Roman city; it had never been colonized by the
Greeks, but had been either Rhodian or independent, though its
later inscriptions suggest that it was a thoroughly Hellenic city;
even in Herodotus' day, five centuries before, its origin had been
forgotten and the Caunians did not know whether they were
indigenous or had come from Crete. Its earliest appearance in the
historical record is in the sixth century BC when it was captured by
the Persians under Harpagus. The sea originally swept up to the
city, but the River Calbis brought silt down from the large lake of
Köyceğiz to the north, reducing the depth of the harbours and
dockyards so much that soon after Strabo's day a rich citizen gave
a handsome donation for the remission of harbour dues in order
that ships should still be encouraged to use the port, through
which there had once been heavy passage of figs, slaves, timber,
resin, pitch, salt and salted fish – enough to make it a very rich
city. A long inscription recording this gift survives on the wall of a
building near the harbour, that has been identified both as a
customs building and a fountain; resembling the cella of a small
temple with a waist-high screen across the front in which there
are water-spouts, it is completely free-standing, though the back
is no more than a foot from the substantial rusticated wall of
another, older structure, of which the corner has been neatly and
curiously trimmed with quadrant sections. It makes sense as a
fountain or the base of a nymphaeum, but not as a roofed customs
building. Water must have been piped from the acropolis hill
behind, which carries some considerable traces of Byzantine
walls and fortifications, and must have had a water supply – a
local guide assured us that the spring still survives, but even in
midwinter we were unable to find it. In our search we found other
things – a huge and lively tortoise with a white patch of dead
shell, wild anemones, swarms of wasps and bees, and a mosquito
that took a bite out of my cheek.

The mosquito came to Caunus with the silt; they must always
have swarmed on the lake to the north, and as the sea retreated

the reeds took root, and so did this small angel of death – even in the fourth century BC the complexions of the Caunians were so jaundiced that they were described as dead men walking the streets. For many centuries the marshes were their breeding-ground, but these are now criss-crossed by broad channels constantly disturbed by the craft that carry tourists and by fishing-boats. Much of the water is a fish hatchery, gated by a timber contraption that must be raised to let craft through, as picturesque as the kind of Japanese print that so influenced Van Gogh – our boatman seemed at pains to cover his small catch of fish as we passed it, and when through, tossed one of them back as an apparent thank-offering (he would answer no questions); the rest he bagged after selling some of the smallest to Ayhan. The Turks, whom I believe to be the most honest people left in the Mediterranean, persist in the absurd fiction that small fish taste better than large – they will offer a choice of bass and minnows, and be disappointed if you do not choose the latter; admittedly you get at least three, but they will have been fried to perdition, while the bass will be succulent – it is a mystery, for the bass is inevitably far more expensive. Ayhan, late in the day, bore his purchase into a restaurant by the harbour and insisted that they cook it for us, explaining, yet again, that we were important journalists from London and that we must be pampered; as a heap of identical minnows lay on show in the restaurant's refrigerator, we were embarrassed by his disagreeable insistence.

The city of Caunus must be a disappointment to the ordinary tourist, who would be best advised to treat it as a boat trip, if he can stand the constant echoing of gunshot that terrifies the moorhens. All three watery approaches have their charm – from the sea, now two miles away, and from the village of Köyceğiz at the head of the lake, both of which induce a sense of repose and avoid the tourist bustle of the harbour at Dalyan, from which the visitor in a hurry will take the shortest voyage – but even that is long enough to gentle and entrance him with the diorama of the temple tombs. The theatre is small, its left wing cut into the acropolis hill, and of the Greek type, noticeably more than a half circle; every five and half paces or so along many rows of seats are circular holes some 25 centimetres in diameter to take substantial posts, suggesting that it was permanently roofed with timber. Little is left of the stage building that Bean suggests 'would repay excavation'; now excavated, it merely provides lavatorial convenience and privacy for those foolish enough to forget that the acoustics of the theatre are little impaired by its ruined condition. Amongst other recent excavations a remarkably pretty white marble *tempietto* has emerged, twelve feet or so in diameter, with perhaps eight columns (it is sadly incomplete) carved with swags and animal heads a foot above their bases, supporting a ceiling with a large central rosette and swastikas in panels flanked by small rosettes, roofed with a single piece of marble carved with graduated scales in a shallow rise; there was no sign of bases, capitals or floor.

Fethiye * Hierapolis

It was almost dark when we reached Fethiye, where it had been raining all day, and the once smart boulevard that leads into the town was awash with muddy water, its surface deeply broken and almost worse than the country roads of Cnidus. The only open hotel was cold and damp, apart from its entrance hall, where half the citizenry seemed to be warming itself over the stove; there was no hot water, the washbasin was hanging away from the wall, supported only by the plumbing, and the taps spun loose – when we went to bed a mephitic smell was billowing from it as a reminder that occasionally the traveller should still be wary of tap-water. The Turkish problem of lassitude and inertia is constant throughout the land – they rarely repair anything, but use it till it rots, and the country is littered with tasteless concrete blocks fallen into immediate desuetude to join the more portable and degradable rubbish; a new small hotel in Istanbul may take five years to sink from its Swedish aspirations to a slum, and with the invasion of Iranian and Iraqi expatriates the decline accelerates appallingly. We tramped round the sodden town in search of the Hamam and the comfort of a hot bath, but it was closed for repair; back at the hotel we washed our various parts in water of a temperature that my notebook records as 'scrotum-shrinking' and changed into our

last clean shirts. My notebook continues, 'Feel a bit of a shit about
losing my temper with Ayhan, he is maddening and cannot see it;
I am reassured that he niggles Petter at least as much with his
constant admonitions – don't drive so fast, keep to the right,
don't overtake – yet he is himself a dreadful, horn-blowing,
hesitant driver.'

  We sat in the hotel entrance, deafened by the clatter of worry-
beads, objects of curiosity constantly plied with glasses of tea that
were no help to my dreadful sense of coffee-deprivation – I
tremble and vomit when I have it to excess, and headaches,
trembling, and a frightening loss of cerebral control akin to senile
dementia overtake me when I have no access to it. There is no
remedy. We summoned enough energy to lead Ayhan to dinner
in a back-street restaurant near the Hamam – not his choice, and
he let everyone there know it. A young man at another table sent
us a dish of nuts to quieten him, and began one of those awkward
smiling, nodding, wordless conversations that receives a boost
every time one accidentally glances in what has become the
wrong direction; at last he left his friends and staggered over to
occupy our fourth chair – 'I am Turkish doctor', he said. He
insisted on English, but he seemed to know only the English that
he knew, responding with blank stares to anything that I said. He
put his arm round Petter's shoulders and began again – 'I am
Turkish doctor. I excuse you. I love you. This night I want . . .',
and at this point ran out of words, though his amatory intention
was clear enough. He was small and dark, with misshapen
clumsy hands, not at all clean; I vaguely hoped that he was not a
surgeon as well as a physician. His friends gathered round and
after repeated and unnecessary apologies shepherded him back
to their table, helping both him and us out of an embarrassing
dead-end, but he escaped them and returned – eventually a
drunken chase round the tables ended with his standing with his
back to the wall pleading not to be thrown out. It was the signal
for us to leave, so that he could stay; he seemed so pathetic and
miserable that I could not resist giving him the friendly reassurance of a hug, but when Petter followed suit he was grabbed in an
ungainly clinch and kissed – and more kisses were blown at us as
his friends detached him and held him down. The restaurant
owner pressed a card into my hand – 'Amintos Restaurant, across
the Turkish Bath'.

Amyntas was a local boy buried in a splendid and accessible

temple tomb just outside the town some time in the fourth century BC. Nine more or less famous men bore his name in antiquity, all Macedonians, but that is not enough to presume a Macedonian origin for the otherwise unrecorded occupant of a Lycian tomb. Telmessos is the ancient name for Fethiye; the origin of both name and city are uncertain, but it is in the Athenian tribute lists of the fifth century BC; it was not then counted as part of Lycia, but was integrated with that country in the mid fourth century under the Lycian dynast Perikles. Its great events were few and widely separated; it submitted to Alexander in 334 BC; in early Byzantine times it was a Bishopric and called itself Anastasiupolis; in 1957 it was the victim of a severe earthquake and the consequent rubble was thrown into the sea, both clearing the devastated town and laying the foundations of the new (and now almost derelict) esplanade. The new town is a characterless agglomeration of concrete blocks set on a beautiful fjord; its few monuments are tombs, of which one, perhaps the finest sarcophagus left in place in Lycia, now stands beside the town hall; it is of the house type, the steep rounded lid acting as the roof, and carved with reliefs of warriors. When the landscape painter William James Müller was working in the area in the winter of 1843–4 he painted it free-standing in the sea, some long distance from the shore – the water having risen since antiquity, it has now fallen again to the level of two and half thousand years ago. Fellows found one large theatre 'of extremely plain architecture . . . in tolerable preservation', and four years later, Spratt, in 1842, found two, of which the larger was 'very perfect'. Nothing remains of either, though the large hollow in the acropolis hill behind the town may mark the site of the smaller – the other stood at sea-level on the western edge of the city. One of Luigi Mayer's Turkish views, published in 1803, may be a more or less unfanciful view of it; this shows the *cavea* hollowed out of the cliff, the stage-building a rank of five simple Stonehenge gateways and some fallen stones, literally on the water's edge. The anonymous text, using the then current name of Macri, describes the theatre as magnificent, and then continues 'But all the art of its [Macri's] magicians, for which it was formerly celebrated, have had no effect in preserving it from the sweeping hand of Destruction . . .'. I can find no other reference to the magicians of Macri, and the unknown author must be heightening the city's reputation as a centre of seers, soothsayers and divination – but even this is in error, for the reputation more properly belongs to another city called Telmessus, in Caria, only seven miles from Halicarnassus. The acropolis is topped by the remains of a medieval castle, credited for no very good reason to the Knights of St John; it contains nothing ancient or remarkable, but the long clamber up to it is rewarded with Nordic views across the Bay of Fethiye.

Some twelve miles up in the Taurus Mountains to the north-east of Fethiye, near Üzümlü, is the site of Cadyanda, an obscure city, mentioned only by Pliny. To judge by the numerous tombs it must have been rich in the fifth and fourth centuries BC, and again in Roman times, for the late ruins are impressive. Üzümlü is 2,000 feet above sea-level, and the city another thousand of hard climbing if the shorter route is taken; the longer, easier route passes a number of tombs carved from boulders, of which one has reliefs of a mounted warrior and a man reclining. The theatre is small, prettily ruined and overgrown – indeed the whole site is obscured by vegetation and fallen into disorder; the most remarkable feature is the long narrow stadium in the centre, of which half the original length of two hundred yards survives, and which seems to have doubled as the city's main street – two athletic festivals are recorded in inscriptions.

The road from Fethiye to Üzümlü is good enough to encourage the foolhardy driver to continue northwards, as I did with Michael. He had thrown pellets of bread into his mouth at breakfast – a sure sign of boredom. I reflected for a moment on my mother's adage that no woman should marry until she has seen her intending spouse eat a kipper, put my diary aside, and asked him what he would like to do.

'There's shit in this water.'

We had swum in it the previous evening, dined with it rippling and twinkling beside us, and had even spent a comfortable night without a mosquito. And now he was glowering at it, and indeed there was shit in the water.

'I want to look at the tombs', I ventured.

'I'm sick of tombs', replied Michael.

'There's no point in our being here if we don't look at tombs.'

'I want to go to Pamukkale.'

'But that's miles away, and there's no road from here.'

'There is. I saw it on the map.'

The distance is 150 kilometres in a straight line over the Taurus

Mountains, and the road is marked as unmade. To argue with Michael in bread-throwing mood is utterly pointless, for he will find a way of spoiling your victory; to give way may endow you with a bargaining counter in some subsequent negotiation. We packed and drove out of town. The sane man approaches Pamukkale from Ephesus, two hours of easy driving on a wide road along a river valley, with cafés and bars to refresh him. Only obstinacy to the point of insanity would take a man further into the mountains by Michael's chosen route once the road beyond Üzümlü narrowed; it consisted entirely of small rocks, many of which had to be removed if the journey on was to continue, and was obstructed by toppled pine-trees; the gradients were so steep and so short that more than once we came to an abrupt halt in a dip with the boot of the car grinding against the road's surface – more than once we had to ease the springs by unloading the boot in order to unhook it from a rock. On one of our pauses to remove a tree-trunk two peasants appeared from nowhere (old Turkish habit) and asked for a lift to Çameli; their help was invaluable, but I remember them more for their curiosity about tennis racquets – no balls were at hand with which to demonstrate, and Michael used a roll of lavatory paper instead (it was one of those days); this catastrophic exhibition took place inside the car, which was at once full of paper unrolled by the solemn and uncomprehending Turks dutifully following Michael's instructions.

Not far from Çameli the road became a river and we drove merrily along its bed hoping not to drown the engine – but we unwittingly smashed the exhaust and emerged from the water totally unsilenced. The noise made by a normally civilized engine relieved of all baffles is hideously beyond imagination, and multiplied by echoes in the mountains our approach must have been audible a day's march away; the damage was too extensive to remedy with my assortment of Coca-Cola tins, wire and asbestos tape, and the journey became an endurance test. North of Çameli we boomed and banged through a white landscape – a slightly grubby white, but astonishing nevertheless to see every tree silhouetted – and at last reached Denizli.

Getting a car repaired in Turkey is comparatively simple. One of the access roads to any sizeable town is lined with garages and workshops, most of which will specialize in one particular motoring malady. At the first of these I was given a small boy the size and colour of a chimney-sweep reeking of black oil, who guided me to an exhaust repair shop two or three hundred yards away. No explanation was necessary; within seconds the car was up in the air and four other small boys were busy removing the metal tatters. I have the impression that all manual work in Turkey is done by twelve-year-old boys whose ambition it is to retire at twenty and grow fat; they care neither how long they work nor how dirty they get (most could audition successfully for the leading role in *The Water Babies*), and then suddenly, at twenty, they grow gold teeth, are immaculate, and sit, watch, and eventually grow fat. Other small boys clambered into the car and leafed through my books – it was here that I learned that nothing could be more useful in the way of tips and modest bribes than copies of *Playboy*, of which I had none and for which the novels of Simon Raven and an assortment of guide-books were no substitute; on a later journey, alone and feeling rather vulnerable in the middle of a petrol shortage that had marooned me for three days in the middle of nowhere, I bribed my way to the head of the queue at a garage by the simple expedient of sitting in its forecourt leafing through a *Playboy*, and then striking a bargain for three copies against a tank of petrol.

Accustomed to English garages I had not expected the repair to be immediate and had only enough money for a taxi back to the hotel, but the gold-toothed youth who controlled the boys, after consulting with a council of elders who suddenly appeared like wraiths, refused my watch or any other security that I offered for the £8 that he had asked. They had fitted an exhaust with a flashy fish-tail, plied me with tea, revealed their stock of ancient girly calendars from Germany and Sweden (what can they have thought of laughing blondes launching themselves on tea-trays down snow-covered mountains with not so much as an ear muff to keep out the cold?), and now they trusted me to return next day – it was the kind of generosity that then surprised me, but now no longer does.

We had fallen for the tourist blandishments of Pamukkale, and were staying in an hotel full of one-night visitors. I shall never go again, but every visitor to Turkey should see this strange sight once, for nothing like it exists in Europe; it is the natural equivalent of a Kurt Schwitters *Merzbau*, an off-white agglomeration of cliffs, basins, rivulets, channels, stalagmites and stalactites, fed by streams that dribble from a hot pool at the top. Pamukkale is Turkish for Cotton Castle, and in its softer profiles it indeed resembles a giant heap of slightly used cotton balls, but to the more romantic imagination it must seem a petrified cascade, a frozen tumble of water to disturb the senses in the heat of a Turkish summer; clever propaganda photographers succeed in blanching it startling white, but the real thing is as stained with rust and ochre as an old-fashioned public urinal. Our hotel had taken possession of a pool that fed it, and we were encouraged to swim in its blood-warm water and to look over the edge at the ossified falls below – a slightly disconcerting experience for the nervous swimmer with an unsteady head for heights. The water tasted vile, and was so heavily charged with lime that no soap or shower could rid me of the deposit on skin and hair – for several days I looked as though I had bathed in calamine lotion, my hair was mousey grey, and my feet resembled those of a corpse.

At the top of this strange plateau lie the relics of Hierapolis, their foundations buried deep in the ubiquitous lime. The city may have been named after Hiera, the wife of a mythical hero called Telephus, a superfluous son of Hercules, who was exposed new-born on Mount Parthenius, there to be suckled by a far-sighted goat and educated as a shepherd. Rising in the world, he almost married his mother (Hercules intervening at the last moment), and played a crucial part in the Trojan War by changing allegiance from King Priam (now his father-in-law) to the Greeks, under the influence of Ulysses, who knew the oracular prediction that the Greeks would not be victorious without the aid of a son of Hercules; an unlikely tale, but perhaps embodying some small element of historical truth. According to Stephanus of Byzantium the origin of its name is much more prosaic – Holy City, called so for the great number of its temples. Historically it seems to have been of no political importance, but to have been rich and prosperous nevertheless throughout Roman times, with industries connected with wool, which had to be washed, dyed and woven, and with iron and copper, and as a centre of pilgrimage.

I found my curiosity deadened by the presence of so many tourists, though the theatre and the great baths with their supposedly sacred warm pool should have lifted the spirit. Rivulets of warm water criss-cross the site, steaming harmlessly in the cool evenings; a deadly steam rises from the aptly-named Plutoneion, the city's chief claim to fame, and still a draw to tourists. In Strabo's day this was a deep but narrow orifice in the hillside, filled with a mephitic vapour immediately deadly to small birds,

great oxen, and all mankind with the exception of the eunuchs of
Cybele – why castration should give immunity to poison gas, no
authority ancient or modern has sought to explain. The cleft was
eventually concealed within a chamber at the rear of the Temple
of Apollo, entered through an arched doorway, surrounded with
an auditorium, and turned into an attraction for the tourists of
antiquity. Present-day tourists are convinced of its deadly reputation by the almost inevitable presence in the forecourt of the
corpse of some small domestic animal whose death may or may
not be attributed to the vapour – the cynical must suppose some
unpleasant commercial reason, and the stinking, bloated body of
a dog when I was there seemed to me to have been strangled.
Chandler intended to try its effects on a chicken, but ran into
difficulties with a local bigwig who had come to the warm pool
with his retinue to bathe, and was forced to leave in haste. The
smell is sharp and stinging, not sulphurous (Fellows describes it
as 'the noxious smell of hydrogen'), brings tears to the eyes, and
in my case, though not a eunuch, was not deadly. I do not
suppose that there is any connection between the gas and the
unusually large necropolis of more than a thousand tombs – of
these, only one is remarkable, and that only for the inscription
that records its occupant's seventy-two journeys to Italy.

   As for famous men, the Apostle Philip was its only notable
resident. This father of four daughters, all of whom embraced
Christianity to become a Salvation Army of the day, and what
Polycrates called 'the lights of Asia', was involved in the feeding
of the five thousand and acted as an intermediary between Christ
and those Greeks who wished to see him in the week before the
Crucifixion, yet seems to have been a disappointment to his
Master – 'Have I been so long time with you and yet hast thou not
known me, Philip?' In the Acts of the Apostles he was elected
Deacon, and baptized the Queen of Ethiopia's chief Eunuch; the
last Biblical reference to him, towards the end of Acts, is to Paul's
long stay in his house in Caesarea on the Samarian coast, and his
four prophetic virgin daughters, but as an educated speaker of
Greek it is not surprising that he should have settled in Asia
Minor; there is a fairly constant tradition that he was martyred in
Hierapolis by the priests of Mars. Philip, who had, after all, early
in his Apostolic career been given the power to cast out unclean
spirits, challenged the serpent or dragon that represented the old
god to come out of the priests' sanctuary – it did, crouched in

obeisance at his feet, and promptly evaporated in a cloud of vile fumes that killed off the heir to the throne of Phrygia and all his pretty friends. Philip immediately restored their lives, for which they ought to have been grateful, but instead they allowed the priests to seize him, tie him upside down to a tree, drive nails through his feet and stone him to death. He was buried at the foot of the tree, to be joined there by two of his spinster daughters (burying the sour remains of a joint, particularly pork, in the roots of an ailing tree has a wonderfully revivifying effect). Early in the fifth century a *Martyrium* was erected; Philip's tomb ought to be in it, but his body had perhaps already been taken to Rome (where it is still supposed to be in Santi Apostoli), and the building was neither church nor mausoleum, but a hall for panegyrics and saint's day celebrations (not, presumably, Philippics). It stood for a century or so, and then fell in one of the many earthquakes that plagued the city more than most.

Laodiceia and Colossae are nearby, both visited by St Paul; to Colossae, of which virtually nothing remains (I can recall no more ruined ruin in all Turkey), he addressed an epistle, and Laodiceia is listed in Revelations as one of the Seven Churches of Asia (the others are Ephesus, Smyrna, Pergamum, Thyatira, Sardis and Philadelphia). Fellows shot a vulture there at nine in the morning, packed it in a leather bag, rode all day with it behind his saddle, and at eleven at night unpacked it in his tent – whereupon it spread its great wings, felling the tent, and attempted to escape; Fellows stood on its back as best he could while his servant beat it about the head with his rifle butt – 'My ignorance of the extreme tenacity of life of this bird must exculpate me from the charge of cruelty.' Misadventures can be much more fun than ruins. Chandler ends his notes on this deserted city, which remained a lively place well into Crusader times, with the suggestion that the Turks finished it off, and 'a fox, which we first discovered by its ears, peeping over a brow, was the only inhabitant of Laodiceia'.

— VIII —

Aphrodisias

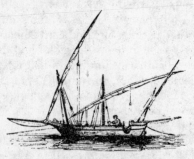

The great site within the wider purlieus of Pamukkale is Aphrodisias. In the beginning were Heaven and Earth, Uranus and Gaea. When Cronus, the youngest of their Titanic children, in league with his mother, cut off his father's penis at the point of penetration, it fell with an almighty splash into the Aegean Sea near Cythera. Never has coitus interruptus been so fruitful, for from the spray and spume of ejaculation and splash emerged Aphrodite, smiling, to become the Goddess of laughter and of sacred and profane love. The Greeks united her with the ancient Semitic Ishtar and with Astarte of the Assyrians and Phoenicians, gave her a beard, endowed her with male and female genitals (still smiling), linked her to the moon, menstruation and the Underworld, and in the Homeric hymn gave her jurisdiction over all things living in earth, air and water. She became the Goddess of gardens and marshes, of passionate sexual impulse, of birth, marriage, family life, and of courtesans and prostitutes; she blessed a man's love for a boy, and a woman's for a girl. As a marine deity, fair winds and prosperous voyages were in her gift, and the dolphin and the seahorse were her emblems. As the Goddess of seasonal fertility, the cypress, poppy, myrtle and pomegranate represented her plenty, and did double duty as remedies for sterility. The tortoise symbolized her marital domesticity (a curious choice when the clumsiness of its mating is considered), and the ram, the hare and the billy-goat her role as a wanton. In her processions, boys strewed the streets with nuts – a symbol current to this day. As a Goddess of War, spear, bow and a crown of city walls signified her role as protectress of her particular place of worship; it was her gift of arms to her son Aeneas that took her cult from Troy to Rome and changed her name to Venus; it was from Rome that the cult of their descendants, the Julio-Claudian Emperors, came to the city that bore her name, Aphrodisias.

In the mid seventies this ancient city was not on the way to anywhere, and the roads to it were bone-shakers. A decade later it has become part of the tourist run from Izmir to Pamukkale, and even the narrow roads across the great belt of the Taurus Mountains make it accessible in half a day from Antalya. It lies a hundred miles east of Ephesus and the Aegean, and thirty miles west of Colosse, but well away from the track beaten between those two cities by the epistle-packing St Paul along the valley of the Maeander; he wrote no letter to it, but could well have had it in mind when he composed his epistle to the Romans, with its diatribe against the sins of the flesh. St Paul has a lot to answer for; the vengeful God of the Jews is an easily understood deity, and the classical pantheon of superhumans with human appetites was one with which ordinary mortals could readily identify, sharing their sensual activities, but their replacement by a Mysterious Trinity beyond comprehension and dependent on faith was only made more difficult when Paul corrupted the humanity and compassion of initial Christian teaching, and ranted against the flesh. In painting, sculpture and mosaics, the effect of Paul's preaching was to de-sensualize the human form, and replace it with a decorative grandeur in which nakedness had no part. Without constant reference to the human body, sculptors fell back on the repetitive formula, and the impetus of realism and the speaking likeness was lost, proportions changed, and the quality of workmanship declined into a thousand years of incompetence, until the artists of the Italian Renaissance turned again to the naked model. Aphrodisias became Christian by slow degrees, and even some two centuries after Christianity was established as the state religion of the Romans in AD 380, the ancient worship of Aphrodite still had its adherents; but with Christian superiority came Pauline attitudes and iconoclasm – the sensual elements of sculpture were eradicated, the heads of pagan figures either smashed or removed, and the sculptors' workshops for which the city was renowned throughout the ancient world were deliberately destroyed. When in the seventh century the city's name was changed to Stauropolis, the City of the Cross, there was no more sculpture, and without Aphrodite there were no more pilgrims in search of sexual remedies, and the city fell into desuetude compounded by a catastrophic earthquake; a thousand years ago it was ravaged by Seljuk and Turkoman invaders, and wiped out.

The Maeander is constantly used as a decorative element in Aphrodisian sculpture, its meandering returns on its track stylized into linked swastikas, but the city lies twenty miles to the south of the river, 1,800 feet up in the Taurus Mountains, behind the peak of Baba Dağ, the Cadmus of antiquity. Twenty miles of steep rough country, and its status as a shrine to the smiling Goddess of what is always uppermost in most men's minds were enough to protect it from the marauding armies using the easy east-west route into the Anatolian heartlands; it built no city walls until long after the birth of Christ. The long valley is typical of that part of the Taurus, fertile and flat as a lake; it is well-watered even in high summer, and there are still substantial traces of the deciduous forest that must easily have supported men as hunter-gatherers before they cleared it and became farmers. Even now the wild figs and pomegranates are too plentiful, and are left to burst and rot on the branch, with only stray Europeans to compete with the birds for their succulent luxury. The site was occupied at least as early as the Calcolithic period, five thousand years ago. In the thirteenth century BC it was known as Ninoe, perhaps after Ninus, King of Assyria, or after Nin, the Accadian name for Ishtar, whose cult may have been established there when Nineveh was destroyed by the Medes and Babylonians. Accad is the Hebrew name of a city on the west bank of the Euphrates, one of the four that formed the nucleus of the kingdom of Nimrod, great-grandson of Noah, and the mighty hunter of the Book of Genesis; hunting was to become one of the great ceremonial pursuits of Aphrodisias, a subject much exploited by its sculptors, and Ishtar, like Aphrodite, was Goddess of War and Love. Pottery of the fourth and fifth centuries BC indicates that a sanctuary of Ishtar-Aphrodite had been established by then. Alexander the Great seems to have paid it no attention when he marched along the Maeander on his way to India, though a few of his coins have been found there. By the third century BC, when the Egyptian historian Apollonius settled there, it bore the name Aphrodisias; and Appian records that in 82 BC, when the Roman general Sulla consulted the Delphic Oracle, it instructed him to send an axe and a golden crown to the 'very great city of Caria named after Aphrodite'. Aphrodite was on this occasion enlisted as a fighting Goddess, for Aphrodisias supported Rome in the wars against Mithridates, the King of northern Anatolia. Caria was the ancient name of the south-west corner of present-day Turkey, seized from the Greeks by the Persian Orontobates, and from him by Alexander; the Seljuk Turks, more than a millennium after Christ called Aphrodisias *Caria*, and the name still survives in the village *Geyre* that occupies part of the site.

In Roman Imperial times the city enjoyed a special status that can only have increased its inherent prosperity. The Maeander valley was a vital route for the Romans, and their hold on it was supported by a zone of free but friendly peoples and strong cities that might control the possibly hostile tribes of the hinterland. The earliest known inscription of political significance there records the alliance of Aphrodisias with two neighbouring cities, all agreeing not to oppose the Romans; it is dedicated to friendship, harmony and Dea Roma, which suggests that Aphrodisias was a Roman client city at least a century before Christ, worshipping Dea Roma as a cult figure. Inscriptions in what has been nicknamed the Archive Wall record that Julius Caesar granted Aphrodisias local autonomy, the right of asylum in the sanctuary of Aphrodite, and immunity from taxation; letters from Augustus and a series of Emperors down to Gordian III in the third century AD confirmed these benefits. The city was looted in 40 BC, and lost a golden statue of Aphrodite's son Eros that had been dedicated by Julius Caesar; this was soon recovered from Ephesus, where the thief had had the impertinence to dedicate it in his own name to Artemis. Augustus wrote, 'I have selected this one city from all Asia as my own . . .'. Trajan promised that the Aphrodisian ambassadors in Rome should, at Games, gladiatorial combats, hunting displays and athletic contests, be seated with Roman Senators. Gordian III, exempting them from some impost, stated that free men may not be subject to orders. Diocletian in AD 301 froze all prices in the Empire's market-places in a vain attempt to halt inflation – the inscription of this edict here blames speculators and profiteers, lists commodities as various as melons, cattle, marble, peas, beans and waggon wheels, and threatens the death penalty for violation.

Inscriptions for these literate people must have been like Chinese newspapers, chronicling the events of the day. Time and again they demonstrate the great wealth of the city fathers, and the prosperity of the people; one priest of Hercules gave enough money to build a hall of sacrifice and another of banqueting, and at his death left twice the sum to endow gymnastic games; families and citizens gave cash prizes for races, wrestling, boxing, armed and unarmed combat and the pentathlon; there were competitions in drama, music, oratory and dance. Aphrodisians had no weekly Sabbath, but the Roman calendar gave them as many holidays as working days; their theatre seated 8,000, and their stadium, nearly three hundred yards long, was one of the largest in the Roman world, and at a pinch sat 30,000. Their hippodrome has not yet been found, but inscriptions prove its sometime existence, and that horse and chariot racing took place in it. Later, the barbarous fights of gladiators were staged in a small circular enclosure at the eastern end of the stadium, and in the theatre the lower seats were removed so that wild beasts could slaughter each other and Christians without endangering spectators. Ritual bull games are also recorded.

Aphrodisias was famous not only for these conventional frivolities, but for medicine (the practices of which it imported from the Dorian islands of the Aegean – an exchange for the slightly oriental influences imported there from Caria) and philosophy; though it conformed to the main stream of Roman Court life, its language remained Greek. All its relics support the notion of life devoted to pleasure, but all is decorous – there are no obscenities, no phallic objects, none of the foreskin jokes of ancient Rome. Yet the city's prosperity came first from the growth of its international status as a shrine; with Ishtar-Aphrodite as an all-purpose deity for sexual and amatory matters, for seasonal plenty, hunting and war, emerging from poly-cultural roots that embraced the whole of the Levant and the Near East, it was for centuries flooded with pilgrims, and the population at its height was perhaps 50,000. Its political and social attitudes were liberal, and it attracted a substantial number of Jews, who, in spite of Hellenized conventions, maintained a synagogue in the city; there were Jewish councillors and Jews in the professions; there are even anti-

Semitic inscriptions, countered by graffiti Menorahs scratched in the approach to the temple.

There was a second source of wealth. When I first saw Aphrodisias what life there was revolved round an enormous spreading tree in whose shade stood a ramshackle tea-house and a clutter of chairs; nearby, a mud hut, painted bright ochre, was fenced about with red and white palings, and the yard thus formed was full of sculpture – not just the conventional sarcophagi, but giant theatrical masks and a high-relief figure of a naked youth, half life-size, surrounded by foliage, in a running energetic pose, striding out of the block, his right arm outstretched, palm outward, to the spectator, as though inviting him to change course and join the chase. There was no indication that it was a hunting subject, and yet some strange connection with medieval tapestries in France seemed to make it certain. It was not a great sculpture in any abstract sense, and the heat, light and brilliant ochre background may have heightened my reaction to it, but it gave me a rare spiritual lift and heightened my expectations of the site. These were soon dashed, for much of the city was closed to visitors, and what was open seemed muddled and confusing. Michael was in an irreverent mood, unwilling to give it time to work a spell, impatient with ground-plans, refusing to walk to the stadium, and when he eventually climbed into a half-buried amphora and demanded to be photographed like the forty-first thief, I did as I was bidden, and we left.

In the summer of 1983, at an archaeological symposium in Istanbul, Professor Kenan Erim made a brief statement on recent discoveries in Aphrodisias that stirred my recollection of the running boy; slides appeared on the screen that showed sculpture of astonishing realism and the promise of an extraordinary processional way unique in the classical world, three storeys high, many yards long, covered with large high reliefs of Gods and classical and historical figures. This *Sebasteion* seemed to lift Aphrodisias to a new and very high level of importance, and I returned to London bubbling with excitement; in October, just as the site was closing for the winter, I spent two weeks there, an amazed and bemused spectator.

After eight years of further excavation Aphrodisias was almost unrecognizable. The great tree remained, but nothing else that was familiar, and where the ochre yellow hut had been there now stood a new, and slightly chill, museum building that might have

sprung from the drawing-board of a Festival of Britain appren-
tice. A boy who reverentially referred to Professor Erim as 'Kenan
Bey' took me across the site to find him supervising the erection of
a column. A man of driving energy, it seemed not to occur to him
that tea, or coffee or beer might be a Godsend, and I stood in the
late afternoon sun subjected to an exhausting dissertation on
the problems of the site and of financing its excavation, all of
which had to be repeated, for at its first recital it was lost to me in
the effort of making polite responses and holding a suitably
attentive and respectful expression. As a young soldier I had
learned to wiggle my toes and clench my buttocks when standing
too long at attention – it was supposed to prevent fainting – and I
did much the same for Kenan Bay, for without caffeine coursing
through me I could not share his enthusiasm. He at last took me
into an enclosure cluttered with sculpture that I recognized from
his slides, and showed me to minute upper rooms in an old timber
house on the far side. The floors sloped like a helter-skelter, and
the furniture was more primitive than in a nunnery; washing was
to be done in the open at an absurdly small sink attached to the
garden wall; showers and loos were in neighbouring cubicles not
quite concealed behind reliefs from the *Sebasteion*. Privacy was
minimal, and so was the water. It was exactly like life in the army,
washing and shaving in only a mug of water, showering under so
few drips that only crutch and armpits merited serious attention –
the only difference was that toads popped out from the dead
leaves and flopped about my feet to catch the little water dripping
from me, and there were sparrows squabbling noisily in the vine
above.

At seven I was summoned to Kenan Bey's balcony and introduced to his two Austrian students, a young Turk from the
Archaeological Museum in Istanbul, a French woman
archaeologist of great distinction, and the burly and dim-witted
Director of the Aphrodisias Museum; we drank vodka and cherry
juice in small measure as moths scorched in the candle flame; I
seemed to be the only one who cared to despatch the wretched
creatures – not the easiest of mercies among the bottles and
glasses on that tiny table, and impossible once they had tumbled
out of the ring of light. The dining-room was a tent of mosquito
netting masked with vines and creepers, autumnal, stagey, like a
set for *Werther*, yet essentially practical, apart from the evening
chill. There was not enough to eat. There never was, and I should

have guessed so from the way that the others fell on their food as Kenan Bey dished the small portions; when the bowls and dishes were empty, I was surprised to see Gerhard and Franz, his Austrian students, scrape them clean with scraps of bread, sharing, almost as a religious exercise, any smear or fragment of food that had any body to it.

I was very hungry after the journey from Izmir; I had stopped for lunch at a fish restaurant where they kept their stock of trout in a concrete pool in which small boys banged a plank of wood to keep it aerated – death must have been a blessed relief to the concussed fish, some of which were bounced out of the water. They were cooked in deep earthenware platters in which the bones continued to sizzle long after the flesh was picked; but there had been a grey kitten with a white face, and a pathetic bitch puppy all paws and ribs, too slow and gangling ever to beat the kitten to a morsel, and all my trout had gone into their maws, and only scraps of bread and fishy oil into mine. After dinner I would have sold my soul for a biscuit, and hunger, cold and the acute slope of the bed towards the middle of the floor conspired to keep sleep fitful.

We had been warned that breakfast was at 7.30, and I woke with ten minutes to spare. It was too cold to wash, and the previous evening's shave would last. Coffee, alas, was inadequate; it did not matter that breakfast was of a small quantity of dry bread with unidentifiable jams that resembled sulphurous mud, I needed coffee, and cursed myself for not bringing Nescafé from London; if all other sources of caffeine fail, a mouthful of Coca-Cola poured onto a spoonful of Nescafé will erupt into a seething froth that can be spooned like a thin mousse – vile, but effective. It was the beginning of a routine that dominated all my actions for the next ten days or so. Professor Erim held court at Aphrodisias as though he were the Prince-Bishop of Würzburg – only the luxury and the Tiepolos were missing. His conversation was as brilliant at breakfast as at dinner – hours of exegesis, the illiberal prejudices of race and class masked, but not concealed, by courtesy, an astonishing memory enlisted as much in the work of sentiment as in scholarship, an incisive mind intolerant of folly, ignorance and woolly thinking, the ability to stimulate, maintain and orchestrate a polyglot conversation, switching to and from French, German, English, Italian and Turkish without hesitation, throwing in the relevant Latin and Greek, drawing guests and staff into the current – it was enough to make me feel an ill-coordinated puppy in a race with a whippet. I had had warning in one of his letters that his attitude would be *de haut en bas* – '. . . I am not particularly eager to have Aphrodisias become a common household word . . . there is enough bad taste proliferating everywhere, and too many tourists currently pestering us . . . if I were one of those aristocratic dilettanti I would keep Aphrodisias as a *chasse gardée* to be seen only by those who appreciate sculpture of the Roman period . . .'

Kenan Bey has been working on the site since 1961. A brief excavation in 1904–5 had uncovered the Roman baths; another, in 1937, had found a magnificent first-century frieze of garlanded heads (now in the museum in Izmir); the city was reputed to have been the home of a significant school of sculpture in antiquity, but there are tantalizingly few references in early texts. On his first visit, in 1959, he found fragments of sculpture embedded in the village houses, sarcophagi in use as drinking troughs for cattle and as vats for the local wine, and every doorstep was a chunk of marble. The problems were formidable; there was not a trace of the theatre, which had earlier been mistaken for an acropolis, for it was completely filled with earth and covered with villagers' houses; the almost perfect small odeon was found under a field of lentils, and a still complete domed bath-house under a patch of artichokes. The earthquakes that had repeatedly demolished the great buildings had disturbed the water-courses, and some parts of the site were flooded – it is an irony that Aphrodite should also be the goddess of marshes. The city's sanctity had been protection enough in Imperial times, but the early Christian Byzantines had to build a wall to protect the old heart of the city, and in doing so dragged masonry from buildings outside its line, which may have fallen in earthquakes or been felled for the purpose – there is now no means of identifying the structures from which inscribed stones, columns and capitals were taken to be heaped higgledy-piggledy.

Early finds were taken to Izmir, but Erim's finds are housed in the new and already full museum on the site, with enough material in the yards of the excavation centre to fill another three. Much of it is conventional – huge and dramatic female figures from the theatre, official portraiture, often more than twice life-size, boxers from the stadium, and copies after such early Greek originals as the 'Diskophorus' of Polykleitos – but even the copies are vital and freshly-observed, as though the sculptors referred once more to the living model before defining the musculature or projecting a buttock, and they are imbued with a quality that distinguishes them from hack reproductions; they are of infinitely better quality than the work of the sculptors who decorated the public buildings of Side, Perge and Aspendos, the great cities of the south coast. As far as I know, no-one has speculated on the problem of how the images of great Greek sculptures were transmitted; every student worth his salt in the sixteenth century flocked across Europe to see the latest Michelangelo, drew it, and went home and did it – and for those who did not go, there was a brisk trade in prints that reversed the image so that feeble paintings of the period are littered with the ideas of Michelangelo back-to-front. But what happened in the ancient world? – no drawings have survived, no paintings – was the traffic dependent on sculptured copies small and large?

The Aphrodisians did not restrict themselves to what we might describe as works of art; recognizing the steadiness of the market, they prepared sarcophagi in great numbers, their decorative swags and putti blocked out in abstract patterns, or drilled and roughly finished, the heads of their portrait figures left blank until their occupants were known. Every building in the city seems to have been decorated with stone swags of fruit, and every flat surface embellished with not only the conventional masks of Tragedy and Comedy from the Theatre, but with heads that suggest the presence in the city of Negroes and Tartars, and that characterize all the moods and ages of man. The city must have seemed constantly in a state of Carnival, and on high days and holidays swags of real fruit were slung across the streets to join the carvings. A great ceremonial gateway with a baroque broken pediment marked the exit to the Hunt, carved with jubilant youths, deer, mastiffs, and a hound pulling down a bear, all interwoven with foliage, as in a medieval tapestry.

The *Zoilos Relief* is the earliest sculpture to suggest that the Aphrodisians were capable of devising a programme for a work of art, that the quality of their invention and technical achievement was at least the equal of work in contemporary metropolitan Rome, and that a long tradition was already well-established – it indicates that much more work of the Augustan and pre-Augustan period has yet to be discovered on the site. Zoilos was a priest of Aphrodite, a magistrate, and the leader who won from

Augustus the city's perpetual tax exemptions and freedom. Greatly respected, he was celebrated with a relief that shows him greeting Demos, the people, crowned by Honour, watched over by the City, contemplated by Eternity – a grossly flattering programme. It is in the Greek and Pergamene tradition of such high relief as to be almost free-standing sculpture set against a plane. Aphrodite in her role as Polis, the city, is crowned with the walls that Aphrodisias did not have; diaphanous drapery clings to her body, sensuously heightening the swell of her breasts and belly, clinging to her ankles as she strides out of the stone. The skeletons found in Aphrodisias are very short, indicating that the inhabitants were rarely more than five feet tall; for them the *Zoilos Relief* was the more impressive for being life-size.

Even more remarkable is the *Sebasteion*, the ceremonial approach to the temple of the Julio-Claudian Emperors, direct descendants (so they claimed) of Aphrodite. This was discovered by chance in 1979, has proved to be unique, and is a treasure-house of sculpture. Entering through a huge monumental gate, the spectator found himself in a courtyard some fifteen yards wide and seventy yards long; ahead were the steps to the temple, and on either side was a façade of applied columns framing, in the first and second storeys, high reliefs that illustrated on the one hand the heroic deeds of Hercules, and on the other such acts of Imperial heroism as Claudius seizing Britannia, and Nero seizing Armenia. The programme on which it was based was begun in the reign of Augustus and finished under Nero, and seems to have been adjusted to fit events as they occurred. Augustus appears most often, youthful and naked, and his acting as counterpart to Hercules is much the same as the medieval and Renaissance Christian system of treating episodes in the Old Testament as counterparts of the New. The lowest panels, possibly once painted, are inscribed with the names of Roman provinces in North Africa, the Balkans, the Crimea, Judaea and elsewhere, as in the Hadrianeum in Rome.

Some of the sculptors realized that their reliefs would rarely be seen from a stationary and central viewpoint, and adjusted their compositions and the depth of the cutting so that they would be more telling from an angle and from below. The variations in the quality of invention and style are astonishing, for some are as smoothly and coldly classicizing as any post-Flaxman war memorial, and others, such as *Prometheus Unbound*, as anguished and

Top William Pars, 1765: the Gymnasium at Ephesus. This view not only gives a very clear impression of the overgrown dereliction of the site (in sharp contrast to its present state in which almost every building is excavated and identified), but of the conditions of the eighteenth-century traveller, writing in his tent, his supper boiling in a pot, his water in a goatskin, and his need for an armoury of shotguns and pistols. *(Trustees of the British Museum)*

Below Patrice Bonnet, 1911: a French archaeologist's reconstruction of Priene from the seaward approach, with the acropolis hill looming behind. The city was built on a regular grid plan, turning roads into flights of steps where the gradients were steep. With its shoulders against the hill, and massive walls on its flanks, it was easily defensible. The Temple of Athena is the large columned building to the left; the Theatre is on the same level, to the right. *(École Nationale Supérieure des Beaux-Arts, Paris)*

Top Albert Thomas, 1874: the temple of Apollo at Didyma, showing the extent to which the huge columns were buried, and the interior completely filled with earth and topped by a windmill. *(École Nationale Supérieure des Beaux-Arts, Paris)*

Below Charles Fellows, 1839: the temple at Euromos, wrongly identified by Fellows as Labranda. It is in much the same condition now, a single row of Corinthian columns (peripteros) that once surrounded a cella, a mere hundred yards from the Milas road in wooded country.

Louis Bernier, 1877: a French architect's reconstruction of the tomb of
Mausolus at Halicarnassus. The fragments of sculpture incorporated in
the Castle at Bodrum are here placed in continuous reliefs above and
below the columns. The body of Mausolus must have been in a
sarcophagus in the lowest part; the temple-like columned structure
would have been used for public ceremonies; the stepped pyramid above
may have been a grandiose enlargement of a Phoenician tomb pattern. It
dates from c.350 BC, stood for 1,500 years until filled by an earthquake,
and was reduced to rubble by the Knights of St John when they
plundered its stones for their castle in Bodrum in 1402. *(École Nationale
Supérieure des Beaux-Arts, Paris)*

Top Luigi Mayer, before 1792: the castle at Bodrum, incorporating in its walls fragments of the continuous relief known to have surrounded the tomb of Mausolus of Halicarnassus, which was plundered for its dressed stones when the Knights of St John built the castle in 1402.

Below Luigi Mayer, before 1792: the harbour of Cnidus, capable, according to Strabo, of accommodating twenty trirenes in its deep water; other boats were beached beyond the harbour walls. The narrow entrance to the harbour could be closed with heavy chains.

Charles Fellows, 1839: the tomb of Amyntas of Telmessus, Fethiye. This is one of the grandest temple tombs in Turkey, but nothing other than his name is known of the occupant. It is in much the same condition now as in Fellows' day.

Top Luigi Mayer, before 1792: the harbour at Fethiye, here called Macri, with substantial remains of the lower theatre still standing. Of this there is now no trace; the shore line was radically changed by devastating earthquakes as recently as the 1950s, and the sea level has risen.

Below Charles Fellows, 1839: Lycian rock tombs in the Acropolis at Tlos, the first sight of the city from the Kemer road. The Turkish Aga's fortifications, now largely destroyed, can be seen on the pinnacle above; the sheer fall of the rock and the valley of the Xanthus river can be seen on the right.

Top Charles Fellows, 1839: tombs at Xanthus. The temple tomb on the left is of a type common throughout Lycia, but the pillar tomb is unique to Xanthus.

Below Charles Fellows, 1839: the theatre at Xanthus as he found it, before his depredations on behalf of the British Museum, heavily overgrown.

Top Luigi Mayer, before 1792: a necropolis at Myra, here identified a Cacamo. Of this there is now no trace, nor does the sea come near the very prominent necropolis surrounding the theatre. Mayer, a diligent and plodding draughtsman, must have had strong evidence for this vi somewhere in the immediate area of Myra, perhaps at its nearby port Andriake.

Below Luigi Mayer, before 1792: the theatre at Myra, here identified Cacamo. It is in much the same condition now, the seats more broker but with no serious falls in the last two centuries. Mayer's perspective separates it further from the rock face behind than is the case.

baroque as the *Laocoön*. They are brilliant enough in the clear Anatolian sun, random neighbours in the sculpture yard, but when they were in their place high above the spectators, and seen at night in the flickering light of processional torches, the effect must have been overwhelming.

There is one comparable relief in Rome, installed high above a door in the entrance hall of the Villa Borghese, from which Curtius and his horse leap into the gulf; set there, it gives much the same dramatic impression as the reliefs of the *Sebasteion* must have made in their time. Glycon's great *Farnese Hercules* in Naples, so devastatingly influential in post-Renaissance art, is now thought to be a copy after Lysippus; whatever the case, either it or the original was cleverly adapted by one Aphrodisian sculptor for his relief of Hercules and the exhausted Erymanthean boar. What seems common to so many of the sculptures is that however conventional the iconography, some fresh observation is introduced, even into the *Three Graces*; *Leda and the Swan*, like windsurfers, do it standing up, she sagging with post-coital contentment, he still clasping her thigh with a clammy webbed foot, and the whole composition supported on his pinions and on a daring invention of drapery that doubles as the swan's tail – the pattern was widespread in Hellenistic times and often copied by the Romans, but the Aphrodisias version has an intense and urgent quality that makes the formula seem original.

Construction began early in the first century AD, was developed in two stages, and was paid for by two families. The programme must have been conceived by a philosopher or priest and adjusted as time passed and Emperors changed. An earthquake demolished the first side before it was completed, and work began again; there is no record of the whole building ever having been finished, and perhaps it never was. Aphrodisias may be littered with inscriptions, but few observations on the city were recorded outside; even so, if the *Sebasteion* was ever completed it is surprising that there should be no record of it, for even by Imperial Roman standards it was a very grand conception, and worth a note of wonderment. It can never have been stable; the great number of original earthenware drainpipes laid in the ground indicate that flooding was a problem even when the foundations were dug, and with each earthquake the watercourses changed; the façades were buttressed at the back by a double series of small rooms that perhaps served as shops or offices, but the large blocks of sculpture had to be very nicely placed between the columns, were very heavy (even though those in the upper registers were much thinner), and, unlike small masonry blocks, had no give or shift in them when earthquakes occurred. It was as inherently unstable as a house of cards. Water runs almost the length of the site now, burrowing under the paving-stones in such depth that it supports schools of small fish, and the flooded western end is the home of a chorus of frogs and the ghost of Aristophanes.

Aphrodisias was a rich source of marble, and exported it in blocks and rough cuts down the steep valley of the local river, the Dandalus or ancient Morsynus, to the Maeander, where it was loaded onto bigger barges and shipped to the Aegean and beyond. There is now some strong suggestion that Aphrodisian sculpture found its way to Jerash in Jordan and Leptis Magna in Libya; we know that it reached Rome. Such connections must be made on stylistic grounds and on inscriptions and signatures, for scientific analysis of marble is not, at the moment, much help – its crystalline quality can vary from quarry to quarry in very short compass. Ancient Aphrodisias produced stone ranging from brilliant white with the surface transparency of sugar, to a soft, warm, pinkish brown, and there was an astonishing piebald vein in blue and white that on a small scale enabled sculptors to produce from a single block figures of which the body was white and the drapery blue.

If they exported the stone, it is reasonable to assume that they also exported the sculptors and masons to work it. When Augustus was a young man, Rome was a contemptible sprawling huddle of bricks; when he died, it was an Imperial city of marble. It had no long tradition of great architecture and sculpture, few craftsmen and masons, no known native sculptors. Sulla, who knew Aphrodisias, was reduced to stealing the columns from the Temple of Zeus in Athens in order to install them on the Roman Capitol; rich Romans habitually plundered the antiquities of Greece, and if they could not get the originals, commissioned copies; foreign sculptors flooded into the city. If Suetonius is right, and Augustus really did find Rome a city built of brick, but left it carapaced in marble, then such a transformation in so short a time could only have been achieved with outside and expert help. Could that help have come from Aphrodisias? Could that be the explanation of the letter from Augustus – 'I have selected this one city from all Asia as my own'?

The days passed in a blur of work and monastic discipline. I slept badly, more for the acute slope of the floor, and in consequence the bed (which more than once pitched me out when I turned over), than for the small and rock-hard pillow; the advantage of the bitter morning cold was that there was every excuse for neither washing nor shaving (best done in the evening, when a day of basking in the sun had warmed the water tank); with all these toilet chores removed, I could stay in bed, wide awake and shivering, until the last moment before breakfast. One night I dreamed about Haile Selassie at some curious reception in the not unsuitable setting of Würzburg – he was so frail that he had to be supported on a wooden framework, adjusted by his minions every time he changed attitude; a tiny negro boy, eightish, entered, dressed as a king, and made obeisance to him – and we all burst into tears; it was an emotional state strong enough to wake me, but I drifted off again, this time to Christie's with Hecate, my whippet, all my other dogs, and a pet rabbit on a string, all in amity. At breakfast after this confusion of images Kenan Bey sandwiched a comment on the meanness of his visitors between an analysis of David Hockney's work on *L'Enfant et les Sortilèges* and a subtle evocation of Turkish intellectual society during the Second World War; I had arrived bearing nothing but my duty-free whisky. In the nearby town of Karaçasu I could find only raki, olives and some rather nasty sweet biscuits, and was taken for German and forced into one of those meaningless conversations that wild Turks seem so much to enjoy – rather more meaningless in my case, for my German is totally without grammar, larded with what passes for an Oxford accent (absurd enough in English, nowadays), and an unfortunate command only of art-historical and barrack-room vocabulary.

I walked and clambered the three kilometres of the walls thrown up against Gothic invasion in the 260s, and later revised and reinforced by the Byzantines. They were certainly in parts built with urgency, but they are not wholly haphazard; they link existing buildings, and columns, capitals and inscribed blocks are frequent enough amongst the rubble, but in places the walls are still faced with thick slabs of marble, and on one stretch these are embellished with neat little swags supporting bunches of grapes. Of the three gates only one remains more or less intact, low and narrow, topped by an enormous inscribed block that supports the full semicircle of a plain pediment, oddly barbaric in its heavy simplicity, and effective in its suggestion of unwelcome; the inscription dedicates it to the eternal survival of the Emperor Constantius II (337–61). This third son of Constantine the Great rehabilitated Arius and Arianism with the same vigour and success as his father had excommunicated the old heresiarch, who had only recently died at the age of eighty-six or so, and was even more responsible than his father for making the Fathers of the Church accept Christianity's role as the Empire's official, established religion – symbolized by his dedication of the first church of Santa Sophia, or Holy Wisdom, in Constantinople in AD 360. He fought from the Danube to Mesopotamia, and died in Cilicia, but did not visit Aphrodisias – just as well, for I suspect that his gate would not have pleased him; he had a long body, but such short legs (and bowed to boot) that overall he was a very short man, yet it was his habit as he passed under the loftiest gates to stoop – and here he would have had good reason. He was not a man to cross; he murdered all relatives who might have threatened his position on his father's death in 337; he pursued with ruthless persistence all whom he *thought* might be his enemies, and executed merciless judgements on them – enjoying it the more if they were fit in wind and limb and their constitutions would stand prolonged and interesting agonies. He had a reputation for chastity astonishing among Roman Emperors, who, ugly as they might be (Constantius, in contrast to his short legs, had a lugubriously long face, with prominent staring eyes), were in amatory matters necessarily irresistible; he always slept alone in a little building protected by a deep ditch, crossed only by a collapsible bridge that he invariably dismantled when he went to bed – a curious sight, the man who ruled from the Atlantic to the Euphrates, from Amsterdam to Alexandria, hauling his plank bridge into the hut as a preliminary to the exercise of the instrument of solitary pleasure at the far end of his long torso, tucked away between his little bow legs.

The stadium forms part of the city wall; the external masonry is largely intact, high and handsome; inside, most of the seating is still in place, the long benches not straight, but slightly curved so that every spectator might have a better view of the full length. At the eastern end, at a time when the Greek tradition of foot-races had fallen into desuetude, a curved wall was thrown across the floor of the stadium to make a circular enclosure for gladiatorial combat; until then, and perhaps continuing concurrently, wrestling, boxing and the pentathlon took place. Games were Pythian rather than Olympic, an altogether lower status of competition that included with athletics and horse-racing, a contest in nomes – the very ancient Greek liturgical hymns that were accompanied by lyre and flute, and which at a late stage were supported by a chorus; from these it was natural enough that contests for harpists and trumpeters should follow, and then in Comedy and Tragedy (the site has produced some extraordinarily beautiful masks), and eventually in sculpture.

Athletics and sculpture go well together. The sculptors of Aphrodisias were able to make constant reference to the naked male, and his stocky muscularity is ever-present within the traditional formula, the little pouch of fat above the hips, the slightly too large heads and straight limbs of the younger boys, the power-packing buttocks of the grown men. The women are altogether less convincing.

I found Gerhard in the *Sebasteion* late one afternoon, numbering stones and noting them in a book – one of the unromantic chores of archaeology; with black hair cut in a Roman mop, broad shoulders, and jeans that promised pretty buttocks, he seemed well-chosen for Aphrodisias. I put it to him that the building was never completed, but he would neither agree nor disagree – I think he was as afraid of my reporting his opinion (if he had one) as I was timid in suggesting to Kenan Bey that the most remarkable thing in what (like Augustus) he had come to regard as his own city, had never actually happened. I sat on the great beam of stone, carved with theatrical masks, that lay in the water at the lower end, watching the speeding minnows and the leaping frogs, picking at an enormous sweet pomegranate from an overhanging tree, brooding, the conviction growing that the *Sebasteion* could never have stood. Sitting at ease in this place of ghosts and spirits, not uncomfortable and disturbing, but melancholy and wistful, I wondered if ESP rather than logic was the source of my conviction.

At lunch one day we were disturbed by a loud and long 'Yoo-hoo' from the gate. Kenan Bey made awful faces at the rest of us – the only time that I saw him relax into conventional bad manners – and yoo-hood back, getting to his feet to greet a large, earnest, professional American woman of uncertain age, dressed in shapeless red and purple as though she had stepped straight from an early painting by Augustus John; she was accompanied by a comparatively small girl, perhaps twenty, blonde, bespectacled and pudgy, called Helga. The woman refused the wreckage on the table, but Helga launched herself at the chilling moussaka with a fierce appetite and her tiny teacup finger stuck straight out (thus depriving the rest of us of the essential second helping); the pupil–teacher relationship seemed a thin disguise for one of a sadder nature. The older woman talked with genuine enthusiasm of Nysa, fifty miles away towards Izmir, describing a complete theatre with the sculpture still in place on the stage building, convinced that it or its sculptors must have come from Aphrodisias; Helga talked of nothing, but munched on everything in sight.

I had been to Nysa, but could not recall the stage building in her terms, and took the chance to slip away and revise my inadequate recollection. Nysa lies on the site of an early Spartan foundation called Athymbra; the mythology is that it was founded by the Seleucid Antiochus I of Syria after a dream, and named after his wife – it was an expensive dream, for his mother and sister also appeared in it and demanded that cities be built and named after them – hence Antiocheia and Laodiceia as well as Nysa; the historical record offers no support for the tale. Apart from a number of philosophers and orators distinguished in their day but now forgotten, it had perhaps two citizens of note – Pythodorus, a friend of Pompey, son-in-law of Mark Antony, father of the confusingly named Pythodoris who was to become successively queen of Pontus and Cappadocia, and Strabo (64 BC–19 AD), who greatly admired her for being a sensible woman, but who is better known for his *Geographica* – seventeen books of physical geography littered with observations on anything remarkable in plant or animal life, partly based on personal observation, partly on sources uncritically plundered, that survived in abbreviated form well into the Middle Ages as a schoolbook (I wish that it had survived into my day, instead of Caesar and Tacitus, and all the other then tedious-seeming texts that were my set books). It is Strabo who tells us that Nysa was a double city, spreading down the line of a river running through a deep ravine, the two parts linked by a bridge (of which little remains), and what must have been a remarkable structure, an amphitheatre spanning the ravine, under which the river ran concealed. Just below the theatre (not to be confused with the amphitheatre) the stream still runs through a tunnel, the name of whose engineer is illegibly recorded in a worn inscription. Bean proposes that the stream was used to flood the arena of the amphitheatre for theatrical sea-battles – the water spectacles of the French King's Court at Fontainebleau were not a new idea.

The site is ravishingly pretty – the road into it very steep and winding, and at points arcaded; the gorge too has traces of arcading cut into the flanking bluffs. But the remains of the gymnasium, library, baths and other buildings are unremarkable. The theatre, at the head of the gorge, looks down into it, almost due south; it is small, its seats disturbed by stunted olive trees; only the lower register of the stage building survives, its five doors leading onto the stage embellished with reliefs of which the second-hand imagery and spiritless cutting make local workmanship abundantly clear – certainly no Aphrodisian sculptor could have been responsible.

There was once a path from Nysa to Acharaca, five kilometres to the west, but it is now too broken to follow and the city is best approached from the main road at Çiftekahveler, taking the side road to Salavatli. Apart from the walls and a bridge in the direction of Nysa (with which it seems to have been a co-foundation by Antiochus), only a ruined Doric temple dedicated to Pluto and Persephone (probably converted into a church by the Byzantines) remains. There is little point in making the effort to reach the city unless it is to make yet another fruitless attempt to identify the cave called the Charonium, which, according to Strabo, was above the temple and had such remarkable curative properties that the sick often recovered after being bedded down in it for several days without food. The cynical might observe that gluttony was common enough in Roman times, and that several days without food would have been of benefit to most of them, cave or no cave. Dreaming and hallucination were part of the process of recovery, but these could well have been the consequences of partial starvation or of the sulphurous fumes that may have filled the place – a nearby stream still stinks of sulphur and is known in Turkish as Sarisu, Yellow Water. As with the Plutoneion at Hierapolis (see p. 103) Strabo tells the tale of bulls dropping dead when urged into the entrance of the cave.

Tlos * Kaş

NEPOYAIYIΩNΩITPAI...
IEYΠAIΩITOΓΠATPIΠAT...
ΦΑΣ ΗΛ

Tlos is reached from Kemer on the road between Fethiye and Xanthus, nine miles or so to the south, and not from the main road along the Xanthus valley. It is signposted in the town, but not once nearer the site; driving south the road eventually forks, and at that point you must return some two hundred yards to a white house on its west side, and take a narrow road on its east side almost opposite. Kemer on a wet January day resembled Piccadilly Circus in the volume and confusion of its traffic; from this hub we could look down the road to Tlos to see that for some hundreds of yards it was axle-deep in mud, wide enough for only one stream of traffic, and occupied by oncoming cars slithering from side to side; Ayhan, instead of waiting out of the way until there was a chance to go forward, stopped the car where it seemed to obstruct all paths, rested his head on the steering-wheel, and refused to budge. He was, I think, having a mild attack of hysteria – I could not follow his argument, though I recognized danger in the rising pitch of his voice, and he would not follow mine that if cars were able to come into town, then cars must be able to leave it – the dispute ended with his getting out of the car and walking away into the rain and out of sight. Petter moved the car, and we sat, wondering what to do, more puzzled than angry. When Ayhan returned he said that we must drive to Xanthus and forget about Tlos; we had argued the point earlier – Xanthus I knew well and did not need to visit again, but Ayhan had never heard of Tlos, could not find it in his guides' Bible, Ekrem Akurgal's *Ancient . . . Ruins of Turkey*, and rather like art historians who cannot find artists in the forty-three volumes of the Lexikon compiled by Thieme und Becker, declared that it did not exist, that I had confused it with Teos (which is in Akurgal), and that his instructions were to take me to Xanthus. Such a use of 'instructions' is calculated to make me obstinate beyond measure.

We stopped at the white house to ask the way, and its owner came with us to be sure; the road climbed rapidly through country that might be the wilder uplands of Derbyshire, and then suddenly, ahead and to the right, the acropolis appeared, a great bluff covered with temple tombs, a sight of such beauty that even Ayhan gasped. We dashed through the pouring rain into the dark tea-house to sort out ourselves and the cameras; it was crowded with young men who shuffled chairs away from the stove, but it was not until my eyes grew accustomed to the gloom that I saw them – at first I could see only the whites of eyes and the glint of teeth. They seemed hostile, but I could not sense whether their coldness was towards us or Ayhan, or both; their only friendly act was the appointment of a taciturn small boy to be our guide. We were waterproof, but he was not – nor was he aware of my slightly fuss-pot distress that he should be so little prepared for our trek in the foul weather. He led us straight to the acropolis; goats sheltering in the tombs confronted us, seeming to hold our eyes with theirs, determined not to give way. A goat's eye is a thing of sinister beauty, the iris made of crushed topaz, yellow and brilliant, each myriad fragment of the jewel reflecting a tiny point of caught light, wide, round and unblinking, horizontally barred by the black line of the pupil; hypnotized, the climber is startled when the beast at last moves, perhaps with an even four-legged spring into the air, perhaps with an extravagant twisting leap that lifts it to another level, facing another direction. Though they corkscrew the air like baroque angels, they have the mien and mischief of devils, and I am never happy until these shaggy black unpredictables are below me; in their book on the lore of rural Greece the Blums report among their narratives the villager who said that the Devil 'has a beard and tail and horns . . . like a goat. That is because goats are so bad . . . always

jumping, jumping here and there. They are bad, so the Diavolo is
a goat.' Their following narrative amuses me more – 'All women
are the sperm of the Diavolo; all men come from God. Women are
born bad, all the sin is theirs. In them is everything that is bad –
that is the Devil's. Men are good – the sperm of God' – odd that
Greece, where the early myth of creation demanded sperm of
Uranus, should still have a peasantry that thinks of its one God as
a sperm-producing deity.

Exploring the tombs was as easy as ducking into cottages in a
village street and induced a sense of complacency that evaporated with a clenching of the bowels on the valley side of the
acropolis, where the fall is almost perpendicular. It is occupied by
the ruins of a Turkish castle, from which rises a rock pinnacle cut
with a stair to a small platform at the top. When Müller visited in
the winter of 1843, only five years after its discovery and identification by Fellows, he had to climb the 'rude rock staircase . . . to
this veritable eagle's nest, where we were received by the Aga – a
sort of feudal chief – with much brusqueness and without the
slightest show of hospitality'. The view from it now, even in
midwinter, is magnificent, and reveals the logic behind the
foundation of the city; mountains offer close protection on the
east, and on the west the valley of the Xanthus lies like a relief
map, with the snow-capped Taurus on the skyline; I can recall no
more dramatic view in western Turkey, and Spratt in 1842
thought it the grandest site in Lycia. We stood, gasping in the
wind and rain, partly with the force of the elements, and (in my
case) partly with the fear of falling – the perpetual dilemma of
experiencing exhilaration at the sight of so extensive and beautiful a landscape, and the nausea induced by having nothing
between me and it.

Tlos is an ancient foundation; Lycian inscriptions call it Tlawa,
and the Hittites of the fourteenth century BC called it Dalawa in
the land of Lukka – the Lycians, incidentally, were among the
sea-people who put so sudden an end to the great Hittite empire.
For Fellows, Spratt and Müller it was not only an ancient city
whose remains were in reasonably good condition, extensive,
with 'extremely massive buildings, suited only for palaces . . .
the theatre . . . the most highly and expensively finished that I
have seen' (Fellows), but a well-fortified Turkish town, with
antique fragments incorporated in its 'strong walls'. Of the
Turkish town and its walls nothing remains but the Aga's ruined

fort; of the massive palaces there is scant trace, and any man visiting Tlos in hope of Ephesian grandeur will be disappointed. To the east of the acropolis is a large flat open space divided into two more or less equal halves with a drop in level to the south – the division, of masonry blocks, appears to be original, but has no obvious purpose – and all is now a cultivated field from which masonry fragments and column stumps have been cleared to mark the borders. Below it there may have been a stadium, but a bustling stream and the dense growth of trees and shrubs have done much damage and impede identification. Between the agora and the road are four handsome Roman buildings with a bath at the southern end, and above them, to the east, is the theatre, so densely overgrown that without our boy we might well have walked past it. Little of Fellows' 'expensive finish' is now to be seen – and indeed the theatre may never have been finished, for among the surviving blocks from the stage building, which was decorated with a system of wreaths and swags supported by putti and male herms (whose carving is as boldly primitive as it is boldly male, and not of sophisticated quality) alternating with panels containing an eagle or a plain uncarved patera, are some very eroded masks, now looking like skulls, that were probably only rough-cut, and others in which the faces are well-finished, but the hair left as plain rough bands around them.

The only other carving of note is on the façade of one of the tombs, low down on the north side of the acropolis, and rather a scramble to reach (it proved easier to climb up from the stream below than down from the acropolis above). It has two doors flanking the carving of a third; each of the high threshold blocks is decorated with an eroded relief of a horse, and above the doors Bellerophon on Pegasus, spear raised, faces a diminutive feline creature that appears wholly indifferent to his impending attack. It has been identified as Bellerophon fighting the Chimaera, but I doubt if any ancient Lycian would have represented that monster so feebly, or been paid for it if he had. The Chimaera certainly had the head of a lion, but it was shouldered onto the body of a she-goat with the tail of a serpent – a far cry from the demure and clearly tom cat of the relief; in some sculptures the Chimaera has the head of a goat emerging halfway along the spine – a corruption, probably, of oriental reliefs of winged animals whose pinions ended with goat-like heads that, when the wings were folded, appeared to grow from spine or flanks. It is a confused

and confusing tale; Bellerophon came from Corinth, and may
have been so called for killing his brother Beller, for that is what
his name appears to mean; he fled to Argos, where the King's
wife took an unrequited fancy to him, and much like Potiphar's
wife with Joseph, then accused him of what, mindful of the laws
of hospitality, he had refused to do; equally mindful of these
laws, the husband could not revenge himself on a guest, so he
despatched Bellerophon to Lycia with a coded message to King
Iobates instructing him to find a convenient way of putting an
end to the tiresome young man. And thus it was that Iobates
sent him off to fight the Chimaera along the Lycian coast near
Olympus, but he killed it instead of succumbing to it. His success
lay with Pegasus, the divine winged horse that sprang from
Medusa's body when Perseus cut off her head (what had she
been up to – were stallions immune to her stony stare?), and came
to rest on the acropolis in Corinth, there to be caught by Bellerophon with the aid of a golden bridle given him in his sleep by
Athena. There were to be other such adventures for this ancient
Roy Rogers before he succeeded Iobates as King of Lycia, found-
ing a dynasty with his son Hippolachus; and his horse was
assumed into heaven after Zeus had sent a gadfly to sting him
into throwing Bellerophon, who was making heavenward too
and was not welcome – some say his fall blinded him (concussion
and severe damage to the optic nerve), others that he broke a leg
and limped ever after.

Some fifteen miles south of Kemer, along the Xanthus valley,
the track to Pinara was deep in mud, and we left Ayhan with the
car, relieved to be without his intrusive presence. The winding
path rises steeply from a right-angle bend, and as we breasted the
top of the hill the city's most astonishing feature seemed suddenly there – a great steep hummock of a hill, 1,500 feet high, its
sloping flat top rising to the left, its vertical sides honeycombed
with tomb chambers from end to end and top to bottom. At a
second glance it is clear that the neighbouring cliffs, hundreds of
feet high, are similarly burrowed. The ancient myth of the city's
foundation is that neighbouring Xanthus sent a section of its
surplus population to colonize the hill for a new city, that the
Lycian for circular is *pinara*, and that the hummock is more or less
round. It is not round, but the story will do, and it is a better tale
than that the founder was Pinarus, the son of Tremiles, the
founder of the Lycian nation. Very little remains of the earliest

city – a few cisterns and rock foundations – but it must have remained at least a defensive position for well over two thousand years, for the relic of a small medieval fort still stands on its south-west corner and it remained a Bishopric till the very end of the ninth century. A difficult and slippery path on the south side is the only access that there can ever have been. The earliest tombs must be those at the top, cut with the aid of ropes from above.

The later city nestles below the acropolis to which the citizens presumably withdrew when attacked. The ruins are extensive, but very difficult to read among the overgrowth and rock-falls. Bean describes its small theatre as 'in wretched condition, utterly overthrown and overgrown', and we failed to identify it with any certainty. The villagers from the neighbouring hamlet of Minara have marked a path of red spots that conducts the visitor to some, but by no means all, the things worth seeing, and as it is in some respects as confusing as the maze at Hampton Court, the unwary will find either that they walk in a circle, or that all paths lead to the village. With difficulty we found the so-called Royal Tomb in which Fellows made the plaster casts, now in the British Museum, of the carved reliefs of townscapes – battlemented and gated walls, with towers, tombs, houses and palaces within them, cut shallow in the living rock. Fellows thought them views of Pinara, but the city was never walled; even so they are of vital importance in two respects – as astonishingly early examples of landscape in art, and as records of the appearance of ancient Lycian towns. Fellows' plaster casts are now of inestimable value, for, since they were made, the originals have eroded so much that they are unreadable without foreknowledge – other reliefs in the tomb, of people and horses, have survived rather better. The tomb cannot be seen until you are upon it, for it is screened by trees when the path to the site runs out, and there it is essential to bear left, cross the river, and climb to the left; if you do not cross the river you will soon come to a handsome group of tombs cut in the jutting angle of a rocky outcrop. Two other tombs are worth finding – one with an entrance of crossed ox-horns cut in the rock, and another with a single relief of a horse and rider high on the right, inside its entrance.

For no very good reason I found it a delightful and moving site; its only other occupant was a stout elderly woman with a few goats, spinning wool with a primitive weight, and nothing disturbed the general melancholy that was reinforced by the rain and the dying light darkened by the shadow cast by the great acropolis. We felt disinclined to leave, and sat in the entrance of the Royal Tomb, smoking in companionable silence. Petter eventually set off the way we had come, but I took a bead on where I thought the car to be and set off in a straight line; almost at once I had my comeuppance with a fall, heavily on my left elbow; there was no pain, but my breathlessness, if nothing else, told me that I'd had quite a whack, and that I'd been foolish to take orienteering risks in the poor light. Ayhan was by now flashing the car headlamps; we thought that he was trying to be helpful, but when we reached him realized that it was only impatience. He let Petter drive, but at once destroyed our contemplative mood and the wish to at least attempt to share with him the reasons for it, with 'slow here', 'go slowly', 'stop, stop', so frequently that Petter quite suddenly stopped, got out, and joined me in the back; we were then treated to a nightmare of stops and starts, mostly on the wrong side of the road, until we reached Kaş.

Ten years earlier, and in late summer, Michael and I, after a day of hot and dusty driving along the unmade and rock-strewn coast road from Antalya, had found Kaş without water and had bathed naked in a nearby cove. It was deserted when we took off our clothes and entered the water, but not when we left it; one of the ubiquitous mysteries of Turkey is the capacity of the Turk to manifest himself from nowhere, and it had happened again – there, by our clothes, squatted a young man, watching. Michael, who is after all a venereologist and should not be shy about private quarters, would not leave the water; I believe that any awkward situation can be saved with actions that express gravity and purpose, and began to walk out of the sea intending to offer a greeting and go about my business as though swimming naked were the most customary thing in the world, but I had forgotten the cruel sharpness of the beach that had ended at thigh depth and now began again, drawing from me curses and the exaggerated gestures of the clown. Gravity was snatched away from me, and the curious Turk had the good grace to grin.

Later, with Jill and David, the little town had again run out of water, and all washing was done under the hesitant dribbles from the stand-pipe in the hotel garden. We had not chosen that hotel – a boy had resolutely stopped the Range-Rover as we drove into town and taken us to it. He reappeared when we were having dinner – and just as well, for he was a diversion in disaster. Jill was in a bossy mood and wanted lobster – not that these two things are invariably associated, but it meant dining at the only halfway expensive restaurant, a concrete platform at the eastern end of the harbour. The waiter, a boy of sixteen or so, took the order for her lobster, and went to the edge of the platform to haul in a piece of string; it came too easily, and ended in nothing. We watched, puzzled by his action and his consternation. He hauled in another string, and another, and another. All four were mere strings. He called another boy, and both stripped off their clothes and dived into the water. 'Oh God. They're looking for the lobsters', said Jill, and broke into the kind of giggle that is self-perpetuating. They found them, eventually. I was for changing the order, but communication with a submarine waiter is impossible, and our gestures when the boys surfaced for air were clearly taken as encouragement.

Dinner was a long time coming, and Jill became assertive with wine on her waiting tummy. A young couple at a neighbouring table were soon divined to be English, but of liberal tendencies, and she trotted out her 'I'm a magistrate. I know', building a wall of hostility between us. The boy who had taken us to the hotel came and sat with us. 'Who's he?' I explained. 'Send him away.' I refused. The boy wanted to speak English and was more amusing than Jill's Conservatism, and we scribbled and sketched all over the paper that passed for a table-cloth in an exchange of lessons that was at least as much for my benefit as his. He was perhaps the ugliest boy I have ever seen in Turkey – big, raw-boned, rough and blunt-featured, with hair a tenth of an inch long, sixteen and ambitious to be a coach-driver – but behind the apparent back-street toughness lay a wholly engaging character. He refused my offer of dinner (Jill groaning in case we had to share a lobster with him), and accepted a Coca-Cola only for the sake of my need to give hospitality. Dinner done, he offered to show us the tombs in the town; David refused, sensibly, for it was night, but Jill accepted – they argued a little, and I then volunteered to go with Jill, unwillingly, while David went to bed.

At the top of the street at the east end of the village, a huge Lycian tomb of the house type stands free on a high podium, picturesque against the falling curve of an ancient tree. In that domestic setting it is not robbed of grandeur, but even enhanced, the more astonishing. Young Mustafa climbed it and crouched in the panel smashed by grave robbers, urging us to join him. We refused, and Jill in any case was far too tipsy for such a jape. He volunteered another tomb and set off up the hill; gently offering Jill his hand. She refused, and then stumbled, and Mustafa put his arm round her waist. I followed, amused to see the arm move, first a little up and then a little down from the waist, the fingers cupping. She was quite unaware of it. When we reached the point where we had to leave the main track and take a rabbit path up the cliff in the dark, she sensibly refused and suggested that she would rest while I climbed to the tomb. It all seemed rather silly in the dark, yet somehow ungrateful, having come so far, to refuse to go further. Mustafa led the way, and in less than a minute we had scrambled to a temple tomb in which I was as blind as a bat in the deeper darkness. As a child in the war I used to stand with my eyes tight shut for a while, so that I might see better in the blackout, and I instinctively did it again. Mustafa took my hand, I thought to reassure me, but he put it to his crutch, to the sizeable erection sporting in the open fly. It was just like the air-raid shelters at school.

Ayhan needed no Mustafa to find an hotel, and lodged us in one that had real white table-cloths in the dining-room – this seemed to reassure him, and he ranted endlessly on the beauties of Turkish food and the splendid atmosphere of the room, which seemed to us bleakly undistinguished. Our clothes were filthy; since leaving Kuşadasi there had been no opportunity to wash them (or indeed ourselves), and after a cold shower down the corridor in pitch darkness (all electricity in Kaş had been struck by lightning in the racketing storm that was about us that night), I had picked through my knapsack looking for the least dirty shirt, peering at collars and snuffling in armpits. I thought I knew all the laundry tricks of travelling, but these had been pointless in the consistent cold and damp, and the schedule of our early rising. And I was long unshaven. I do not like my beard – it grows in all directions, is as wiry as a doormat, and glints with ginger and silver – but I knew where to find the barber in Kaş, and was filled with the pleasure of anticipation. Tomorrow I would feel better.

Tomorrow dawned with Ayhan drinking tripe soup for breakfast with much noisy slurping – the remedy for too much raki again. We had some difficulty getting tea; a despairing note in my journal – 'Somehow everything is slow and incompetent. Turks are willing, put enormous repeated effort into the slightest service, but never look ahead. First a journey with the tea glasses, then another with the spoons, and a third with the sugar – and all before the water has been poured into the urn to boil. Getting extra blankets last night meant talking to one man, who sent another to fetch a third, who took the key of the empty room next to ours and stripped the beds – something that we could have done ourselves with a tenth of the trouble in a tenth of the time.'

I made a beeline for the barber. He used the word *cicatrice*. It is not in my Turkish dictionaries, perhaps pruned from the language under Atatürk's reforms, when Greek and Latin, Persian and Arabic words were replaced by inventions deemed to be pure Turkish, or other bastards fathered by European tongues; one sad consequence is that young Turks in love no longer understand old love songs, knowing only from the music, not the words, the tenor of the tale. Pruned or not, he said *cicatrice* when I leaned back in his chair and he saw the scar on my throat. This is a tall T with a Devil's punchbowl of tough hair curling in the junction, and I invariably skin its cobbled unevenness with the blade, and waste five minutes of the day mopping blood or changing a shirt put on too soon; it gave me perverse pleasure to see that a Turkish barber skinned it too, and had to work with styptics as the whisper of it reached the small boys of Kaş, some of whom looked tactfully at its reflection in the mirror, while the bolder spirits came to the front to touch it with doubting forefingers. The razor work done, the barber set about the real business of his trade, massaging temples and behind ears, and then plunged his hands inside my none too clean collar to pinch and squeeze what tendons he could find knotting in my shoulders, leaving me as relaxed as a cosseted tom-cat and almost as randy.

We had our boots cleaned of their caked mud, with much laughter from the boys who did it. I cannot understand the gaiety of bootboys who year-round tout for custom in all weathers and at all times of day, whose hands are often the actual instruments of their trade, delicately applying polish with their fingertips and massaging it into the leather, and who are paid a pittance. I have often given a child (for some are no more than six or seven) the price of his labour, feeling guilty in expensive sandals or suede trainers that do not need his care. I have often wondered why

Turks persist in wearing polished leather shoes in streets that within fifty yards will scuff and cover them with dust; in far-off Hakkari, where tarmac is as unheard-of as the Trinity, and the mountain winds constantly whip the dust into scurrying whirls, all shoes are polished leather and half a dozen boys scout for custom in the tea-garden; it is a symbiotic relationship, and as long as the boys charge so little that they will for ever be in penury, shoemakers will eschew suede and canvas and all the other fashionable and unpolishable materials of the West, and keep them in business.

Kaş in winter is a bleak little town; it was raining, and the wind whipped the sea over the harbour walls, and the little lighthouse had been knocked askew. The scant ruins seemed wretched, and finding them no more than a duty. And then we met the boy with the ram. It was a big strong animal, jibbing at the rope, and he was a big strong boy; the steep gradient was in the ram's favour until the boy picked it up in both arms and tottered up the hill with it for fifty paces – then the tussle began again. The poor beast was to be an *adak*, a votive offering, and knew it. The boy's family was about to begin building a house, and the ram was to be sacrificed on the land that afternoon; he invited us to the event and to the feast that would follow it. Petter asked if we might take photographs and got a very matter-of-fact assent; I said that I would again act as his dogsbody, but that I would not look – I had the stomach for a circumcision in Cappadocia, and the blood-stains on my white trousers to show for it, but not for slitting the throat of a hapless animal. Such sacrifices are still commonplace, and are offered in advance of examinations, marriages, starting a business or any other enterprise; *adak* can be the gift of a carpet to the mosque, or it can be any animal from a cock to a camel – though during *Bayram* a cock is considered insufficient for any cause.

We had time to kill before the sacrifice at three, and bought a kilim, reducing Ayhan to a state of hysteria by bargaining so hard that the carpet dealer refused him a commission. In high dudgeon he took us to lunch and another quarrel; we could either eat inside, his preference, or out, in the wind, under a ramshackle tarpaulin that discharged its lying water when sufficiently ruffled, watching the world go by. The *lokanta* was within sight of the barber and the bootboys, and within sight of what passes for a market square and a bus station, and all the little world of Kaş was there to see. So we sat outside, cameras primed, and Ayhan grumbled, shouted at the waiter, ordered and disordered, and broke into a rage when the salad was brought. It was an inoffensive salad of chopped tomatoes, onions and parsley, the so-called shepherds' salad that is automatically brought in Turkey whether you are in a workman's café or the Hilton (the only distinction is that the Hilton's portions are less generous); we had eaten it twice a day since we arrived; but the sight of it turned Ayhan's face a purplish red, and he upturned his chair as he left the table and stumped off into the market square. He returned, bearing tomatoes which he gave to the waiter with long instruction and repeated gestures – 'These are real good tomatoes and should be sliced instead of chopped. When you have important visitors you should always slice the tomatoes, not chop them. You don't know how to treat tourists.' I noted that we had come down in the world from journalists to tourists. The waiter looked chastened until he caught my eye, and then grinned; but when he brought the neatly sliced tomatoes Petter and I resolutely refused to eat them, and there were far too many for Ayhan. Then there was a quarrel with the boy over the bill – the sort of thing that makes me freeze with anger, though Petter, with skilful seeming-innocence questioned Ayhan into embarrassment and confusion, and eventually into paying it; the sum of money was minute in English terms, and the boy was right – but had he been wrong I would still have paid.

It was trivial, and would not be worth recalling except that it was yet another episode to widen the rift between us. It had long been clear that Ayhan was not interested in ruins and despised the customs, dress and behaviour of the ordinary Turk; we had nothing in common, but that was no reason for failing to establish a working relationship – and the purpose of our journey was work, and the purpose of his presence was to relieve us of obstruction or delay. That he would himself become the obstruction, the drag anchor, the time-consuming irritant, no-one could have foreseen, and as he and the car were the inseparable gifts of the Turkish Government, the obvious remedy of paying him off was not an option. I mistrust my own foul temper in such matters – it is explosive (monumentally so), and fills my lungs with anger that emerges not as a shout but as a parade-ground bellow, pitched hard as a weapon; in circumstances where I retain enough control to recognize that this unleashed rage is something for which I shall soon have to apologize, I occasionally manage to freeze, and once the trembling is done, can isolate the cause – an exhausting business. Others might think this sulking, but it is not, for the anger is still active, revived by each fresh sighting of the man who brought it about.

In this condition it was a disaster to be sought out by the boy with the sacrificial ram and to be told that the weather was too unpleasant for the deed, which must now be delayed until the same time the following day, or the day after that, or . . . Turkish time had taken over. It was indeed pelting with rain, but we had to shed Ayhan and do something useful. We dumped him at the carpet shop, where he would at least be warm and dry and given tea, and hijacked the car.

In the mountains behind Kaş is the ancient city of Comba, so obscure that I know of it only from Bean, and even he says that 'the effort of reaching it is poorly rewarded', for nothing remains but the ruin of a church and some late walls. Comba's only distinction is that it remained at least until the third century AD the centre of the cult of the Twelve Gods of Lycia, who appear to be known only from primitive reliefs found in the area. These unnamed deities stand in a row full frontal, behind square shields with a central boss, flanking either the figure of their unnamed father, or of Artemis; below them, flanking a portrait of the donor, is a row of twelve dogs with heads like human skulls, each engagingly lifting a forepaw – quite enough to set me off on a lunatic journey into the mountains. Relieved of Ayhan's lugubrious presence, or perhaps as part of the relieving process, Petter threw the Renault about in Scandinavian rally style until, up in the mountains, we passed a couple of old men trudging uphill through the rain. They clambered in the back, shook hands, steamed, offered cigarettes, and shouted at us in much the same way as London bus conductors with uncomprehending tourists. They had walked some eight kilometres and were drenched, and they stayed with us another ten, underlining yet again the toughness of the Turk, imperturbable when his legs are the only form of transport. We put them down in the village of Gömce – not on the map, and we were not sure that it corresponded with Bean's directions to find the site above the village of Gömbe; *Gömbe* is obviously a survival from Comba, *Gömce* is not, but the old men insisted that their village was Gömce and knew nothing of any ruins. We refused their invitation to drink tea, and drove on; the climb grew steeper, and as we crossed a pass at perhaps 5,000 feet the rain changed to snow as suddenly as magician's work, and within seconds we were deep in a Christmas landscape with the car ploughing into a drift. To look for an obscure ruin in these conditions, with, if Bean was right, an hour's stiff climb of another thousand feet, was to court death, and no ruin is worth that – even turning the car was impossible, and by the time we had manhandled it out of its drift the bitter Poyràz from the north-east had hard-driven the snow against us so that we were both thoroughly chilled in the numb, fatigued way that signals danger.

We retreated to the tea-house in Gömce, but were prevented from leaving the car by a band of snarling dogs in the company of a flock of sheep and some shepherd girls. Shepherds in the Taurus wear the *kepenek*, a strange tent-like hooded coat made of thick, stiff felt, surrealist in its enlargement and distortion of the human frame, sometimes seeming in its bulk and shadows to contain nothing; in its traditional form it is the basic instrument of survival in foul weather, but these girls wore transparent plastic replicas of it, ankle-length, over their ordinary skirts and jumpers, beaded and trickling with condensation. Inside the tea-house our two old men were still drying out, and there was more shouting and hand-shaking, and chairs were shifted away from the makeshift oil-drum stove to give us room. A boy of about fourteen brought us tea, and then more tea; the village dandy in a white jacket came to look at us, and tiny children, sodden from the rain. Here there was poverty and wretchedness not seen since the War in western Europe, not a waterproof garment, nothing dry under the leaking roof. Men and boys came in to steam like damp toast by the fire for a few minutes; they wanted only our company, and to be photographed, but in this we met yet again the standard Turkish problem – confronted by the camera the Turk, be he three or ninety-three, stands ramrod rigid, arms straight by his sides, shoulders upped and squared, expressive eyes (and they are expressive, speaking) dulled in a direct stare. Ask him to smile and he will processed-cheese you with a gold tooth or a gap. Atatürk took away his regional costume and dressed him like a Yorkshire miner – even the boatman at Caunus wore a three-piece brown suit, Cecil Gee, circa 1960 – and his early education stands him at attention every morning vowing to his country; to be photographed is a formal occasion, and he responds in the only way he knows, and is as photogenic as a beanpole without a bean.

The streets of the village, covered with ankle-breaking stones the size of bricks, were streaming with water draining from the mountain-side; the timber houses seemed makeshift, or derelict, or both; women, their long skirts trailing the sodden ground, drove sodden horses into sodden shelters; the only sign of wealth was a petrol-driven saw. The bleak misery of it was oppressive. Back in the tea-house we gave our store of oranges, dried figs and biscuits to the children; the boy who ran it took me by the sleeve and out to the car to ask for my map. I had had it for eight years, but had treated it well so that its folds were unbroken; it was a familiar tool; it had careful notes and corrections penned in; I remembered giving my Oxford Turkish dictionary to the school-master in Hakkari, leaving myself with the return length of Turkey to travel with no source of words, and then discovering back in London that the book was out of print; and then I saw the pleading in the boy's eyes, and gave it to him. Back in London I found that the map too was out of print and irreplaceable.

— X —

Xanthus * Latona

'It has been killed by Swan's tourists' said the guardian at Xanthus. I could see what he meant – at the end of a long summer season the city ruins are a melancholy sight, dusty, littered with all the signs of trampling European hordes. But if tourists are responsible for the Kodak cartons and the broken shrubs it is Charles Fellows who must take the greater blame – the unfettered enthusiasm for the city and its monuments and inscriptions expressed in his journal of 1838 brought a marauding British battleship to Xanthus four years later, and for two months Fellows, Lieutenant Spratt and Captain Graves urged British sailors (hardly qualified archaeologists, even by the standards of the day) to ravish the site, dismantle and pack its monuments into seventy-eight great crates of which the contents now reside in the British Museum. It is indeed fair to suggest that a better impression of Xanthus is to be had in Bloomsbury than in Lycia, and that the belated rage of the Greeks over their loss of the Elgin marbles seems absurdly histrionic (as well as wholly unjustified) when compared with Turkish losses from Xanthus – to say nothing of the worst loss of all, the Pergamon altar in East Berlin. It is now impossible to share to the full Fellows' excitement – nothing can detract from the beautiful situation of the city above the wide sweep of the Xanthus river, and nothing can remedy the

effect of earthquake or the Byzantine depredations as they stripped the theatre and other monuments to build their defensive
wall, but he found the city full of tombs, inscriptions, reliefs and
free-standing sculpture, and he ripped them from their settings
and carried them off to London.

D. G. Hogarth in an account of Xanthus written in 1911 uses the
word 'robbed' – 'The well-preserved theatre is remarkable for a
break in the curve of its auditorium, which has been constructed
so as not to interfere with a sarcophagus on a pedestal and with
the Harpy Monument which still stands to its full height, robbed
of the reliefs of its parapet . . . the best of the tombs are in the
British Museum, as the result of Sir Charles Fellows' expedition;
only their bases can be seen on the site.'

There are fewer excuses for Fellows' behaviour than for Lord
Elgin's – the Parthenon marbles had been turned into mortar,
provided targets for pot-shots, had lost their parts as souvenirs,
and both Greeks and Turks were indifferent to their fate. Indeed
the Greeks continued to be indifferent to the Parthenon even
when they gained their independence and adopted young Otho
of Bavaria as their first King, for they invited the great German
architect Karl Friedrich Schinkel to design a royal palace on the
Acropolis, incorporating the Parthenon as a monumental folly;
only the outrageous cost of a structure that would have been of
much the same extent as the British Museum prevented the total
redevelopment of the Athenian Acropolis. But that was in a city
that had been continuously occupied for at least three thousand
years and was recognized as the capital of Greece – Xanthus in
1838 was uninhabited, under no threat from local villagers, and
had lain undisturbed and unravaged for over a thousand years. It
was indeed Fellows' claim to have rediscovered it (though it had
been published by Sir Francis Beaufort in his *The South Coast of
Asia Minor and the Remains of Antiquity* of 1817, and again by
William Leake in his *Journal of a Tour in Asia Minor*, recording a
journey made early in the nineteenth century, but only printed in
1824), and that perhaps excuses his proprietorial response – it
was there for the taking, almost. The publication of his journal in
1839 so excited the Trustees of the British Museum that they
persuaded Lord Palmerston to ask the Sultan of Turkey for
permission to remove an unspecified number of Lycian sculptures. It was hardly an opportune moment – Palmerston was
pretty brisk in 'getting the affairs of Europe into trim', as he put it,

but the Sublime Porte was not to be so bullied and bustled even when it was under appalling threat from Mehemet Ali, the wild Albanian who had contrived to become Pasha of Egypt, and Turkey seemed about to become the melting-pot of European power politics with Russia, Prussia, Britain, France and Austria all scrapping for influence.

Late in 1839 Fellows set off without the firman from the Turkish authorities necessary for excavation and removal but with George Scharf to make drawings of the journey, this time to lay claim to thirteen more Lycian cities, and another journal was published. In October 1841 the British Museum asked him to make a third expedition to Asia Minor, but provided neither funds nor firman; Fellows put up the money himself (he was the son of a banker) and went to Constantinople in person to apply for permission to remove antiquities from Xanthus. He cheated in his application for a firman, and asked permission to retrieve and take only *buried* stones. The drawings made by Scharf indicate that the stones of the Nereid Monument were less buried than lying about in the vicinity, and that other tombs were intact. He knew what he was doing (the emphases are mine):

> I felt sure that, if properly explained, no objection could be made to the removal of the *buried* stones in the almost unknown mountains of Lycia. I therefore resolved to go to Constantinople and *ask for these only*, and, if I failed, then to return to England. To assume an appearance of authority, *of which I had but little in reality*, I requested Captain Graves to accompany me . . . leaving his ship at Smyrna. We arrived on 21 November, and on the first application to the authorities I was gratified in finding that I had judged rightly. *Riouf Pasha observed that he was glad that the other part of the request had been withdrawn, as he feared it never could have been granted*; that no difficulty now remained, and a firman should now be given forthwith for the marbles from Xanthus . . . The following is a translation of the Authority:
>
> A letter from H.H. the Grand Vizier to Hadgi Ali Pasha, Governor of Rhodes, dated the 15th of Sheoval, 1257 (the 29th of November, 1841).
>
> The British Embassy has noted by a *tairer* [a note in Turkish] that there are some antiques consisting in sculptured stones lying down, and of no use, at a place near the village of *Koonik*,

in the district of Marmoriss, which is one of the dependencies of Rhodes, and not far from the sea-shore; and has requested that the antiques aforesaid should be given to the British Government, for the purpose of putting them in the Museum. The British Embassy has in the meantime represented that the distinguished Captain Graves has been ordered by the British Government to embark those stones and to carry them to England; and that as he is going himself to the spot a letter was asked in his behalf that your Excellency may give him every assistance on this occasion.

The Sublime Porte is interested in granting such demands, in consequence of the sincere friendships existing between the two Governments. If, therefore, the antiquities above mentioned are lying down here and there, and are of no use, Your Excellency shall make no objection to the Captain's taking them away and carrying them on board; and to that effect you will be pleased to appoint one or two of your attendants to accompany him . . .

Such are the Sultan's commands, in conformity to which you will act. . . .

Fellows then adds:

The knowledge of the boundaries of the various Pashalics of the remote districts is very limited in Constantinople. *I therefore myself gave instruction for the letter*, and although imperfect I could then obtain no better authority. On my return to Smyrna I learned more, and, fearing verbal irregularity, *I provided a present for the Pasha* to whom it was addressed.

From all this it is clear that he wittingly deceived the Grand Vizier, who knew neither the whereabouts of Xanthus nor the vital importance of its remains, dictated his own firman in such terms as he knew would pass scrutiny, and bribed the provincial Governor.

The day after Christmas, HMS *Beacon* (Palmerston's contribution to the affair) landed Fellows, Spratt and their sailors at the mouth of the River Xanthus, and they trudged upstream to begin their work of depredation. In midwinter he found the Xanthus a wild and unmanageable stream, powerful enough to drown two of his sailors; he built a camp immediately below the ruins, played cricket when the weather improved, and in June 1842 set sail for

Malta leaving the site stripped by six months of unskilled labour. It is reasonable to assume that the Turkish authorities knew nothing of the extent of the removals – they had as an act of friendship to the British Government given a firman to a private gentleman acting on behalf of the Museum, and certainly not to a vandal with a battleship in support. Getting away with it once, Fellows made a similar raiding expedition in 1844, with a hundred sailors from the Royal Navy, masons from Malta, Roman experts in casting plaster, cooks and carpenters; he raided Xanthus again, Patara, Pinara, Tlos, Myra and Olympus, and sent back to the British Museum a further twenty-seven crates of antiquities.

Later that year he also deposited in the Museum such papers and portfolios as applied to his work in Turkey, together with natural-history specimens found in Lycia – he shot wolves, jackals and hares while there, none of which now survives in the area. The British Museum's Register was not compiled until 1848 and makes no distinction between the antiquities brought from Xanthus in 1842 and 1844, but the Register of the Natural History Museum is more specific; in 1841 Fellows deposited four birds from Asia Minor, including, perhaps, the battered vulture from Laodiceia; in 1842 he gave thirty-seven reptiles from Xanthus, of which the condition was poor; and in 1844 he deposited a group of sixty birds, mammals and reptiles, some from Xanthus, including foxes, a dog, a pig and a mongoose. Some of these specimens still survive, but none, surviving or not, was regarded as at all remarkable in the 1840s; most, inexpertly cured, have mouldered away.

In May 1845 Queen Victoria knighted Fellows 'as an acknowledgment of his services in the removal of the Xanthian antiquities to this country' – it was his only reward and it cost him dear, for all his journeys had been made at his own expense. He did not have to endure the censure and ridicule heaped upon Lord Elgin, accused as he was of both aesthetic and financial overvaluation of his Marbles, but there was perhaps criticism enough to persuade him into publishing a pamphlet in 1843, *The Xanthian Marbles: Their Acquisition and Transmission to England*, in which he documented his enterprise.

Because it was unique, Fellows took the Harpy Tomb – that was his name for it, interpreting as Harpies the corner figures framing the dynastic reliefs that formed the funerary chamber; he could not take it all, for most of it is a rectangular pillar some twenty-five feet high, and that he left in place, just by the theatre.

The Harpies are now thought to be Sirens carrying small-scale female figures that represent souls. I wonder. Sirens merit a place on tombs in that one of their functions was to sing dirges for the dead, and accompany them into Hades; on the funerary monuments of girls, women, poets and orators, they symbolize beauty, eloquence and song. A Siren beats her breast and tears her hair above the stele of Ariston in Athens, and another, less distressed, is on Sophocles' tomb. In the National Archaeological Museum in Athens a Siren four feet high, with a face of perfect tearful dolour, is an unfortunate blend of fat girl and plump chicken – below the knee she tapers too soon to talons, wings spread behind the lost arms and frame the plumpest thighs in pre-Christendom, accentuated by the deep dimple of her rima; in the Louvre another of her kind is fully feathered from the crutch. They have a mixed reputation – in Odysseus' day they seduced men with their siren song, and then, presumably, ate them, for their island was littered with men's bones (a late explanation is that they were notorious prostitutes so good at their work that men never, having once tasted their pleasures, returned to their wives and children – a notion that finds some support in Attic comedy, where their role is often erotic); yet they are also described as the playmates of Persephone, who grew wings so as to extend their frantic search for her when she was carried off by Pluto; Hera took away their wings as punishment for losing a song contest with the Muses – unfair, as ever, for she it was who had suggested it (of what, I wonder, would she have deprived the Muses?).

The problem with Harpies is that all early illustrations of the breed are line engravings of the winged creatures on the Xanthus tomb – a visual syllogism – and they have thus entered the Victorian imagination (and mine) in the form of egg-shaped creatures with female heads and breasts, great wings and feathered tail, small human arms, little taloned bird legs that are absurdly out of proportion, and posteriors ideal for ovipositing. Virgil more or less supports this invention with his description of them as birds with the faces of women, rather than the half-and-half imagery of the Sirens. The Harpies too had associations with death, for at an early stage they were considered to be the servants of the Erinyes, the ancient personified curses who were the spirits of punishment, particularly for murder, for which the punishment was death. (The Erinyes were offended by Hera's giving the power of speech to one of Achilles' horses, and promptly silenced the animal when it rebuked him for a cruel chiding and forecast his imminent death – it is a curious coincidence that it was named Xanthus.) The Harpies are best known from Charles Kingsley's tale in *The Argonauts*; pausing on the shore of the Bosphorus to feast with Phineus, King of Bythinia, Jason's men saw their food snatched from the table by these shrieking monsters, and two of their number, Zetes and Calais, sons of the North Wind, took wing and did battle with them, and drove them south, beyond the Cyclades. It is in memory of this that a breeze blows on the Bosphorus even on the hottest summer day.

What Kingsley omits is the unpleasant gloss that just as birds have no control over their sphincters (the best of arguments against allowing pigs to fly), so the Harpies were likely to defecate at random, and did; what they could not snatch in their talons was spoiled by their droppings, and poor Phineus was left with tainted food that stank. An eighteenth-century French writer of the Enlightenment suggested that the Harpies were locusts, insisting that the words came from the same Greek stem, and that the tale of the great battle with Zetes and Calais was no more than a picturesque description of a horde of locusts being blown to their deaths out at sea. The tale of the Argonauts, one of the oldest of Greek sagas, may be associated with the trade link between Miletus and Colchis; it was known to Homer, but its earliest complete telling was by Apollonius Rhodius, an Alexandrian poet spanning most of the third century BC; it has been suggested that Apollonius knew of the filthy habits and fierce appetite of the Indian fruit-bat, and used them to embellish the character of the Harpies.

Harpies or Sirens, they do not seem malevolent in the British Museum; they grasp their little female burdens with obvious tenderness, and are rewarded with a chuck under the chin – the playful and affectionate gesture of the Christ Child to the Virgin in so many Renaissance paintings, and one of great antiquity in Egypt and Greece; in one relief a watching female figure displays no more agitation than the gesture of putting her hand over her mouth as though in astonishment.

The four main reliefs are equally enigmatic. On the north side a

warrior offers his helmet to a seated chieftain – a moment of
formal dignity disrupted by the appearance of a pig rooting about
under the throne; on the east a boy offers a cock and a pomegranate to a second enthroned chieftain, who sits sniffing at a flower;
to the south a woman, perhaps, offers a pomegranate and a bird
to yet another chieftain – the Museum describes it as a dove, but it
more resembles a hawk; and on the west side two seated women,
their long dresses elegantly trailed under their thrones, their feet
on stools, frame a procession of three more women bearing an
egg, a pomegranate and what may be a lobster (the Museum
avoids identifying it) – one seated woman sniffs a flower, and so
does one of her visitors. In so far as it is possible to understand the
programme behind these reliefs, it seems to be the hope of
resurrection; the pomegranate is associated with the tale of
Persephone, who, carried off by Pluto, ate six pomegranate
seeds, and was thus only permitted to return to earth for six
months in the year, a summer of regeneration. The cock is
another attribute of Persephone, as he plays an essential part in
this regeneration in one way and another. The egg is a symbol of
creation, again associated with spring festivals of revival and
rebirth; the helmet may symbolize the wisdom of Athena, and the
hawk was sacred to her brother Apollo as the symbol of divination – a better idea than a dove, which at this early stage did not
suggest peace, but stood rather for lust. If, as an alternative, the
helmet is the helmet of invisibility, then it is the attribute of Pluto,
whose rape of Persephone was the cause of winter. With so much
suggesting Persephone, it is perhaps she and her mother Ceres
who are enthroned in the relief on the west side, and that may
just explain so much flower-sniffing, for she and her companions
were picking flowers in a meadow when Pluto (suddenly shot by
Cupid) snatched her; and if that is so, then the Harpies are much
more likely to be Sirens, for they were her companions.

The reliefs, carved in marble from Paros in the far-off Cyclades,
and painted (traces of blue paint are still to be found in the
backgrounds, and on the west side the thrones and dresses are
patterned in paint), were capped by a hugely overhanging
stepped coping of great weight; the Museum suggests that it was
built in honour of Lycian chieftains but hazards no guess at how
many may have occupied it, nor how, if they died at different
times, the tomb was opened to receive them – no easy task under
that coping if it were at ground level, and virtually impossible at

the height of twenty-five feet. Perhaps the bones of many members of a dynastic family were gathered for a single honour. The Museum notes that the reliefs are 'certainly the work of Greek sculptors', implying that they were brought from Attica in 480–470 BC. This raises interesting points: who decided to commission Attic sculptors? How was the commission given to them, and at what diplomatic or social level? Who devised the programme and its imagery – Greek or Xanthian (if Greek, then surely there would be parallels in Attica, and the identity of the Siren-Harpies would not be enigmatic)? And why the assumption that Xanthus, which must have supported a native school of sculptors to satisfy the demand for more conventional Lycian tombs that are still scattered far and wide over the hillside, carved with dancers, acrobats, lion and bullfights, had produced none capable of executing a major commission?

What early historical evidence there is suggests that the Lycians had for centuries resisted Greek influence, and certainly Greek invasion; though they are honourably mentioned by Homer, their land was not colonized by Greeks during the great migrations of the heroic age, yet there are Greek foundations enough in Caria to the west and Pamphylia and Pisidia to the east. In their own language the Lycians did not even call themselves Lycians, but Termilae, and only adopted the Greek name when they adopted the Greek language. Xanthus was not called Xanthus ('the Yellow'), but Arna. Ancient Lycian as both language and script was preserved in use into the fourth century BC, and the slow adoption of Greek came about through commerce and other peaceable means of exchange, and not by invasion. Politically the Lycian states were bound to each other in a federal organization long before even the possibility of Greek influence, and indeed were successful where the Greeks failed, for they had no difficulty in reconciling the autonomy of princely cities with the unity of the whole nation. When the cities lost their princes and became republics, they still maintained their national federation, made formal in the Lycian League, and even Aristotle recognized the virtue of their constitutional development. With such independent spirit, holding too to their own religion, I cannot see why the princes of Xanthus should send to mainland Greece for monumental sculptors.

We know the appearance of the Harpy Tomb when Fellows first saw it, for his draughtsman Scharf made a detailed drawing of it in more or less perfect condition. His British sailors left it in the damaged and precarious state in which Professor Henri Metzger found it when French archaeologists began work on the site in 1950 – tottering, and in need of a makeshift scaffold of tree-trunks; the pillar is now straight and erect, the reliefs replaced by cement casts, the crowning slab in position above them, and once again it makes visual and functional sense in relation to the theatre.

The base of the Pavaya Tomb is still in situ, its reliefs too in the British Museum; Scharf's drawing offers devastating evidence of mishandling by Fellows' men – it shows the tomb cracked, but complete and standing on its pillar; as reconstructed in the Museum, concrete infill far outmeasures the original fragments knitted into it. The reliefs are illustrations of Pavaya's life – a fragmentary inscription reads, 'Pavaya, son of Ad . . . secretary of A . . . rah, by race a Lycian'. Fellows also took the funerary chamber of the Lion Tomb, an oblong chest cut from a single piece of white limestone, with reliefs carved on all four sides; its nine foot high base he left in place, damaged, with its two handsomely realistic feline beasts prowling towards each other.

By far the grandest Xanthian antiquity is the Nereid Monument, a confection of Ionic temple architecture, free-standing sculpture and narrative reliefs. When Scharf drew it, nothing remained in place but the monumental base set into a steep slope to the south of the city, overlooking its main approach; one row of relief carving remained in place at the back – the rest had fallen. Fellows found it in 1838, felled by earthquakes, its reliefs and architectural elements widely scattered. After he had recovered it piecemeal in 1842 it proved difficult to reconstruct, and it was not until 1951 that French findings on the site enabled the Museum to offer its present convincing interpretation. Again they claim that 'to build a monument that is thoroughly Greek in design and detail, artists must have been brought from the Greek world; Athenian influences in the detail of the architecture and in the style of the sculptures have often been noted and are probably to be explained by the presence of Attic masters'. The platform supporting the elegant Ionic *tempietto* is roughly twenty by thirty feet; it was decorated with bands of reliefs of different heights and very different styles; the largest are conventional episodes of combat, rather dull, offering poor competition for the Elgin Marbles in the next room, but the smaller scenes of siege, with armies crowding at the city walls, the citizens and their defenders within, with pleading hostages, men shouting news from the battlements, the suggestion of figures contained within architectural space, are much more realistic, pictorial and narrative, and infinitely more exciting – indeed they seem to me to be imbued with a representational truth to which I would look for documentation of architecture, costume and the way things were done. The columns supported pediments that were capped with three-dimensional figures of naked men carrying off women, and between the columns stood the Nereids. These six standing figures, three-quarters life-size, are ancient Isadoras to whose limbs transparent draperies cling in wind-blown movement, billowing like slack spinnakers. Indeed they are now identified as *Aurae*, personifications of winds, instead of Nereids, whose element was water. The degree of detail finish is greater at the front, the treatment broader and more general behind, but they are realized fully in the round, with movements of the legs and gestures of the arms that actively induce the spectator to circulate about them. If the monument was to honour victorious Lycian chieftains, the connection of the wind imagery with what appears to be detailed historical narrative in the reliefs below, has no obvious explanation.

Dwelling on the bowels of the British Museum is not to suggest that the city itself is not worth visiting. A few of the monumental tombs and heroa that so impressed Fellows were left in place for others to take; beyond the agora is an almost completely preserved pillar tomb dating from late in the fifth century BC – the dynastic statue that must once have capped it is missing, but the reliefs from the funerary chamber below it, showing the occupant's victories, are in the Archaeological Museum in Istanbul. The pillar is inscribed with a little Greek and much Lycian, the letters covering all its four faces, and, in 250 lines, extending to far the longest known Lycian inscription. The twelve Greek lines record that the tomb was dedicated to the Twelve Gods in the agora, and that its occupant was an heroic son of Harpagus, in his youth a champion wrestler, a victorious soldier remorselessly sacking cities and pillaging them for trophies, and that he once slaughtered seven heavily-armed Greek infantrymen in one day. In so far as it is intelligible from its expansion of these lines, the Lycian inscription throws light on the detail of local Xanthian alliances and enemies, and on a significant victory, in partnership

with Sparta, over the Athenians at Jasus in 412 BC. The presence
of a Greek précis may imply that Xanthus had an Hellenic
minority living within its walls.

At the foot of the acropolis hill is another pillar tomb, intact,
presumably because its funerary chamber is in plain white marble
– without reliefs and inscriptions it held no interest for Fellows,
but it may raise the point that the funerary chambers were carved
after they had been erected on the pillars; this example dominates
a group of rock tombs of the commonplace Lycian pattern, much
less dramatic than at Tlos or Pinara.

Identifiable but unrewarding (apart from a gate dedicated to
Vespasian), remains of public buildings litter the city; the theatre,
of Roman type, is not well preserved (though many writers claim
it to be so); the agora, again Roman, is dedicated to the Twelve
Lycian Gods (see p. 136). Early Christian and Byzantine
churches, and a large Byzantine monastery, confuse the palimpsest. The trouble is that the city lasted too long and was successively redeveloped, and if the Romans were reasonably respectful
to the buildings of their predecessors, the Byzantine Christians
were not; the seventh-century Arabs devastated the remains of all
previous populations, and Fellows and his men behaved as
Goths and Vandals. Xanthians appear in Homer's account of the
Trojan War, which suggests that they were an established community long before 1200 BC; in Herodotus' day Xanthus was
pretty well synonymous with Lycia – his tale of its siege by
Harpagus ends with a scornful comment on the Caunians who
'generally followed the example of the Lycians' by which he
means the Xanthians; the city submitted to Alexander, and fell
successively into the hands of Antigonus, Ptolemy I, and Antiochus III before passing to Rhodes. Of these invasions only the
Persian siege seems to have been disastrous – only eighty families
survived, and that because they were not at home when it
occurred, but in the mountains on their summer pastures; the rest
of the population was gathered by its menfolk on the acropolis,
together with their goods and chattels, beasts and babies, and
burnt – and as the heavy smoke and stink of charring flesh wafted
over the city walls, the men burst from them to die in one last
desperate assault on the Persians. Self-immolation was again the
Xanthian solution to a siege by Brutus in 42 BC – they first burnt
the farms and houses that lay outside the city, and then, after
fearful complications and confusions in which the Xanthians

contrived to get themselves locked *outside* the city gates, and the Romans attempted to take it by swimming *under* water (only to be caught in nets set up by the Xanthians), and even when a small party of Romans did succeed in clambering over the walls they could not open the gate, so that there were parties of them attempting to batter it down from both sides – only then did the Xanthians surrender to Brutus, promptly rushing off to slaughter their wives and children. Brutus, apparently deafened by the weeping, wailing and general perturbation, offered a truce to save these civilian lives, but the Xanthians would have none of it, and threw their corpses, their possessions and themselves onto a monumental funeral pyre and perished.

A little to the south-west of Xanthus lies the sanctuary of Leto, perhaps better known as Latona; the site is occupied by the floors of three temples, and a well-preserved Hellenistic theatre that has lost its stage building but preserves sixteen masks in one of its vaulted passages that give perhaps some idea of the quality of its decoration. Leto, pregnant by Zeus, was driven away by Hera to wander from place to place until she gave birth to Apollo and Artemis on the island of Delos; in Lycia, herdsmen watering their flocks would not let her drink at a fountain, and unforgetting and unforgiving she returned after the birth of her children, and clutching them both under one arm, splashed the herdsmen with water from the fountain and turned them into frogs. A pretty gloss to the tale is that wolves took pity on her thirst and guided her to the River Xanthus to assuage it, and as a memorial she changed the country's name from Termilis to Lycia, from the Greek *Lykos* for wolf. Leto, Apollo and Artemis were the national deities of Lycia, and the priests of this sanctuary were the chief priests of the Lycian League. Swimming in the River Xanthus is safe enough in high summer, and a blessed relief after the shadeless exposure of the city, but I would not recommend splashing one's face in the dribbling spring of the Letoum.

Cyaneae * Myra * Phaselis

High above the main road to the east of Kaş lies Cyaneae, signposted (if you are quick enough to see it) Kyenea; a very handsome temple tomb cut in the sheer rock face that forms the skyline gives warning of it, and with field glasses and foreknowledge it is possible to identify a well-camouflaged cluster of rocks as house tombs. The guardian of the site, leaning against the yellow signpost, obscuring it, was surprised to have winter visitors and scurried into his house to search for the peaked cap of office that would convert him from peasant to proprietor. For some eight hundred feet we followed him up the cliff-side, twisting and turning on the fragmentary cut steps of the ancient approach as the view of the distant Mediterranean drew its tight curved horizon line, broken only by Kerkova Island lying like a crusty meringue offshore. Ayhan, puffing and purpling, gave up after ten minutes and returned to the car; Petter stripped off all the many layers with which Norwegians invariably protect their bodies from the winter elements, and climbed naked to the waist with vest, shirt, woollies and anorak insecurely tied about him looking as though real flesh had burst from the body of a scarecrow; I plodded, keeping pace with the guardian and attempting to place my feet where he had placed his. Europeans have a tendency to skip and trip and leap on rough tracks, compelled to treat them as stepping-stones over water, always sticking to the high points and the clear surfaces of rocks – it makes for irregular progress and irregular breathing, worsened on a steep climb; our guardian strode up the cliff like a camel, his large feet in large misshapen shoes with broken laces always placed wherever they happened to be at the end of a natural stride, the ankles seeming to swivel to accommodate whatever irregularities and gradients lay beneath them. A heavy man, his unhurried progress eventually outpaced us, and all the time he smoked without puffing.

Towards the top, the first tombs appeared – small and tumbled, often carved with heads, swags and figures, nice enough but unremarkable, flanking the rising steps and framing the always-changing view; overhanging the cliff at one point a rock outcrop has been sculptured to form a house tomb complete with fixed lid, hollowed through a hole in the western end to accommodate the bodies. The great surprise is the wall that surrounds three sides of the city – the fourth, the south, ends at the cliff face and required no protection; its lower registers are decent ashlar, more or less regular, and bossed, but late rebuilding shows all the signs of panic or wanton purpose, for fallen masonry has been re-used higgledy-piggledy, and supplemented by column drums and Lycian tombs turned on their sides – an engineering feat of some wonder, for a by no means large Lycian tomb recently removed from Cyaneae to the museum in Antalya weighed some eighteen tons; this late rebuilding was probably a Byzantine defence against the Arab invasions – the city was a Bishopric under the neighbouring Metropolitan of Myra. The Lycians, who lived at ease with their dead, lining the streets with their tombs – and the main street in Cyaneae, running from the theatre to the acropolis, handsomely wide, is almost awesome in their number and scale – would not have so abused them. The guardian blamed the Arabs, but could offer no authority for his assertion.

Within the wall is chaos. The site is densely overgrown and confused, and the foundations of many buildings are full of earth and trees – nothing stands to any height. The column drums in the wall suggest that there were handsome classical buildings here, but no temple foundations have been identified, and even the so-called baths seem doubtful – an arched subterranean chamber, very long, and with only one chamber off one side, and that too small – this is not the pattern of the five chambers of

apodypterium or changing-room, frigidarium, tepidarium, caldarium and sudatorium. The site is littered with bell cisterns, and
there is also a large vaulted reservoir; a similar structure cannot be
a reservoir, for it has a passage cut through the wall near its base,
leading to a steep stair out and down the hillside – a granary
perhaps. Below the acropolis, on another, lower hill, stands the
theatre, small and very ruined, but recently cleared of rubble and
undergrowth; nothing is left of the stage building.

The early history of the city is better known than the late, but
there is little of either. Its name is Greek for the blue of lapis lazuli,
but I saw no sign of the stone that was until post-Renaissance
times precious to painters – perhaps it was a reference to the
colour of the sea on the southern horizon. The few coins found on
the site date from the period of the Lycian League after perhaps
150 BC (the cities of Lycia formed a number of federations – in
Strabo's day twenty-three were in the League), and from the time
of Gordion III, Emperor for the six years AD 238–44. Murdered on
the Euphrates at the age of only nineteen by treacherous soldiers
campaigning against the Persians who preferred an adult man as
their leader (a sad and brutal end to 'a light-hearted lad, handsome, winning, agreeable, merry, and distinguished in letters',
who had already proved himself capable of resisting Shapur I of
Persia, King of Kings, and his incursions into the Roman Empire
as far as Antioch), it is unthinkable that Gordion ever visited
Cyaneae, but possible that he paused somewhere in Lycia on his
way to Antioch, and that coins spent then in Kaş or Myra found
their way to the city on the cliff-top. The Lycian League was of
ancient standing, but came to prominence when the Roman
Senate declared Lycia a free country in 167 BC; more than a
millennium earlier they had fought for the Trojans in the great
war; seven centuries after the Trojan War they were defeated by
Harpagus, and when Xerxes invaded Greece they fought for him;
with Athenian victory then, they paid tribute to Athens; with
Athenian defeat by Sparta they once again became Persian; with
Alexander the Great they became Greek; with Alexander's death
they joined Ptolemy and his new dynasty in Egypt for a hundred
years, and then in rapid succession passed to Antiochus of Syria
and to the Rhodians as a gift from Rome. What is given can be
taken away, and when Roman friendship with Rhodes grew cold,
and the Lycians sent ambassadors to Rome complaining of
Rhodian oppression, the Senate declared them free once more.

According to Strabo, in the time of Augustus, the twenty-three
cities that were voting members of the League held their meetings
in whichever of them had been chosen for each congress, electing
a leader whom they called the Lyciarch for their system of
democratically representative government; Pliny, a century later,
observed that thirty-six cities then functioned in Lycia, but that
there had formerly been seventy. At least forty cities are identifiable still from their remains, and other smaller sites may
perhaps be added to the list, but of the remainder there is not the
smallest relic.

Cyaneae's earliest monument is the handsome temple tomb
that can be seen from the road far below. My 1975 photographs
seem less concerned with it than with the road, a track littered
with large shards of the red rock through which it had recently
been widened, and which, in the mere hundred kilometres
between Antalya and Myra, had starred my windscreen and
shattered my exhaust. There was no question then of reaching
the tomb or the city, dismissed by my comprehensive guide-
book with two lines and only a probable identification; the tomb is
still inaccessible directly from the road, but it is easy enough to
scramble down a steep path from the city and enter the Ionic
façade of a pediment on three supports. I can understand that an
early Italian Renaissance architect, discarding his Gothic roots,
might make the mistake of plonking a column in the middle of an
entrance – Alberti misunderstood the Roman coffering of ceilings
and vaults, and made the opposite error of failing to centre his
coffers – but that a Lycian of the third century BC, capable of
producing correct Ionic capitals and evidently aware of Greek
exemplars (the inscription is in Greek), should place them on two
pilasters and one column far too widely spaced, is a minor
mystery. It is a very large tomb, with the sarcophagus of the
owner and his wife installed above the pediment, and the rest of
the space reserved for their family. The Lycians were prickly
about grave-robbers, though the penalty was only a fine, payable
to the city treasury until Roman times, when it became payable to
the Imperial Treasury – the city was then responsible for the care
and maintenance of tombs (for similar penalties at Termessos, see
p. 208).

The view from Cyaneae over the valley of Yavu, is, as it were,
the view of the kitchen garden – a long wide bowl of flat fertile
land contained on all sides by mountains, well watered – that

must always have provisioned the city. Here they still plough the small fields with yoked oxen and ploughs made of bifurcated tree-trunks fitted with iron shoes, unchanged since the early years of the Byzantines (and before), when a pair of oxen was a unit of tax assessment. The camel may be the ship of the desert, but here it is the personal transport of the older peasants – the younger have motorcycles that may cut a dash with the girls, but the camel's inexorable capacity to cross rough country un-hindered, whatever the load it carries, its limbs hidden by the low walls and the tall wheat, demonstrates its resemblance to a ship in full sail seeming to breast the land instead of the sea. The tree-trunk plough is not the only recollection of ancient Byzantium – Strabo wrote of olive plantations, but here oc-casional olive trees are mixed with random fruit trees, almonds and walnuts, with crops of winter wheat or barley grown among their trunks, and green vegetables and pulses grown in small open fields; this may seem unremarkable, but it conforms to patterns of agriculture suggested in Byzantine texts that enshrine the practices of the early Eastern Empire much more than a thousand years ago.

Myra, or Demre, was a scruffy little town when I first saw it in the midday heat ten years ago. We were parched and filthy with the dust from the road, and deafened by what seemed the total destruction of the car's exhaust system. I did not care a damn about tombs, theatres or Father Christmas (see below) – I just wanted the unbearable noise to stop. Demre is too small to have a street devoted to the repair and maintenance of decrepit cars, and we stopped in the centre of the little town to ask where we should seek a workshop. The first man asked a second, and the second a third – or so I thought, until small boys were sent running and returned with a fourth; he said he would repair it within an hour. 'How much?' 'That's up to you.' I hate this response and don't know how to deal with it even in my own country; I produced the equivalent of £3.50 as the base-line of my bargaining, and to my surprise the mechanic snatched it from me, threw the notes on the ground, spat on them, and slapped my hand with a resound-ing thwack. I had no idea what it meant, and Michael's assertion that it was an old Greek custom for cementing a bargain seemed unlikely – but he may well have been right, for the mechanic then got into the car and drove off with everything we possessed. I made at once for the barber's shop, had my hair washed, was

shaved, massaged about the temples and given tea. I can think of
no other country in which I would, as a stranger, give the charge
of all I had to a man whose name and address I did not know, and
expect to see him again an hour later – but such follies in Turkey
involve no risk.

In the warm sunshine of January 1986 the town seemed much
rebuilt and refurbished, and no longer the sort of village where
the mechanic would collect and deliver; I experienced acutely the
very opposite of déjà vu – much more the feeling of the old
woman in the children's tale who woke to find that an unfriendly
pedlar had stolen her skirt, leaving her legs quite bare, and cried
out at the unaccustomed sight, 'Lawks a mercy, this is none of I.'
Even the church of St Nicholas, Santa Claus, Father Christmas or
Noël Baba had had a wash and brush up, with a new garden of
that municipal type in which a floral clock may be expected, and a
new over-life-size bronze statue of the saint in hooded gown,
with a robin on his shoulder and a clutch of children about his
skirts, with that heroic air favoured by revolutionary sculptors
whose work exhorts a groaning populace to greater efforts and
the acceptance of greater suffering. Inside, the church was much
its old self, and, lying as it does many feet below present ground
level, it was flooded – the reflections dappled the winter sunshine
onto its shadowed walls and up into its roof like a Canaletto
drawing of the underside of London Bridge, and we spent many
idle minutes tossing pebbles into the shallow water and watching
the light ripple into new recesses.

It is, no doubt, a very old foundation, but what can now be seen
is largely the work of 1043 or thereabouts, with some mid-
nineteenth-century restoration by the Russians (St Nicholas is
their patron saint) and an even more modern upper storey and
campanile. A large late classical sarcophagus is quite certainly not
his tomb, in spite of the enormous hole in its long side through
which his bones are now supposed to have been retrieved by
merchants from Bari when Myra was occupied by Saracens in the
tenth century – by which time the cult of Nicholas was widespread throughout Europe and the Near East. All that is known of
him is legendary, and not even that he was Bishop of Myra in the
time of Diocletian (and thus almost certainly a martyr) can be
confirmed historically. Diocletian was Emperor from 284 to 305,
and spent most of his time in Asia Minor and thereabouts, having
ingeniously devised a Tetrarchy of a secondary Caesar and a pair

of Augusti to safeguard the imperial borders in the West, with himself in sole charge of the East – he visited Rome for the first time in AD 303, after reigning for nearly twenty years. If Nicholas was indeed then Bishop of Myra and an active worker of miracles, then it is not surprising that the legend records his persecution, torture and imprisonment, for both Caesars and both Augusti agreed upon a savage persecution of Christians in 303. When Constantine the Great became Emperor in 306 he was too much engaged in battles on the Rhine and in Italy itself to pay much heed to a tiresome Bishop imprisoned in Lycia, but when he decided that Rome was no longer central enough for the proper management of an Empire that spread from the Rhine to the Euphrates, and established in 324–30 a new capital in the ancient Greek city of Byzantium, Asia Minor became a Christian land along with the rest of the Empire. AD 311 must be assumed to be the year of Nicholas' release, for the Edict of Serdica then issued by Constantine and his co-rulers Galerius and Licinius guaranteed freedom of worship to all Christians. Nicholas is supposed to have been present at the Council of Nicaea in AD 325 – that august occasion when Constantine is reputed to have banged the Bishops' heads together in order to establish the beliefs of the Church and enshrine them once and for all in the Nicaean Creed – but St Athanasius (who was not, as might be supposed, the author of the Athanasian Creed – that was probably written a century later by St Hilary of Arles), who was the Sydney Smith of his day and knew all the Bishops and their bruised heads, never once mentions a Nicholas of Myra.

The legends are Grimm and pretty tales, beginning well enough with his own late birth to ageing and fruitless parents, whom he immediately amazed by standing up in the bath in which the blood and confusion of birth were being sponged from him to give thanks to God. He refused his mother's nipples on Wednesdays and Fridays, and constantly uttered words of profound theological wisdom. His parents relinquished him to the priesthood, and then died, leaving him wealthy – which led directly to the most important of the myths surrounding him; like Mr Gladstone he took to prowling the streets by night, and discovered three pretty young sisters whose impoverished father could give no dowry, and who were thus destined for a life of prostitution; on three successive nights Nicholas tossed a bag of gold through the window to provide each with the dowry that would make them respectably marriageable, and in so doing he established the notion of Santa Claus as the secret and surreptitious visitor with presents, and the three golden balls of the pawnbroker. When famine overwhelmed his see Nicholas stole a hundred hogsheads of corn from every grain ship that called at the ports of Lycia, yet miraculously their tallies stayed correct and the thefts were never noticed. Three handsome lads, the sons of a widow unable to feed them during the famine, set out to make their fortune abroad, and spent their first night away from home in the company of a wily butcher, who slit their throats and put down their tender bodies in a barrel of brine; but their guardian angel was watching, and winged his way to report this predecessor of Sweeney Todd to Nicholas, who promptly invited himself to dinner and was given a roast leg that, at the sign of the cross, rose from the platter and danced its way to the barrel in the cellar, so that the saint might restore the other bits and pieces to life and send them all back to their mother with a fine tale to tell. Perhaps one of these lads in gratitude relinquished profane life for the church and himself became a bishop – in medieval England the feast of St Nicholas on 6 December was marked by the election of boy-bishops who performed all the rites and offices except Mass, accoutred with mitre, cope and crozier, and whose authority lasted until Holy Innocents' Day on 28 December. Henry VIII put an end to it in 1542, Mary revived it ten years later, and the Great Eliza finally abolished it, rendering the Church of England joyless for ever. The reversal of the roles of choirboys, bishops and clergy was the ecclesiastical counterpart of the secular revelry of the Lords of Misrule which finds some reflection still in the Christmas traditions of army officers waiting on soldiers, prison officers on their charges, and the Royal Family on their servants (though this last may now be legend). Other aspects of the Christmas celebrations we would now find deeply shocking – the Mass of the Ass whose manger the infant Christ usurped ended not with the priest uttering *Ite missa est* and the congregation responding *Deo Gratias*, but with an exchange of three Hee-Haws apiece; on the Feast of the Circumcision, vespers was sung falsetto, suggesting a slip of the knife, the precentor was drenched with water, and the adolescent sub-deacons celebrated a mock Mass with obscene songs and dances, and indecent shenanagans with sausages that were then eaten on the altar.

Nicholas also saved from execution three unjustly condemned

men, and from drowning three sailors off the Turkish coast –
three girls, three boys, three prisoners, three sailors, three balls.
He became the saintly *vade-mecum* of children, sailors, scholars,
merchants and barrel-makers, but not of butchers; he was invoked by travellers as a protection against robbers and a support
for St Christopher; his cult almost usurped the Feast of the
Nativity; yet the only early foundation recognizing him seems to
have been the Church of Sts Priscus and Nicholas built in Constantinople by the Emperor Justinian, AD 527–565, two centuries
late and far away from Myra. Priscus is not much help in this
context – an obscure worthy of Besançon, martyred during the
persecution of Aurelian in 272 or thereabouts. It is as foolish to
ignore early traditions as it is to place credence on their late
accretions, but Justinian would surely not have yoked to Nicholas
a minor martyr from far-distant Doubs if Nicholas had been quite
so distinguished as legend suggests – but most of that legend
dates from a fictitious biography written by Methodius in the first
half of the ninth century, when Myra was occupied by the
Saracens. Methodius, a Balkan saint, spread the tales of Nicholas
westward – including the slightly discreditable story of the saint's
appearance to a group of Saracens who wanted to destroy his
tomb, ensuring that they destroyed another (perhaps the damaged sarcophagus still in the church); in both Bari and Venice
merchants realized that his bones must have great thaumaturgical value – but the boys from Bari got there first, in April 1087
(that is, more than fifty years after the departure of the Saracens
and the restoration of the church), dug up the newly-paved floor
of the church, discovered a marble sarcophagus, smashed the lid,
were overwhelmed by the smell of myrrh, found the bones and
stole them. The Byzantine historian Nicephorus Callistus, writing more than two centuries later (but an insistent user of early
sources), gives a graphic account of the Greek clergy rending their
vestments in grief and causing such a hullabaloo that the Italians
had to tie them up and gag them before they could go about their
business. As for the myrrh in which the bones were said to be sub-
merged, the Greek clergy had made from this much profit selling
phials of the liquid straight from the tomb, claiming that no matter
how much they took from it, Nicholas always generated more;
the cynic might suppose that their distress was at least as much
at the loss of their cottage industry as from the loss of the relics.

Myrrh is a gum resin used in the manufacture of perfumes,

incense and ointments; a Byzantine romantic called Constantine Porphyrogenitus seems to have been responsible for the assumption that myrrh is the eponym for Myra (or the other way about), but no earlier source mentions the city as an important source of unguents, and the connection is quite certainly false. When the Venetians eventually arrived, they carried off other bones, the Russians others still, and in the Museum in Antalya is a pathetic handful of bones attributed to Nicholas but never known to have had thaumaturgical effect (they were useless on the elbow that I had cracked at Pinara). According to the sailors from Bari whose ship the merchants had hired, Nicholas appeared to them in rough weather and promised a safe journey of twenty days, setting the seal of his approval on the theft.

The only other event of note in medieval times was the brief appointment of Eustathius as Bishop in 1174, one of the clergy of Hagia Sophia and a teacher of rhetoric in Constantinople; too brilliant a scholar to stay in Myra long, within a year he was to become Archbishop of Thessaloniki. He made critical compilations of Homer's Iliad and Odyssey, wrote commentaries on a text by Dionysius Periegetes in which otherwise lost material by Arrian and Stephanus of Byzantium is preserved, a life of Pindar, an account of the Olympic Games, and *The Reform of Monastic Life* – a near diatribe that astonishingly anticipates most of Luther's denunciations. Had he not been elevated to the see of Thessaloniki we would have been deprived of a most entertaining account of the pillage, rape and torture that characterized the Christian Normans' capture of that most Christian city in 1185.

We lunched in a bleak *lokanta* crowded with men who gave the impression of having worked themselves to exhaustion – that hollow-eyed drawn state in which the body demands food and drink before it will respond to any stimulus. Kebabs slid off their skewers into envelopes of hot unleavened bread and we ate them without cutlery – easy enough, but the onions were not; these were small and in their blackened skins straight from the grill, scalding hot; if we peeled them we burned our fingertips, and if we squeezed them, then they shot from their skins like scalding cannon-balls and we lost them among the table legs; those that we managed to control were crunchy and sweet and delicious in a way that no European onion has ever been.

In good temper we set off through the orange groves to find the site, lying almost five kilometres inland from the sea; it is now impossible with the clutter of the new town of Demre and its vast spread of greenhouses to conjure any impression of the city's original appearance from the distance of its ancient port of Andriake, where St Paul once stopped long enough to change ships, but close to, the first sight of the theatre and the tombs, low and accessible, virtually at sea-level, and perhaps never visible from a great distance, is as astonishing as the first sight of the stage when the curtain rises on a grand opera. Nothing but a late wall survives on the acropolis hill, but below it we found the Roman theatre, the much earlier Lycian tombs, and, by chance, a man who had once worked with George Bean and who turned to a photograph of himself in *Lycian Turkey* to prove it to us; as we sat in the sun eating his oranges, the old digger said that a statue of Bean should have been erected instead of Noël Baba, who means nothing to the Turks and was only put there to please the silly tourists (I wondered for a moment if we would have fallen into the same category had I not been carrying Bean's book). We climbed the seats of the theatre and looked down through the broken vault into the passage below, full of golden sunshine that seemed to suffuse the stone with warmth as the trapped light reflected from surface to surface.

The face of the rock behind the theatre, a mass of temple tombs, all facing more or less southward, all gentled and coloured by the sunlight, seemed almost within reach from the upper seats. These splendid tombs are divided into two main groups; those just to the west of the theatre honeycomb the cliff-face in a densely-packed repertory of types, of which some are carved with reliefs on which survive extensive traces of colour – as sculpture, they are provincial and undistinguished, suggesting extensive dependence on standard prototypes and no original study or observation, and in some cases the relief is so shallow and the outline so stressed that the carving could derive from painted rather than three-dimensional sources, as perhaps from decorated pottery. In the less extensive group facing north-east, round the corner of the acropolis hill, the sculpture is rather more remarkable – one of the tombs shows eleven members of the dead man's family in indoor and outdoor pursuits, almost *vita activa* and *vita contemplativa* prototypes, in which the tomb represents a house rather than a mausoleum. In Fellows' day both figures and tomb were painted in purple and the primary colours, but these have since almost faded away and indeed in afternoon light are virtually invisible. Quite why they should have survived so well for two thousand years and then faded to almost nothing in fewer than two hundred requires an explanation that I cannot offer – as well as further speculation on the absence of colour from the tombs of Tlos, Pinara, Cyenaea and elsewhere; a little cynicism may not be out of place.

The Chimera defeated us, as its monstrous embodiment defeated so many before meeting death at the hands of Bellerophon (see p. 127) – but only in the sense that we failed to reach it. Hereabouts, fifty miles or so nearer Antalya on the road from Myra, was the ancient home of the monster – an opening in Mount Olympus that was lit by perpetual fire; you may take your choice between the gloomy comment in a recent guide-book that the gases of the ancient volcano 'are not normally to be found burning nowadays, though they can be lit artificially', and Pliny's assertion that all the neighbouring mountains would explode with fire if put to the torch; when Bean last saw the flames in 1967 they were about the size of a small bonfire in a pit, and best seen at night. I like best the account by Dr Edward Daniel Clarke in his *Travels in various countries in Europe, Asia and Africa*, written between 1810 and 1823, but recording journeys made at the turn of the century – early in 1801 he was in Troy with Tito Lusieri, Lord Elgin's draughtsman, in June in Cyprus, in July in Jerusalem, and in October in Athens, and his observations of the Lycian coast were probably made between these last two. I observe wryly that he was paid £6,595 for his *Travels*. Of the Chimaera he says:

> The first land we saw was ascertained to be part of the mountainous coast of Lycia – here we were becalmed; as the evening advanced, a land breeze carried us again from the bay; but before night came on, it blew only in hot gusts; and, being on deck, we were in utter astonishment at the indescribable grandeur of the Lycian coast, and the awful phenomena by which we were surrounded; stupendous mountains, as the shadows increased, appeared close to the ship, towering above our top-masts; the higher parts being covered with snow, or partly concealed by the thick clouds; the air around us becoming every instant more sultry and stagnant; presently the whole atmosphere was illuminated; the mountains seemed to vomit

fire; a pale, but vivid lightning darted innumerable flashes over every object, even among the masts and rigging; never surely was such a scene elsewhere exhibited! The old Greek pilots crossed themselves, but comforted us with the assurance that this appearance of the kindling elements was common on this coast, and that it denoted favourable weather; we heard little thunder, but streams of living light ran continually from the summits of the mountains towards the sea, and seeming to separate before they reached the water, filled the air with coruscations; since reflecting on this circumstance, as characterizing the coast, it seems to explain a fabulous notion, which the ancients entertained of the Chimaera disgorging flames on the Lycian territory . . .

I can vouch for the fury of storms on the Lycian coast, but it seems clear that Clarke saw more than mere thunder and lightning in his 'streams of living light'.

We had, I thought, judged it nicely to reach Bean's 'bonfire' in daylight and then settle down to see what it looked like at night – and if all the earth about was riven with cracks through which more gas escaped and more flames might be induced, then these would be most visible and dramatic at night. We had no fear of being consumed by fire, for we had the third-century assurance of old Bishop Methodius (the only local worthy ever) that the flames were too cool to burn flesh. Guide-books are evasive at this point, and it is clear that none of their authors has been to the Chimaera. Bean merely says that trudging up the shingle for an hour and half from Olympus and then climbing to almost 1,000 feet will get you there quite easily – he also says that a jeep can be driven along the shore, but then he cannot have experienced our difficulties in reaching Olympus (see p. 165). Another account suggests that the Chimaera can be approached from the main Antalya road, reducing the walk to a mere two kilometres and a rather shorter climb, but no signposts indicate it. We drove up and down looking for a likely turning, or a likely peasant, but it is a wild stretch of country, deeply forested, and without villages or hamlets; in more than an hour of casting about we encountered only one living soul, and he was an idiot. I do not mean that unkindly – he was in his early twenties, conventionally unshaven, wearing only a sleeveless pullover, shirt and trousers (the flies undone), and he was barefoot – yet it was January and raining; he was without doubt one of the most beautiful young men that I have ever seen, but when we spoke to him, there was not only no response to the question, but no response to our presence – he did not even run; the eyes were blank, the dark sensual face expressionless, the effect chilling. A few minutes later we found another man, but all that he did was to gesture towards the forest and the sea, and say 'Down there'.

The next turning 'down there' was signposted 'Çirali 7 kms.'; it is narrow and steep and did not commend itself to Ayhan – we had passed it several times in retracing our steps, and as it is only three or four kilometres from Olympus on the Antalya side, and is the only turning in the right direction, I had been convinced for an hour or so that we must attempt it, however unwelcomingly steep and narrow it seemed. We learned later that it was the right road and that we should have followed it all seven kilometres into the village, but within two or three we had all turned to cowards. It might not have been so bad if Petter had been at the Renault's wheel, but Ayhan would not relinquish it – and the road was not just wet, but running with water; it was not just steep and twisting, but acute enough in its bends and changing gradients to deal an almighty blow to the car's boot as we plunged in and out of dips, and finally it confronted us with a passage of gravel on which the car slid inexorably down, turning broadside as it went, and then came to a halt facing more or less uphill. Had we wanted to continue, the road was too narrow for the car to turn, and I am superstitious enough to believe (occasionally) in divine intervention – as the car was now, without any effort on our part, pointing back the way we had come, it seemed expedient to return to the Antalya road (if indeed the car could be persuaded to climb its way up the gravel), and to the consolations of a very comfortable hotel that had been conjured from an old custom-house overlooking the harbour in Antalya, and which, to my delight, I recognized from a watercolour by Max Schmidt, painted in October 1843, bought in Christie's some years ago.

We thought to tackle the Chimaera again the following day, from sea-level, following Bean's footsteps along the shore from Olympus. This city is posted on the Antalya road as at a distance of 9 kilometres, and the path down the mountainside, though steep, is seductively broad and in places covered with concrete. Children sat by its side offering live ducks for sale (which I wanted to buy and release, but was prevented by a more realistic

Petter – and they had probably been pinioned), and strings of yellow mushrooms that looked delicious – had we been staying in a less respectable hotel I would have bought them and begged the use of the kitchen – even now my mouth waters at the thought. But at 9 kilometres there was not the slightest sign of Olympus, and we eventually halted in the square of a village that is not on the map and seemed to have no exit other than the road by which we had come. It was not Deliktaş, which is the Turkish name for Olympus that may one day be inscribed on a yellow signpost indicating an ancient site. We were advised to return to a ford and turn right before crossing it; in reverse this means driving only 5 kilometres from the Antalya road, and taking an unmarked turning to the left immediately after the ford, which was deep under water in January, but may well be dry in summer. After a hundred yards or so, we came to a real river and had to stop. An old man emerged from a house on the far side and volunteered to guide us to Olympus. Ayhan began one of his 'How much? How long? How difficult?' conversations, but Petter and I forestalled the impending arguments against the trek by leaping from stone to stone across the river onto the old man's side, but we were wearing boots, and Ayhan was immaculate in patent leather shoes, newly polished in Antalya. The old man, whose face was shadowed by a great flat cap of tweed pulled well down between enormous ears that looked as though they had been moulded in the red leather of Victorian bookbindings, rolled his trousers to the knees, walked through the stream in his shoes (he had neither socks nor laces), hauled Ayhan onto his shoulders pick-a-back, and carried him. We set off down the river bank single file until we had to cross the river again – four times more, each requiring Petter and me to take off our boots and socks, while the guide carried Ayhan; each time the river was deeper – well up the thigh, nibbling at our rolled trousers – and colder, and our socks grew soggier from being hauled onto wet feet; each time the stream was swifter, and tugged at our legs to make our footing unsure – it is a strange feeling to take the weight from a foot and feel it whipped away by icy water, and is the more unsteadying when it is the upstream leg.

At the site we found the guardian – why in midwinter was he there, miles from anywhere, five river crossings from the nearest road? He greeted us without surprise and with the same reserved courtesy as though it were mid-season, and set off at a brisk pace through the helter-skelter of the waterlogged city. There are points at which the scribbler should not attempt to turn his notes into decent writing, and this is one – 'A real mess of Byzantine rubbish over some faintly findable Roman stuff. A very few Lycian tombs, of which only one is interesting – much carved decoration, and the exposed end (the other is stuck in the mud) carved as a closed door, with a knocker in the left panel.' This immediate impression is likely to be shared by most visitors, but it is not wholly fair; with a little industry, a clearer picture of the city begins to emerge – a Hellenistic foundation as a decent harbour with a constant supply of fresh water (Bean diffidently repeats a suggestion that the sea-level was then perhaps much higher, allowing ships to sail into the river mouth, but that would have drowned most of the land on which the city stands, and it is now deeply waterlogged – the evidence elsewhere is that the sea-level is higher now than it was in antiquity), important enough to be a member of the Lycian League. Cicero described it as an ancient city, rich and well-furnished – it certainly had a theatre, of which only a few seats and one arched entrance remain, but it was small; and it must have had one very grand temple, for its one decent monument is a short stretch of fine smooth masonry framing an enormous door more than sixteen feet high dating from the time of Marcus Aurelius. This single door poses a problem, for it stands within a few yards of a shallow marshy lake, and on neither side of it is there now room for the substantial building to which it must have given access. Bean proposes the hypothesis that the decoration and the statue (of which only the inscribed base remains, giving the clue to Marcus Aurelius) were on the inner side of the door (contrary to common practice), but it would surely make more sense to assume that the lake, formed with the rise in sea-level since antiquity, drowned the foundations of the temple.

In the main necropolis on the south side of the river none of the great number of tombs is of Lycian type, and in the 217 inscriptions (Fellows found only two) neither the names nor the language is Lycian. The city is, of course, on the very eastern edge of Lycia, and Bean does not include it in *Lycian Turkey*. Its later history is lost. The chief deity in Roman times was Hephaistos, to whom a small temple close to the Chimaera may have been dedicated. If Plutarch, who died in AD 120, is to be believed, the city tried Mithraism, but by AD 300 or so, it was a Christian centre with a Bishop, St Methodius; quite why he should have become a saint I cannot imagine, except that he seems to have been slaughtered during Diocletian's general persecution that was for so many Christians the passport to sanctity. He was the author of *The Banquet of the Ten Virgins*, extolling virginity with Christ as arch-virgin, promoting the notion that its loss brought corruption and separation from God. Elsewhere he concerned himself with man's progress from incest to monogamy, leeches, leprosy and Old Testament food laws, and supported Free Will against Gnostic fatalism; among his lost works is a commentary on the *Song of Songs*, Solomon's anthology of erotic and anti-virginal love songs, no doubt interpreted as allegories of God's feeling for the Church or the soul – though another theologian, not distant in time or place, Theodore of Mopsuestia (Antioch *c.* 350–428) was bold enough to insist on its literal interpretation. Methodius was also curious about the Chimaera, commenting that the flame was hot but did not burn the flesh, and that bushes grew close to it and seemed to thrive as though close to water.

The guardian maintained that after the Byzantines, the city was taken over by Saracen pirates – a not unreasonable suggestion, but it may have been a confusion with a period in Pompey's time, a thousand years before, when it was quite certainly usurped by a pirate chieftain called Zeniketas or Zenicetes for some twenty years, or perhaps with the raids of marauding Goths on the Lycian coast in AD 253. Zenicetes was master not only of Olympus the town, but of Olympus the mountain, and of nearby Phaselis; one of the most powerful chieftains of Turkey's long southern shore, he paid no heed to the weak and corrupt officers of Roman occupation. Control of the mountains as well as the coast suggests that he was a well-established ethnic Lycian ruler rather than the pirate into which Roman historians have changed him, and this is borne out by his alliances with the Cilicians, formed in an attempt to protect his eastern flank, and their willingness to fight a great naval battle for him against Servilius Isauricus, the new and vigorous Proconsul of Cilicia, in his long campaign to subdue the coast during the years 77 to 75 BC. When Servilius eventually captured Phaselis and Olympus, Zenicetes fled to his mountain, and when that too was overrun, he set fire to himself and his family. His self-immolation again confirms his status as a Lycian chief, for the Xanthians too, at the other end of Lycia, burned themselves in defeat.

It was, of course, easy for the Romans, experts in propaganda and self-justification, to distort the historical record and convert their enemies from worthy chieftains into unworthy pirates. In one quarter of the Mediterranean theirs was the long-established view – twelve hundred years before Sevilius began his campaign, the Pharaoh Ikhnaton (*c.* 1375–1358 BC) had complained bitterly of the annual plunder of Egypt by raiders from Lukki, and it apparently continued for some century and a half, with the Egyptians persisting in their view that the Lycians were pirates and not the military and naval allies of their Libyan invaders. But the Lycians also contributed to the fall of the Hittite Empire, of which the heartland was in central Anatolia. Perhaps the supposition can only be that they enjoyed warring for the sake of it. With the Roman suppression of the ancient Lycians, the Lycians themselves became the occasional victims of piracy, and with the decline and depopulation of the coastal cities under the Byzantines, there is every reason to suppose that pirates could take them over and use them as their bases. Perhaps the guardian was right after all, and the Saracens did occupy Olympus.

Servilius Isauricus had a young man of great distinction serving under him in his campaign against the pirates – Julius Caesar, who, by chance, was later captured by pirates when on his way to Rhodes; they wanted a ransom, and he threatened them with crucifixion – a fate that they eventually suffered. Crucifixion, beheading, and being thrown to wild beasts were the official Roman punishments for piracy; in Turkish times they had been replaced by burning alive – a penalty executed officially by Pashas and unofficially by any body of peasants and fishermen strong enough or lucky enough to capture a corsair; in so far as records of these executions exist, they suggest that the fires were slow-burning and that, turned on a spit, the pirates took as long as three hours to be roasted to death.

I was glad that it was midwinter – Olympus in the summer must be plagued with mosquitos. Bean, with a note of regret, records the presence of a coffee-house and an abandoned motor-car on the beach, but neither is there now, and I cannot think how any car could have been driven there, even if in summer the stream is quite dry, for its bed is alarmingly uneven. Its banks are lined here and there with groves of oranges, on which we feasted, and half way back to the car we were overtaken by a tractor hauling a trailer laden with them at what seemed an astonishing pace upstream and midstream, with great wings of water flying from its wake, and much high-pitched giggling from the girls and women clinging to it. Some minutes later we came upon it, stuck at an alarming angle where it had attempted to leave the river; its churning wheels had dug deep and lessened its chances. Ayhan was carried across, and we followed barefoot; we, not he, tried putting our shoulders to the trailer, but the tractor wheels continued to slip; as despair seemed to have unmanned the driver, Petter and I began to pile large flat stones hard against the driving wheels, filling the pits that they had dug and offering some chance of grip (there is much to be said for the experience of National Service) – the driver's mate, a boy of about fourteen, joined in, but Ayhan suggested that we should leave them to it – still immaculate and quite dry, he said, 'Shall we go on?' It was Petter who said that we couldn't and wouldn't, forestalling an explosion from me. When the driver started the tractor again, Petter and I and the boy got back into the deep water behind the trailer and heaved; nothing happened; my eyes were screwed tight shut when we heaved again, and when again nothing happened I yelled 'Move, you bugger' at the top of my voice – and it moved, and I opened my eyes to find a touching look of astonishment on the boy's face, three inches from my own. To this day I do not know whether he had been astonished by my shouting in his face at such close quarters what he may well have taken to be some appalling imprecation, or by the success of the trick with the stones. (I should not be surprised if he shouts 'Move, you bugger' at every seemingly intractable problem, and it may slowly enter the Turkish language after the fashion of Veriko grapes in Cyprus – Veriko is neither place, nor man, nor botanical description, but the peasant corruption of 'very good', shouted by street vendors for the benefit of English army wives.) When we eventually reached the car we found the tractor waiting by it; the girls put more oranges in the boot than we could eat in a month, and parted from us with much waving and shouting, and a damp eye on my part for their generosity and gaiety.

Phaselis, the second city of Zenicetes' brief rule, is 21 kilometres from Olympus, north towards Antalya. In the mid seventies the track from the main road was rough, even for the Range-Rover, and stopped short of the unmarked site, then densely overgrown and heady with the perfume of wild herbs and pine saplings; we drove across a shallow marshy stream, and parked within a few yards of the sea. Only swimming in what appeared to be a harbour convinced us that we were indeed in Phaselis – both Jill and I could see under the water what we took to be a marble mole, with a few scattered column drums and capitals. Three villainous boys appeared and broke the idyllic mood; they carried large catapults and wanted to sell us bunches of dead birds threaded on a wire through their eyes – I had seen Jill bully and sulk on many occasions, but never blaze with anger as she did then. I suppose such pathetic little corpses end in the pot, though they can hardly be worth the trouble of plucking and drawing. When I was a boy I knew the shiftless son of a country doctor who claimed to get sixpence from Shippams, the fish-paste manufacturers, for every hedgerow bird he shot; when I raised the objections of plucking and drawing a tomtit, he told me that they didn't bother, but that feathers, gut and bones all went through the mincer, and if the mixture came out dark, then it was anchovy, if pale, then chicken and ham. I have never discovered the truth of the matter, and have ever since eschewed vicarage tea parties. But catapulting in Turkey (and I have since seen it all over the country) cannot compare with the wholesale slaughter of migrating birds in Cyprus, to be pickled in jars like plums and walnuts, or the autumn jamboree in Italy, when anything that moves is peppered with shot and then left to rot in the undergrowth.

Bean, rarely drawn to describe the natural beauties of his sites, introduces Phaselis with a brief passage of evocative prose that conditions the visitor's response. It has since been adapted for the demands of mass tourism; the rough track is now a wide tarmac road, barred by an automatic gate at the entrance to the site; beyond it is a huge and hideous administration office touched by the worst of Costa Brava fantasies, with a lacing of decorative street lights strung round the vast coach park. The site itself has been cleared of overgrowth, and its sad ruins neatly labelled with poker-worked cross-cuts of barky, varnished timber, more suitable for *Mon Repos* and garden gnomes. Straight line stretches of the neighbouring hillsides have been brutally stripped of their forest trees, stumps uprooted, leaving nothing but bare rock, ripe for erosion. No development (if that is what it is) could be more devastating, stupid and short-sighted.

Phaselis is both Lycian and Pamphylian. Its ambiguous situation may give another clue to Zenicetes' reputation as a pirate

rather than a chieftain, for the Lycian League lent their army and
navy to Servilius Isauricus to crush him, though in controlling
neighbouring Olympus, Zenicetes had three votes in the running
of the League and was part of it; but his real strength lay in ruling
Phaselis too, and in an alliance with Antalya, both cities of
Pamphylia. The Lycian League preferred its eastern border to be
clearly defined, and was happy to have its integrity restored with
Zenicetes' defeat, when Olympus was expelled from the League
and passed, with Phaselis, to the new and enlarged Roman
province of Cilicia.

The early history of Phaselis is confused. One tradition has it
that the Rhodians were its founders in 690 BC, as the principal
commercial port on what is now the Bay of Antalya (the later
foundation of Antalya itself was to usurp this position); this
confirms the idea of Lycian resistance to colonization, for Phaselis
was the first suitable site for a major harbour east of the great
jumble of 10,000 foot mountains that is Lycia bellying into the sea,
and the last for shipping from the east before it must swing away
to the south to round that hostile coast. Another tradition, less
reliable, has Mopsus as its founder – but then he is the posthum-
ously adopted parent of far more cities than could ever have been
established by a single roving hero, and has a wide-flung reputation quite irreconcilable with either the historical record or the
whimsies of mythological chronology – indeed his foundations
are the antique equivalent of 'Queen Elizabeth slept here.' Herodotus, a reasonably disciplined historian, groups it with Rhodes
in the fifth century BC, and inscriptions as late as *c*. 300 BC are in
the Rhodian dialect; to the Rhodians, who were, it seems from
Strabo, early colonizers in Spain and Italy, and even further
afield – their pottery has been found in Libya, and their graffiti
scratched on the legs of one of the giant statues at Abu Simbel –
Phaselis at a distance of only 150 miles must have seemed very
much within the parish bounds. Phaselis too had early links with
Egypt, as a city contributing to the foundation in the sixth century
of Naucratis in the Nile Delta – the great commerical centre that
welcomed Alexander, and whose citizens built Alexandria. But
whatever Greek claims there may be to the foundation of
Phaselis, it is probable that the Phoenicians were first to develop
the site as a staging-post in their astonishing expansion westward
to Spain – if indeed they founded Cadiz on the Atlantic coast in
1100 BC, then they must have been in Phaselis much earlier;

one small cultural link with the Phoenicians survived for many centuries, the *sisoe* (see p. 175).

The history of Phaselis in the grand sweeps of Greek and Persian conflict, in the brief empires of the Levant and the long dominion of Rome, offers little to relieve the tedium. The Phaselitans more or less welcomed the Persian invasion in the mid sixth century, but when Cimon of Athens tried to relieve the city in 469 BC, they rejected him – his response was an early example of propaganda warfare, for his Chian allies attached leaflets to their arrows and shot them over the city walls. When Persian rule was re-established, they came under the rule of Mausolus of Halicarnassus until his death in 353 BC. Twenty years later, Alexander arrived, spending some months there in the spring of 333, and after his death there was a long period of weak Egyptian control, then Syrian, then Roman, then Rhodian (a Roman gift), then the freedom of the Lycian League (even though Phaselis had never before been considered a Lycian city, but Pamphylian), and, finally, independence. But that was brief, and for most of the duration of the Roman Empire, Phaselis, though once more Lycian, was wholly subservient and of little importance. The city had a reputation for being unhealthy, feverish, and full of strange smells that may have emanated from the shallow lake recorded in antiquity, but now no more than marshy ground just to the north; its inhabitants were disreputable (citizenship, when once Phaselis fell on hard times, could be bought for 100 Drachmae), notorious for their dishonesty, sharp practice, failure to repay borrowed money, and accomplished lying.

In terms of grandeur the ruins are wholly unremarkable, and with its recent taming by German scholars and the Turkish Ministry of Tourism, the city has lost what Bean described as 'a charm beyond most others'. Even in midwinter, utterly deserted, it had the neatly dead quality of the ruins of Bury St Edmunds, and it was impossible to recapture the floundering excitement that had earlier come of swimming in the three harbours. The north and south harbours are wide and shallow, with breakwaters; the central harbour is small, almost circular, closed on the east by a mole, with a south bank that is a forty yard stretch of ancient quay with horizontal bollards to which ships moored. Apart from this harbour, which is just enough to raise a vision of the grand arrival of the Emperor Hadrian in AD 129, the visitor must conjure for himself the magic of past events. Jill, knowing the tale of

Alexander's march along the coast, was inclined to follow it, and had to be restrained, for the reports are in conflict. His destination was Perge (Antalya was not founded much before 150 BC), which could only be reached by an indirect and difficult march through the mountains, or, as he believed, by a quicker march along the shore. He hedged his bets, sent part of his army into the hills with local guides, and himself marched northward up the coast, having been told that a north wind made passable those stretches where the mountains plunged straight into the sea. According to Arrian, all went well, and he was swiftly in what is now the wide sandy Bay of Antalya that would today still be the beginning of an easy (and dull) coastal march to Perge, and indeed far beyond Side and Alanya. But Strabo tells a different tale, suggesting that the passage might be easy enough in fair weather, but that Alexander did it in foul, and spent much of his time up to his waist in water. A third account has it that Alexander and the whole of his army set off on the slow route through the mountains, and that, growing impatient, he rode down to the sea, whereupon the onshore wind stopped blowing and a way opened through the waters – Callisthenes, Aristotle's nephew and Alexander's tame historian, converts this into an image not unlike that of a successful King Canute, with the retreating sea bowing to its new master. Bean reasonably suggests that all accounts are inaccurate, and that Alexander attempted the coastal route, but made at least two inland detours.

Alexander must have liked Phaselis in spite of its smells, mosquitos, wasps, hornets and rascally inhabitants, for he stayed far longer there than in more important cities, and for no clear reason. Though it was renowned only for its possession of Achilles' spear, as a principal harbour it may have offered him those customary pleasures of a Levantine port to which he was not averse, and it had surrendered to him with golden crowns of submission. One revel is recorded in which, merry with wine in the main street, Alexander took the chaplets from the brows of his companions and tossed them onto a statue of Theodectes, the city's only famous son, whose expertise in riddle-me-ree casts doubt on the high intellectual seriousness of some of Aristotle's followers. Plutarch, in piety, converts the episode into a neat compliment to Theodectes, Aristotle and Alexander himself, but a drunken jape seems more probable, with a suitable measure of irreverence for the foolish ancient worthy who stood hoop-la for a conqueror. I have often wondered if Theodectes wore his hair in a *sisoe* when it was fashionable in Phaselis, and had thus seemed absurd to Alexander – alas, neither he nor any other man survives in sculptured form to prove the point. Quite what a *sisoe* was we do not know, but it was bad enough to be forbidden in Leviticus in the chapter that demands the ex-sanguination of animals slaughtered for food, forbids tattoos and prostitution, and talks of the unclean three-year uncircumcision of young fruit trees. The word *sisoe* is used only in the Septuagint, that body of Old Testament law and lore translated into Greek, it is said, by seventy scholars for the library of Ptolemy Philadelphus at Alexandria; in the English of King James' Bible it is revised to, 'Ye shall not round the corners of your heads.' The only useful comment on this curious custom was made by Robert Jamieson, a Glasgow divine whose *Eastern Manners illustrative of the Old and New Testaments* was published in 1836–8; he suggests that it is a reference to the worshippers of Baal, who shaved their heads leaving only a circular topknot of long hair. If this is so, then it is yet another of the many indications of eastern influence in Anatolia, though it is odd that it should have been restricted to Phaselis, unless, as Bean suggests, the Phoenicians, whose chief God Baal was, were the city's true founders, and their Levantine influence prevailed. Phaselis, coincidentally, could be a name of Semitic origin, meaning 'God saves' – a good deal more sensible as the name of a port at the homeward end of a hostile coast than its nearest Greek word, *phaselos*, the chick-pea.

— XII —

Antalya * Side

I do not care for Antalya. It was founded in the second century BC by Attalus II, King of Pergamum, has a fine marble gate built in honour of the Emperor Hadrian, a picturesque harbour in which fishermen still have their moorings and their market, and a rambling old quarter that in winter is smogged with wood smoke from chimneys that emerge from the house façades at not much above head level. At all seasons of the year it is dirty, scruffy, noisy and nasty; it gives the impression of having been generally modernized and brought up-to-date in the appalling European taste of the sixties, with pavements of cheap mosaic and tile, but these are now broken and uneven with patches of cement, tarmac and aggregate; most of the buildings are concrete, the fringes of the city are littered with characterless tall blocks, and only with tremendous effort of will may the visitor find the picturesque old bones of the town. As with so many deliberately modernized cities, the rot has already set in, and it has to be said that the new rots much less prettily than the old, and seems infinitely more sordid. The new museum is a good example – its contents used to be housed in Seljuk buildings above the harbour, but they are now in a hideous modern structure that was promptly closed for a programme of refurbishment that involved the exclusion of daylight and the erection of floodlit timber niches

– an effect calculated to take all the life out of the marble sculptures; outside, most of the sculpture is under a substantial raft-roof of concrete on feeble supports, and will be crushed in the first earthquake tremor. The exhibits are from nearby Perge and elsewhere in the immediate area, and it has to be admitted that their quality is largely abysmal – suggesting, as was no doubt true, that much Roman work was for theatrical effect and not for aesthetic experience.

An episode of no importance, as is so often the case, soured Antalya for ever; a gipsy girl jumped down from a cart and grasped my hand, pointing first to her very pregnant belly and then to her mouth; my reaction that had she spent less money on gilding her teeth she'd have more to spend on her hunger was no doubt uncharitable, but it changed to blind rage when she got back on the cart and her girl companion goaded their very old white and starving horse by whipping a knotted rope on its hind flank where a harness strap had worn a deep sore – anywhere else it would hardly have mattered, but on the raw flesh it was painful enough to make the horse miss its stride. I shouted at her – she knew what she'd done, and did it again, so I made a Sicilian evil eye sign at her as a last resort, and consoled myself with the thought that as a gipsy she was not a true Turk, for Turks seem to me, although perhaps indifferent to animal suffering, never deliberately cruel.

Antalya was not always as I find it; Fellows preferred it to all other Turkish towns:

> Every house has its garden, and consequently the town has the appearance of a wood – and of what? – orange, lemon, fig, vine and mulberry, all cultivated with the artificial care of a town garden, and now in fresh spring beauty. I see in the bazaar small green almonds; and among the fruit trees barley is coming into ear . . . I find the town is small, but clean, and more agreeable as a residence than any that I have before seen in this country. The town stands on a cliff rising sixty or eighty feet above the sea, which has no beach, but breaks against the overhanging rocks; these are apparently formed of, or in-crusted by, a stalactitic deposit of lime. I have returned from a walk laden with flowers . . . It is impossible to find points at a distance from which to see Adalia, as its walls hide it, and these are completely concealed by its rich growth of trees . . . I have never seen mountains so beautiful, so poetically beautiful.

I cannot argue with him over the beauty of the mountains, but the rest is unrecognizable – except in one small respect, where he writes that 'in the courtyard for the house in which I resided there were eighteen wooden pillars supporting the building above, and each of these had for its base an inverted capital of a Corinthian column', for I think that house still stands in the old quarter, occupied by a family whose young sons inevitably used our prying as an excuse to introduce us to the nearest carpet dealer.

Like it or not, Antalya is the natural centre for exploring the sites of eastern Lycia and western Pamphylia, but my preference lies with Side, fifty miles on down the coast – though it may not stay so, for the continuing process of turning the village into a resort has imported many tiresome aspects of tourism. Turning off the main coast road, one is at once among substantial and picturesque fragments of the aqueduct and other buildings, aware that the scattered guest-houses must lie on ruins that now will never be explored. The village itself has grown piecemeal and too fast – swinging through the great gate to find the vast theatre on the left and a line of marble columns on the right should be a breathtaking experience, and it still is, except that the columns give way to a parking lot, the bus station, a ramshackle café, a mephitic loo, taxis and a stand for a dozen *dolmuş*. A few taxis are permitted to enter the village street, which, otherwise restricted to pedestrians, leads straight down to the harbour; it is flanked by a number of houses that date back to the beginning of this century, part stone, part timber, with a centre gable, that are characteristic of Side. These were built by Muslim exiles from Crete, who were dumped among the deserted ruins in 1900 or thereabouts and left to fend for themselves. In 1896 civil war had broken out in Crete with a successful Greek Christian insurrection against the governing Turks; the French, British and Austrians intervened, a Christian Governor-General was appointed, reforms were instituted but not carried out, the Greek Government in Athens encouraged discontent, and early in 1897 the island was again in a state of insurrection, with the Greek Navy mobilized in support followed by a Greek invasion in the name of King George (National Servicemen at the time of the Cyprus crisis will recognize familiar elements in this dispute). This Greek intervention caused great excitement among the Christian population, who felt encouraged to carry out what even

James Bourchier, a Member of the Order of the Saviour of Greece and a noted Greek sympathizer, reported to *The Times* as 'terrible massacres of Moslem peasants'. The international powers eventually secured the withdrawal of both Greek and Turkish forces, with the promise of Cretan independence from both Turkey and Greece, but then appointed Prince George of Greece as their High Commissioner on the island – though peace was restored, the Muslim population, which had been reduced to extreme poverty by the civil war, began to emigrate to Turkey in large numbers, some of them to Side, and continued to do so, dwindling from 88,000 in 1895 to 40,000 by 1907, the year in which they asked the British for some remedy for their continuous ill-treatment at the hands of the dominant Greeks. Sir Edward Grey assured the House of Commons that their complaints were exaggerated, and continued to arrange the withdrawal of the small forces put on the island by the major powers to support the Greek High Commissioner; when these began to leave on 27 July 1907 the Muslims rioted, believing themselves abandoned – as indeed they were, for in October the Cretan Assembly voted for union with Greece and began to administer the island in the name of King George. There are now no Muslims in Crete.

The oldest inhabitants of Side still speak Greek. Osman, still in his twenties, speaks a little in order to communicate with his grandparents. He speaks and writes English, and has a smattering of French and German; he is a graduate of Ankara university; intelligent and ambitious, his frustration tempered only by Turkish fatalism, he is typical of many of his generation. I met him in 1976. He was then a skivvy at the Motel Turtel, so low in the complicated hierarchy of house-boys and waiters as to be invisible – certainly I had not noticed him, though he had noticed me, and at the very moment of departure in Jill's Range-Rover he stepped from a shadow and in perfect English wished me well. The English was astonishing from this tiny waif with a plain and solemn face, and stopped me short; I promptly gave him an incomplete set of the complete works of Somerset Maugham and a dictionary, and we have been corresponding ever since – I treasure particularly a description of life at Ankara university during the worst of the social and political unrest of the late seventies, when he wrote that work was constantly interrupted by 'exploding bums' (I have learned since that students learning English are taught many of the distinctions between the

European and American variants, but are nevertheless confused by them).

In the Army he became a subaltern and commanded a platoon on the troublesome Syrian border. And then, with education and experience under his belt, he returned to Side, to his father who bakes bread all day and most of the night, and his brothers who walk miles every day to sell sesame rings on the beach. It is another Turkish dilemma – a social system that allows a peasant boy to achieve education and authority, and then confronts him with the insuperable obstruction of no suitable work. Now a town councillor, he runs free classes in English for any villager who wants to learn, and sees his village as ruined by the rampant tourism of large hotels that are an invasion by big banks and big business from Ankara and Istanbul. In the winter, when the tourists die away and the village population sinks back to its permanent 900 or so, there is nothing to do except sit in the one café that stays open and play an exceedingly noisy numbers game with other boys, for the restaurants and shops are permanently closed, and the awful souvenir shops are wrapped and roped in plastic sheets like expensive works by Christo.

In summer, with thousands of tourists milling through the village, the boys must earn enough in the short season to last for the full year – but the opportunities are confined to work in the hotels where most of the plump tourists on package holidays do not expect to tip, and the salaries from May to October are no more than we would pay an English boy for a month. The Turtel – which I first thought (and still wish) was Turkish for 'turtle' instead of a fashionable hybrid – was Michael's discovery in 1975. I once drove round Spain with a man who had only to arrive in Seville or Santiago for his nostrils to twitch and lead him at once to the most expensive and exclusive hotel – I was then in love with an old, enormous and very distinguished open Daimler, with the grandeur to match any hotel, but now my tastes and priorities have changed, and I prefer to slum; I recognized the same extra-sensory process in Michael, the trance-like state in which he uttered directions, the refusal to answer questions as we drove along the sand past Turkish peasants and their strange beach houses, and his relaxation as we swept into the grounds of the motel, to be greeted by a flurry of white-jacketed boys. The Turtel was then run by what I would have described as a grandee had he been Spanish; as immaculate as a retired English colonel (even to the liver and white spaniel), and as well-spoken, Mardin Bey was a relic of Ottoman courtesy, and his German wife a relic of Robert Musil's *Young Törless* (as Michael was to find when he blocked the loo with melon skin – doctors deprived of nurses to skivvy for them can be such fools) – a combination of old-world charm and ruthless efficiency.

In 1975 the Turtel was an oasis among Turkish hotels, one of the few in which it was not essential to dowse the bed in flea-powder, repair the mosquito netting with plastic bags and sticky tape, or pray for water, hot or cold, and for a decade it has drawn me back to Side like an old friend after rash wanderings in the east. In 1984, running out of money, Petter and I deserted it for the cheapest of *pansyons* on the Turkish side of the village, and discovered a different world – of Turkish families holidaying on a shoe-string, of flutes and sad love songs in the moonlit theatre, of wild Turkish dancers in the ruins, and where time slowed and lost its European disciplines. Petter fell in love with a pretty Turkish girl staying with her mother and brother in what passes for a youth hostel. They spoke a little English and wanted to practise – Ali, the son, would lose patience very quickly, and turn cartwheels or pull faces, but Mama (whom I describe as a 'crazy woman with two children' in my first diary note on her) perse-vered with such gambits as 'The Russians are so romantic' (she had just made the café owner substitute a Rachmaninov tape from her handbag for the Chipmonks' version of 'The Dead March in Saul') and 'I am Utopian, but not Communist.' Bengisu, her daughter, spent most of her time just gazing at Petter.

With use, Mama's English began to flow easily. In the course of revealing an aversion for all things American she said 'Son-of-a-bitch' and 'Mother-fucking' – neither of which she understood either as an idiom or literally, and when I explained their indeli-cacy, she found the first more shocking. At lunch on the second day of her inescapable company, an old man walked by playing a flute – she bought it from him, explaining over her shoulder in mid-negotiation that one should always buy the demonstrated instrument, for it will be the best. Disinfecting its mouthpiece in *my* glass of raki, she gave it to Ali to play – it was as well for him to be distracted, for she next hissed at Petter, 'Don't let my son see what you are doing – the consequences will be terrible – Turkish men are like animals when they are angry.' As far as I could see there was no cause for anger – Petter was innocently nursing a cat in his lap, and Bengisu was joining in; what in fact was happening was that she was masturbating him under the table, and they were desperately holding onto the cat as camouflage. It was the first of a number of such follies, none of which was noticed by Ali (who seemed not the slightest bit interested in girls, and least of all in his little sister), so that there were no terrible consequences.

In the dark theatre, listening to love songs late at night, Bengisu lay on her back and let Petter tease her breasts and crutch – her white blouse rose and fell with the movements of her breast and his hand, as though it had a fluorescent life of its own. 'Brian can see', she whispered (but no whisper is private in that theatre) – 'It doesn't matter', he answered. And it didn't. Very late one night we plunged through the hole in the Byzantine wall above the sea and found Mama and Bengisu swimming in moonlight that made the shallow water look like a sheet of mercury; they came towards us and urged Petter to join them, but as he strode into the water in his shorts Mama shrieked at him to take them off and swim naked – and then she sat with me, watching, first while he stripped, silhouetted against the moonlight, and then while he swam to Bengisu and stood waist-deep with her, kissing and fondling. Bengisu took off her bra with a flamboyant gesture and set about the business of Petter's underwater climax, while Mama and I sank into an involved and tedious philosophical conversation about giving in friendship with a good grace – broken when without warning she plonked a kiss on my mouth.

I assured her, without conviction, that Petter would never do anything remiss with Bengisu (whom we now knew to be only sixteen), and she replied, 'I know. We have no secrets. We are mother and daughter.' But the next morning, Friday the thirteenth, when they arrived in the middle of our frugal breakfast with enormous bunches of flowers stolen from local gardens, mistaking it for my birthday, Mama launched into a catechism on the Virgin Birth, with some particular anxiety that the hymen should survive the birth intact. I expressed the view that this is impossible. She was convinced that vast quantities of sperm are left in Turkish baths, lying in wait for women's day, and that the Virgin Birth was thus a fairly common occurrence; my experience of Turkish baths offers no support for her notion, but she must have got her ideas of rampant ejaculation from somewhere, just as I, on the reports of three woman friends in London, of widely different ages and physiques, harbour the notion that women's days in the baths are riots of lesbian amusement.

I have heard many tales of homosexual mishap befalling Westerners – the dark warning that no blonde man or boy should venture into the baths – but Petter survived unscathed, apart from a scrap between the attendants as to which should scrub him, and that turned out to be less a matter of lechery than of the expected tip. I have only one reliable witness to an unfortunate but scarcely damaging episode in his case, and he was no blonde. He had the misfortune to take a bath in mid-afternoon when there were no other clients; it was his first, and he had no idea of the ritual, and was thoroughly baffled first by the mummifying effect of the towels in which he was wrapped, and then by the force with which bowls of hot and cold water were alternately flung at him by the two attendants, who soaped, scraped and scrubbed him everywhere but his groin, which remained demurely covered by a thin towel until they told him to scrub it himself. They then spread a towel on the marble floor and indicated that he should lie on it, face down, while they stood on his ribcage in their bare feet, and yanked his arms and legs into impossible backward positions; the painful process seemed to separate him from his body, as though this inanimate thing on the floor, still capable of feeling pain but unable to react to it, was no longer his, and it was in this detached state of mind that the first entry began; one attendant was squatting on his shoulders, seeming to mas-sage them and his neck with the broad weight of his buttocks, but in reality holding him down while the other set about the busi-ness of sodomy; and then they changed places, and the new man on his shoulders crouched forward and whispered 'Baksheesh' in his ear, and with his finger wrote exorbitant figures in the soap-suds on the floor, while my witness cried 'Yok! Yok!' with as much energy as could be summoned in the circumstances. He remains convinced that they asked for *baksheesh*, but it is not a Turkish word, and he described the man who asked for it as looking like a Tartar. It seemed to me in the telling that he resented the demand for money more than the assault on his backside that must have been encouraged by some sign or pleasurable response to what was happening. This was no tale to tell Mama, who was by now talking about Homer; as she fre-quently slipped from English into French I took the new subject to be lobster, and was completely confused by its connection with

Turkish baths – after a bout of helpless giggles at the confusion with *homard* I found myself unable to explain 'lobster' and took to drawing one, but realized with horror that what was appearing on the paper resembled nothing so much as a whiskered penis, and the giggles began again.

Petter became increasingly bothered about Bengisu's innocence; convinced that she was largely ignorant of the mechanics of sex, and of the female orgasm, he found her sensuality disturbing and forbore to comply with her urgings that they should conjugate. Sex seems to be full of problems for the young in Turkey. The boys in Side, exposed to Europeans, do not do so badly – they light fires on the beach near the hotels, and any passing girls are asked to join the 'birthday party' that with wine, music and a little luck will end in the girl or girls servicing them all. Osman, whose English can take surprisingly direct idiomatic forms, maintains that they regard compliant girls as prostitutes, 'no more than holes to fuck', and owe them neither the respect nor affection that they might have for virginal Turkish girls. This attitude obtains towards Western men; homosexuality exists in Turkey at least as much as among Western nations, perhaps more, but there is in addition a widespread element of homosexual opportunism by heterosexuals who regard Western men in much the same way as Western women, and given the opportunity for sexual activity, will take it, offering nothing but scorn for their partners. In the villages where there are no tourists, the donkey may well introduce most of the boys to the pleasures of intercourse; one young Muhtar told me that his mother had found him masturbating at the age of thirteen and had told him to 'Go and fuck the donkey – but don't blame me if she kicks you and breaks your leg'; he said that the boys tended to do it in groups – one might say, 'Hey, come on, let's go and fuck the donkey', and they all would, never watching each other, but quietly waiting their turn outside the closed stable door.

The Family Planning Association of Turkey has issued in English a research paper on *Sex Information and Attitudes of Youth in Ankara*, where, as capital city, a degree of sophistication might be expected. The authors of the paper are a professor and the Director of the Social Services Academy in Ankara, yet their statements are often astonishingly naive; Case V of the section dealing with 'Problems related to the anatomy and the functioning of the genital organs' makes the point:

A young girl of 12 years old was brought to the doctor by her parents because she very strongly refused to get married in spite of all the pressures put on her. During the examination her development and genital organs were found perfectly normal. At the end of some enquiries made by the doctor the girl confessed that, when she was six years old she had some childish sexual plays with a boy of her age, and now she thinks that she is no more a virgin. At the age of six erection of the penis cannot occur and for this reason a six years old boy cannot deflore the hymen.

Two matters arise from this report, that girls of twelve are marriageable in the fullest sense, and that the authors, one of whom is a doctor, do not believe that it is possible for a boy of six to have an erection – a manifest absurdity of which most British nannies could disabuse them, if they are too old to recall their own pre-pubertal experiences. Most of the quoted cases relate to girls anxious about their virginity after lesbian experiences, the insertion of leeches, the insertion of 'an empty tube because of her curiosity', and of amulets. But boys and young men, particularly in the first few months of marriage, also reveal astonishing ignorance, mistaking nocturnal emissions for gonorrhea, threatening divorce because there is no blood on the wedding night (a pretty picture that, of two families wailing over clean sheets until the doctor demonstrates that the hymen is still intact), and complaining that normal intercourse, and therefore conception, was impossible, when, as the doctors were to point out, the wife was three months pregnant and they had been 'having normal sexual intercourse, but due to their ignorance they were not aware of it' – the report does not, alas, tell us what they thought *was* normal.

In spite of the tourists, Side still has a life of its own. At weekends rural Turks come to the water – a larding of rich Turks from Ankara and Istanbul is always to be found in the better hotels and restaurants, but these are distinguishable from European visitors only by their greater courtesy and decorum – the peasant Turk ignores them, and us, and goes his own way; the men swim in loose knee-length pantaloons, often pyjama-striped in brown and beige, clinging and perhaps transparent when wet, covering all and concealing nothing – they are for the most part shaven-headed and lean, with deep-socketed eyes, and they swim with noisy flapping movements, unlike the local men who swim as efficiently as fish after the first rushing, splashing, shouting plunge. The country women rarely swim; they enter the water fully clothed, their loose dresses ballooning as the wet hems trap air in them, their heads covered, and sometimes their faces too; they stand in the water, islands of safety for the mobs of small entirely naked children that surround them; occasionally they play with an inflated inner tube, using those of tractor size as bottomless and very unstable dinghies. They bring picnics which they supplement with the nuts, fruit, ices and sesame rings that can be bought from pedlars traipsing the beach, and they build shelters of twigs, bits of cloth, leaves and anything else that can be found on the sand, to huddle in their scant shade, and they dig shallow pits in the sand and bury themselves. They used to build ramshackle stilted shelters, roofed with branches on which the leaves quickly died, which lasted the summer through, and were then carried off in the autumn storms; their semi-permanence brought a village atmosphere to the beach, with the smells of cooking and the bedding thrown over the rails to air, but German tourists found their lavatorial use of the sea offensive, and it is no longer permitted to build a shack or erect a tent on the beach. There is a byre in the village – the cows are normally driven inland to pasture, but occasionally they are taken for a plod along the beach, causing outrage to the inevitable yapping poodles of Germans who have driven all the way from Bad Oeynhausen. West of the Turtel an old man, naked but for vest and pants so worn and torn that they look like flakes of skin, waters his cattle at a brackish well in the sand, and sometimes lets them wander towards the village – the well is connected with an equally brackish stream that is the haunt of dragonflies. Once in a while, within the village, old men will walk with a sheep as though with a dog. On my birthday I had the serendipitous gift of a boy on horseback riding through the Roman harbour wall, his saddle a worn scrap of *kilim*, and on into the sea until the stallion was swimming – he slid from its back and swam with it, as though with a friend, and then in shallow water curried and combed it until, satisfied, he vaulted into the saddle and rode in proudly from the sea and through the Roman wall again. It was a handsome image, bold and timeless.

— XIII —

Seleucia * Etenna * Termessos

In the hills behind Side are the ruins of Seleucia, some seven miles to the north of the neighbouring market-town of Manavgat; they are not easy to find, for it is not an enclosed site, has no guardian, is not signposted, and no-one in Manavgat seems to know of it – the village of Şihlar lies within an hour's walk, but with discreet persistence it is possible to drive an ordinary car to the very edge of the city. It may have been an early foundation whose old name was lost when it was given its new dynastic name under the Seleucids, who controlled the whole of Pamphylia (in which this Seleucia and Side lie) and, to the east, Cilicia, reaching beyond St Paul's armpit, where the greatest of the many cities called Seleucia still survives as present-day Silifke; the founder of the dynasty was Seleucus I, one of the generals to inherit a substantial part of Alexander's empire. The Pamphylian Seleucia has no historical importance, but the few standing remains round the agora are monumentally impressive; they are market buildings, with a basement on the west side where the site falls away steeply, a well-preserved wall of shop-fronts, a semi-circular building that may have been an odeon or council-house, and some standing columns from the colonnade that once surrounded the open agora. There is no theatre, even though the site is very steep on three sides and could have accommodated a *cavea*

quite easily, and the only building distant from the agora that can be identified in a small temple to the north of it. We could find no trace of any Christian occupation, but it must have had an early Byzantine after-life for it sent its Bishop Quintianius to the Council of Nicaea in AD 325, where he gave his assent to the Nicene Creed; it is amusing to think that the Creeds recited by the Catholic and Anglican churches of the West, in North and South America, Africa and Australia, were first established in the East by eastern theologians – of the 318 Fathers attending the Council of Nicaea only two represented the Pope, and of the five others from western sees, one was the Bishop of Carthage.

The site is remarkably cooler than Side, which can easily be seen, and seems always to have a slight breeze to rustle and creak the pine-trees that perfume it. In a cave that is embellished with the wreckage of ancient masonry that once formed a pool or fountain, the city's source of water still springs, and, nearby, a local peasant grows tomatoes, peas and melons in a small *bahçe*. Perhaps it was always a Sidetan suburb, and not independent, a cool retreat for the wealthy from the seashore heat and bustle, yet within easy reach of the theatre – there is no doubt that if the theatre could accommodate the 40,000 spectators now claimed for it, their roars could as easily be heard in Seleucia as are the roars of Fulham football supporters in Kensington.

Still further to the north of Side, to the west of the road from Manavgat to distant Beyşehir, is Etenna. It is exactly thirty-one kilometres from Manavgat (and that is worth noting), but seems more because of its height in the Taurus Mountains and the slow rough track that leads to it. In the office of the Side Museum the staff, after much humming and hawing, sketched a crude map in my diary – their road passed through the villages of Şişeler, Dolbazlar, Evrenler, and Sahir before reaching Sirtköy, the modern village on the site, and the distance they estimated at twenty-two kilometres. None of them had ever been there. In Colin's elegant air-conditioned Ford we drove north out of Manavgat, and at rather more than twenty-two kilometres found only a high and very pretty Seljuk bridge in fine condition, with a woman watering two cows in the brackish green water below. She fled when we enquired the way. We drove on and asked some children; they directed us to return the way we had come – and we were almost back in Manavgat and in despair when we saw the sign marked 'Sirtköy 31 kms.' pointing to a narrow road

on the west. At half that distance the rough track suddenly
deteriorated to dust and boulders too prominent for sump and
exhaust, and we gave up, returning to Manavgat in search of
easier pleasure.

We found it in the market-place, a vast emporium for so small a
town, part open, part tented, in which the noise was deafening
and yet had a quality that at once induced a comfortable excitement. Here almost anything edible or wearable could be found –
whether one would want to eat decaying medlars or wear straw-
hats bedecked with plastic cherries is another matter, but both
were there. Peasant women in ballooning trousers, their hair
tight-trapped in bright kerchiefs, weather-worn faces grinning
with gold teeth, sold us chunks from wet white cheeses with
hands that were none too clean, and made us taste their butter –
salt, or rancid, or tastelessly greasy, and in all its variants wholly
unlike the butters designed for English palates. Greengages,
peaches, plums, grapes, apricots, oranges, and cherries black,
creamy-white, pink and cherry-red, lay piled on the stalls;
women sitting on the ground offered small deep baskets of black
or green figs, and old men sat with branches of the tiny local
bananas in every shade of ripeness from dull green to glistening
suppurating black. Gipsy women sold bunches of wild herbs and
the delicious *ada* – a dried weed that smells a little like hops and
makes a refreshing alternative to tea. I was tempted to buy, for
their sheer nastiness, a pair of transparent plastic shoes in
fluorescent green, with the moulded stitches and laces picked out
in gold. Women and small girls, mothers and daughters, I
thought, wondering why no teenagers or young women were
there, dipped noisily and with much laughter into a huge basket
of brassières of all shapes and sizes – odd, in a country where
feminine modesty is so highly prized. Pegs, biscuits, nuts, plastic
baths and buckets, iron saucepans and cauldrons, zinc pipes and
chimney-pieces, lamps, mirrors, haberdashery, soap, blankets,
fish and scissors . . . I decided to have my hair cut, regretting that
I had already shaved and would thus miss the massage of
temples, ears and neck that always follows the blade – but it was
not so, for after the delicious surrender to a boy who not only
washed my hair but washed my face with the tenderness of a
mother, his fingers delicately retrieving soap-suds from the perimeter of my mouth, swabbing the sockets of my eyes with warm
flannels as gently as though they were wounds, he eased my taut

temples, found the pressure points behind my ears, manipulated my neck until I could have danced *Swan Lake*, and then gently pinched my lips and the line of my jaw, reinforcing my notion that the Turks, however scruffy they may seem to us, are both inherently vain and aware of erogenous zones that the West has never explored. Gwen John, I recalled, pinched her nipples before bedding with Rodin, and I looked at my lips with new interest.

In Side I hired a jeep for a second assault on Etenna, and we set off in the early morning of the following day. Within fifteen minutes, even before eight, I was burning in the wind and sun to the point where I had to relinquish the wheel to Petter and sit huddled in the back swathed in a bath towel – without a hood, exposure in the jeep was as near as I have ever come to cooking, and I felt not far behind St Lawrence, a corsair caught by Turkish peasants, and Tom Brown. We followed the road that we had found the previous day, reached the point where it had become too rough for the car, bumped on another hundred yards or so, and stopped. Not even a jeep could go further – a tank certainly, but not a jeep. We backed, and returned to the last group of houses, where a tractor driver told us to go back still further, to the unmarked village of Dolbazlar, and piled water-melons in our laps for which he would take no payment. In Dolbazlar con-flicting help was offered, and we found ourselves driving in and out of what passed for the square without ever leaving the dusty purlieus of the village – a man in pyjamas directed us the first time round, and we waved to him in embarrassment on our second, third and fourth passages past his house as we made our way back from various farmyards and dead ends. A boy on a motor-cycle eventually offered to take us, jettisoned his machine against a hedge and climbed into the back of the jeep. From the centre of Dolbazlar the main road is the one that we had already followed, and we now followed it again, but only to the edge of the village – on the right, at a right angle, is a narrow track that we had taken to be private, but it was the unmarked turn to Etenna. Further on, at a fork, again unmarked, the road bears to the right – the only confirmatory indication is a small graveyard a little along on the left; at yet another fork, yet again unmarked, you must again bear right. We passed through no other villages, and saw no sign of the Evrenler and Sahir that we expected from the Sidetan map; the road eventually ran out in Sirtköy, whence a steep ten-minute trudge leads to Etenna, on the ancient border of Pamphylia and Pisidia. At no point, though rough, would the road have been impassable to the air-conditioned Ford, and indeed a couple of Turkey's ubiquitous Fiats were parked in the village.

The city was once ringed by a wall of irregular ashlar, well made, but most of the ruins contained within its traces are unidentifiable – neither temples nor theatre have been found, and only one apse-ended church, reservoirs, cisterns, granaries and rock-cut tombs can be recognized. Unlike nearby Seleucia, Etenna had a long and independent history, with shards of the Classical period (very rare in inland sites) and evidence of the continued minting of coins from the fourth century BC to the third AD. It makes only two appearances in the historical record. In 218 BC it supplied the astonishing number of 8,000 troops to Garsyeris, army commander to the then King of that general area of Asia Minor, Achaeus, the uncle of Antiochus III of Syria – Garsyeris was supporting the citizens of the lost city of Pednelissus, north of Perge, who were under siege from Selge (see p. 196); it was hardly an important event, but it brought so many Pamphylian and Pisidian cities into the record at the same time that it helps to conjure a picture of the political complexities of the day, as well as to suggest quite substantial populations. There is then a gap of six hundred and fifty years before Etenna is mentioned again – and then it is only as being represented at the Council of Ephesus in AD 431, called to settle the controversy caused when Nestorius, Bishop of Constantinople, mooted a human as well as divine person in the body of Christ (poor Nestorius was exiled to Upper Egypt, but his church survived into this century in Kurdistan). After that, silence and ruin.

The site makes little sense – the very broken ground and steeply climbing hillsides could never have accommodated grand buildings; we would not have found many of the cisterns and granaries (if indeed that is what they are) had it not been for the band of small boys that immediately formed our company, scrambling with caprine agility where we could see no toe-hold, shaming us into pursuit. Two young men appeared, small and fine-boned as boys, dark-eyed, moustached, one with a stick of stripped poplar rather shorter than an English walking-stick, the other with a shotgun (with no sight) and an endless supply of acrid Libyan cigarettes that burned fast as a fuse. They found easier ways than the boys, but still difficult, and gradually insisted on carrying our knapsacks and cameras – if we put anything down while we were looking at a scrap of sculpture or inscription, even my notebook, they promptly picked it up or slung it over their shoulders. We found the apse-ended church, the broken remains of perhaps two large columns, part of a small column in polished rouge marble that looked very like something from a High Victorian church in respectable north London, column bases, a crude Ionic capital whose carver had completely misunderstood the origin of the design, an inscribed door lintel, and a worn relief of a bull's head flanked by swags, all hard by or jumbled into a vaulted cistern. Without thinking how we might get out, we dropped into every subterranean chamber that we found; in some there was only rubble, in others the walls were carved with what seemed to be random patches of decoration, or the floors littered with architectural fragments in white marble. Colin, still the only one of us capable of reading ancient Greek, hung upside-down to transcribe two long inscriptions on a fallen stone, the men and boys holding onto his legs, until I thought he would die of apoplexy. Nothing makes any sense. Nothing, except an inscribed stone in the city wall, seemed to be where it belonged. The small boys disappeared, bored, we thought, by our long pauses and much puzzling.

If there had ever been buildings on the east face of the hill, they had long since slid into the valley; we skirted it, aiming high to compensate for slipping in the patches of shale, grateful for trees to hang onto when there was no clear path to the necropolis on the north side. Here again there had been rock falls, but a few tombs remained undisturbed, high up; as we stood working out a route to the highest, skulls, thigh bones, a pelvis and rather less identifiable bones suddenly erupted from the ground at our feet – we were standing on a ledge of earth and rock, part of an old fall that had blocked the entrances of lower tombs, and the boys had scrabbled their way into one of them to lie hidden and play a joke on us. The shock was momentary but multiple; there we were, a bunch of Europeans on an errand of high seriousness, perched on a patch of ground no bigger than a bathroom floor, with a mortal fall only a step back, having to come to terms with a heap of bones whose sudden and absurd appearance offended ancient taboos, disturbed by irreverence for the dead, wondering what archaeological or historical evidence might have been destroyed in pursuit of this childish jape – and at the same time wanting to

laugh. We made the boys return the bones to their tomb, thinking
that they might do so with care, but as the joke was over and they
had other things to do, they merely booted them back through
the small hole, and we heard them land with a melancholy thud.
Et in Arcadia ego, indeed. In one of the upper tombs we found
three stone beds, complete with pillows, and, in another, room
for six in double-decker bunks, again all complete; the hole
through which the children had kicked the bones was too small
for any adult, and we could not tell if they had lain on beds for two
thousand years until our coming.

Etenna was supported by the small, flat and very fertile valley
that now supports Sirtköy. A spring still rises on the site, but the
flow is feeble and the old cisterns are not even damp – that there is
water on the hill is indicated by the wild hollyhocks, thyme and
thorny scrub that cover the site, as well as the tall pines that grow
on the east side. It is cool and windy, even on a very hot day, and
high enough to see the sea, some thirty kilometres away to the
south.

The two young men, brothers, took us to their parents' home
for food; the house nestled against the steep slope below Etenna,
and we entered it by walking over its roof and climbing down
amid a rampant vine. Giggling younger sisters brought us ice-
cold water, and then watched us we sat on the floor eating our
way through the great heap of hot unleavened bread, a scramble
of eggs and tomatoes, salad and cheese; they came in to gather
what we had left, with care, as though, as I suspect, the remains
were their share of the meal. Yet again we had found ourselves in
receipt of hospitality for which there can be no payment, for
which all uttered thanks are inadequate, and for which gratitude
can only be expressed by deep eye contact and the physical
warmth of hugs and kisses. These are, at first, uneasy contacts for
the Northerner, to whom touching is taboo; in Turkey he must
learn to take it with grace, and give as good as he gets – and then
he must learn to give it with grace. The man who carried the
shotgun kissed me on the lips; his brother gave me his rough
poplar stick, and I have it still.

When I first went to Selge it seemed that we drove through
country wilder than I had ever seen – a constant climb from what
might have been the lower Alpine slopes of Switzerland into a
fairy-tale of erosion – but a later visit followed immediately upon

our hikes and climbs in Cappadocia, whose Bosch-like fantasies tamed it. In the Range-Rover, with Jill, David, Klaus, Susannah and Michael, we had, we thought, the ideal vehicle for the appalling road which recent rain had turned into a river, but on the return journey all four wheels lost their grip, and it went into a slow inexorable slide over which David could not regain control – it was as though we were in the grip of a current. I do not now recall how the decision was made, nor how with so many in the car we achieved immediate unanimity, but the doors were opened and everyone jumped out, convinced that it was heading into the precipice – except for me, who, with no sense of heroism, but a profound irritation that such a vehicle should let us down in precisely the circumstances for which it was designed, clambered behind the wheel and somehow halted it. It was the beginning of my conviction that my old Peugeot 404 was as good for Turkey as any expensive and fashionable machine, and that a Range-Rover only made one *feel* better. With Petter at the wheel of a Turkish Fiat I was not so certain, for we bottomed its springs and bumped its sump unmercifully, until I was convinced that we were on the wrong road. We were not; no map adequately indicates the way to Selge. In 1976 we picked up two small boys who had hitched lifts from school in Antalya – one eight, the other twelve – on their way home to the village of Zerk that lies just below its ruins, and Ali, the elder, directed us; he was learning English, and spoke it with surprising fluency as long as he was holding the reins, but he could not understand any thread of conversation that we initiated, and greeted every question with a loud staccato 'Wut?' I remembered his directions well enough; to anyone following my footsteps from the coast, the road is signposted to Beşkonak; beyond that village – which hardly exists – the traveller is confronted by a fork, of which the upper right looks convincing, and the lower left not at all – but it is the lower that leads to a narrow Seljuk bridge high above the gorge through which runs the River Eurymedon, Kodak postcard blue; beyond the bridge the road turns back in the direction from whence it came, and then divides, and it is the upper fork, to the right, that eventually reaches Selge. The distance from the bridge to the city is only twelve kilometres, but it takes well over an hour of determined buttock-busting and increasing disbelief.

The village of Zerk is on a flat site some 3,000 feet above sea-level, with the old city on the hill behind it. In 1976 it was a miserable collection of hovels, with every sign of extreme poverty; Ali insisted on our meeting his family, all with coughs and sniffles even in midsummer, and Jill identified tuberculosis and fled, taking the others with her before the tea-drinking could begin. My fatalistic view of such matters stems, no doubt, from sharing the Communion cup, and having those qualms quashed at an early age by a resolute parish priest. Bean, writing in 1968 of a visit in 1951, describes the villagers as desperately poor, so short of food and water that the visitor should, out of charity, take his own; in 1976 my observations were the same, but in 1984 the village was transformed, and Coca-Cola had reached it. The hovels have been replaced by houses, laden vines clamber over their red roofs and into the neighbouring trees, and the wide saucer of land gleams gold with the harvest – it may now reflect the heavy cultivation that Strabo recorded in his *Geographica* two thousand years ago when its population was 20,000 and large enough to do battle with its neighbours.

One tradition is that it was founded by Calchas, the seer who accompanied the Greeks to Troy and caused the sacrifice of Iphigenia, but it seems improbable that between the end of the Trojan War and his foolish death at nearby Colophon, he could or would have journeyed into so remote an area of the Taurus (he competed with Mopsus, the founder of Colophon, to guess the number of figs in a tree, failed, and died of mortification). Another tradition has it that Selge was founded by the Spartans; Bean dismisses this as a wishful claim to status made in Hellenistic or Roman times, but the Spartans were, after all, present as near as Xanthus. Nicola Bonacasa, of Palermo University, recently asserted, 'It is certain that the city was settled by Lakedaimonian (Spartan) colonists.' If only we knew how the ancients of Selge treated their dogs – for Colophon and Sparta are the only cities of the Greek world that used them as sacrificial animals, later eating them, and in Colophon dogs were trained as auxiliary troops – to find that the Selgians too sacrificed their black bitches to Hecate on dark nights at the crossroads would suggest some solid pudding in both old traditions. According to Strabo's contemporary, Pollio, the Selgians were fierce and tenacious mountain people; strictly speaking, they were Pisidians, but they considered themselves closer to Aspendos in Pamphylia, and seem to have shared a related coinage, and, in very early times, related names in a pre-Greek language. Selge volunteered

friendship to Alexander in 333 BC when he was camped near
Termessos (see p. 205), but nothing came of it. In 220 BC they
were defeated by Garsyeris while besieging Pednelissus (see
p. 191), retreated to their own city, parleyed, were betrayed by
their ambassador Logbasis, fought and won a bloody battle within
their own gates, defeating both Garsyeris and his King, Achaeus,
and slaughtered the traitor and his family – it is an irony that in
all this long history only the name of Logbasis is remembered
among Selgians. In the middle of the second century BC Attalus II
of Pergamon came south to absorb them under his rule, and may
have been assisted by the people of Termessos, who were their
almost local enemies. With the first Romans Selge regained her
independence, but she was later absorbed as the gift of Mark
Antony into the client Kingdom of Amyntas of Galatia, who
struck coins in Side; under the early Emperors she was completely
absorbed. The city seems to have had no Christian role, though it
has a Byzantine basilica, and is last mentioned by Zosimus, a
fifth-century Greek historian, who tells of its resistance to the
Goths in the third century.

　Savage though the Gothic reputation is, it is difficult to believe
that they are responsible for the present very ruined condition of
the site. Only the theatre can be described as standing, the Greek
cavea cut into the hillside, but the seats are disordered and the
stage building is a tumble of masonry; it is overgrown with *Arum
italicum*, whose English variant is known as 'lords and ladies' or
the 'cuckoo plant', a sinister creature whose glistening cone of
currant-red berries is fatal to man and beast, but not to birds – but
in the whole of Selge we saw nothing of the iris from which the
Selgians made an unguent for massage, nor the resinous storax
from which comes incense. Below and to the west lies an abbreviated stadium, too short for full-scale games, also cut into the hill
on its north flank, but the rest of the city lies above the theatre on
three connected hills that demand a measure of scrambling. It
was at this point that a tiny boy appeared from nowhere, the size
of a European six-year-old, and appointed himself our guide – or
rather mine, for he took my hand and would only release it when
it was needed to climb or take notes; he wore black leather town
shoes that would have been too big for me, without laces and
without socks, yet his agility far outstripped mine in Adidas
sports shoes with soles that are supposed to grip like leeches. He
took us to the agora, high above the village, a windy open space,

still paved, that was once closed on three sides by buildings, and showed us the life-size head of a calf in eroded marble, and in the necropolis below he pointed out one small figure on the gable-end of a more than half-buried sarcophagus lid – but apart from these and the two carved stones recorded by Bean, there is very little evidence of decoration. But then there is very little evidence of anything – there are the remains of an encircling wall (but none of the city gates through which Logbasis invited the enemy), and scanty traces of a stoa (at one end of which stands a handsome pillar with inscriptions), of a gymnasium and of a Byzantine basilica. On the third hill the outlines of two temple foundations, possibly of Zeus and Artemis, are hardly recognizable.

Nothing is known of the city's later history, but the survival of its name, corrupted to Zerk, suggests continuous occupation since antiquity. The present population is now eight hundred, an astonishing rise in less than a decade, and a reflection of the civilizing measures that have transformed its appearance. Our infant guide accepted his tip with gravity, pocketing it, as do all Turks, without inspecting it, and then with lightning speed caught something and gave it to me with a grin; I had always thought grasshoppers green, but this four inch monster was black and white – what could I do with such a parting gift but open my cupped hands and let it go? With a helicopter clatter it sprang away, and we drove off down the hill. Climbing, one is only aware of the formidable surface of the road and of its twists and turns – it is only in descending that the views are apparent, and they are a spectacular combination of mountain peaks, pinewoods, a profusion of pink hibiscus, and weird heaps of grey eroded rock. On the lower side of the Seljuk bridge, just as the road turns away from the river, is a restaurant hidden from sight; it is no more than a shack above a shelf of rock on which are set benches and tables shaded by huge trees; in their spreading branches, perilous over the water, are timber platforms on which the local lumberjacks spend their bachelor nights – the restaurant is their canteen – and their blankets were spread about to air. We were welcomed like old friends, invited to wash in a spring gushing ice-cold from the rock, and given fish straight from the river; later, either overcome with beer and fatigue, or lulled by the plashing of the river, we slept on the hard benches like Plantagenet princes on their tombs.

As a ruin Selge is not for beginners, for the winds have filled it with dust that rain and snow have consolidated; no excavations have ever been carried out, no fallen stones re-erected; it is desuetudinous and sad; yet from the very moment of leaving the coast road, following the line of the wide River Eurymedon that runs past Aspendos to the sea, halting here and there to let a swirling host of goats engulf the car, on and up into the wild mountains, there is a lightening of heart that has nothing to do with ruins and much with the folly of adventure. Fellows ident- ifies with Selge a site south of Isparta and east of Bucak, about thirty-five miles to the north-west; as he constantly complains of the inadequacy of maps this discrepancy might be of no conse- quence, but he describes a city of such grandeur that it cannot be Selge, for there is no reason why it should have declined beyond recognition in less than two centuries, even though the use for agriculture of any flat space within the city has the ring of Selge about it. The city must in fact be Adada, twenty-five miles south of Egridir, which in the mid second century BC was in alliance with Selge's enemy, Termessos (see p. 203). His description is uncharacteristically enthusiastic:

> I was at the end of a ridge of mountains of white marble, which terminate abruptly in a deep and rich valley . . . rising perpen- dicularly, perhaps a thousand feet. Upon this promontory stood one of the finest cities that probably ever existed, now presenting magnificent wrecks of grandeur. I rode for at least three miles through a part of the city which was one pile of temples, theatres and buildings vying with each other in splendour; the elevated site for such a city is quite unaccount- able to me . . . the scale, the simple grandeur, and the uniform beauty of style bespoke its date to be the early Greek. The sculptured cornices frequently contain groups of figures fighting, wearing helmets and body-armour, with shields and long spears; from the ill-proportioned figures and general appearance, they must rank in date with the Aegina marbles now at Munich. The ruins are so thickly strewn that little cultivation is practicable, but in the areas of theatres, cellas of temples, and any space where a plough can be used, the wheat is springing up. The general style of the temples is Corinthian, but not so florid as in less ancient towns . . . I can scarcely guess the number of temples or columned buildings in the town, but I certainly traced fifty or sixty . . . vast arched vaults . . . strong walls . . . partly . . . in the Cyclopean mode . . . I never

conceived so high an idea of the works of the ancients as from my visit to this place, standing as it does in a situation, as it were, above the world.

Never was there a description less applicable to the real Selge.

In 1986 Petter and I returned to Selge with Colin and were greeted, to my astonishment, by Ali. I at once recognized the boy in the man, but he took a little prompting to recall our ten-year-old first encounter, and it was not I but the Range-Rover that had lodged in his memory. His English was larded with American-isms, and he had the constant ill-informed patter of the experi-enced guide who deems it his purpose to numb his clients into submission while he shows them worthless things to which he has attached a tale. I could not blame him – Selge is hard work for little obvious reward, and in his unofficial and self-appointed position as guide he was making up in words for what most visitors would miss in sights; but I could neither halt him, nor turn him aside to see what interested me. I did at last stem the flow by asking if it were known how the ancient Selgians crossed the mountains to join Alexander at Termessos; he paused, con-sidered his answer, and said, 'I don't know the whole way, but it should not be difficult to find, and should not take more than three days.' He seemed disturbed by the question and fell silent. The straight line distance is 70 kilometres, no distance for three days' walking in the Hartz Mountains, but at Selge there is a peak rising to more than 6,000 feet only 12 kilometres away to the south-west, and even in late July plenty of snow still lies on much lower hills. Ali then told me that he had been some distance in that direction, walking to Sillyum, and had found a small theatre, Roman houses and some very angry wild boar on the way – that trek had indeed taken him three days, sleeping rough, and it is only 30 kilometres as the crow flies.

As with Selge, it is as well to know something of Sillyum before visiting it, for it is even more ruined, and could well be mistaken for a cleared demolition site – the unwitting visitor might stand there in despair, wondering why he had come. It is easy enough to see from the coast road between Perge and Aspendos, a huge flat-topped oval rock, grey in midwinter, darkly silhouetted against the misty silver of the Taurus Mountains, brown in midsummer, with no hint that a great city once capped it – but it is not easy to find, for the roads that look as though they might lead to it veer away and leave it floating like a mirage on one side or the other. Even Bean says that it is hard to find beyond the village of Kocayatak (which means literally Great Bed) and that one should pick up a guide there, but the sleepy villagers in the shade of the tea-house merely wave the visitor on. On my first visit, our Sidetan taxi-driver, in exasperation when the road ceased to be identifiable as a road, drew a bead on the great hill and drove across the open fields in as straight a line as he could manage among the bumps and humps and ditches, and Petter did much the same; when we left to return to Side we found ourselves without conscious effort on a road that ran for some considerable distance parallel with and within sight of the Antalya–Manavgat road, and, when it joined it, was signposted Kayaburnu 1, Bügüs 15 – and that is the road I shall follow on another visit.

Mopsus appears again in Sillyum (see p. 195) – no more than a name on a statue-base, but even that is enough to suggest that he may have been credited with its foundation during the mytho-logical-historical migration with Amphilocus and Calchas after the Trojan War – Perge also claimed him as its founder, as did eponymous Mopsuestia, more than three hundred miles to the east as the crow flies, beyond Adana, though establishing, con-solidating and maintaining Colophon in the part of Anatolia most troubled by the aftermath of the siege of Troy must surely have taken all his time. Quite why so many cities in Anatolia claimed Calchas and Mopsus as their founders has never been satisfac-torily explained – it was, perhaps, a kind of ancestor worship, a claim to the respectability of age as absurd as Englishmen who claim to be of the direct line of the Normans of 1066. Whatever the case, Sillyum's foundation must have been ancient, for it is so obviously defensible in the same way as Peçin Kale (see p. 64), yet is surrounded by a fertile plain capable of feeding it, that was once much better watered than it is now, if Strabo's record of a large lake nearby is to be believed and identified with an area of marsh east of the city towards Aspendos. Its sole historical achievement was its successful resistance to Alexander – unique among Pamphylian cities – under what Arrian (see p. 205) describes as native barbarians and foreign mercenaries. The problems that deterred Alexander from mounting a second attack may well today deter the casual visitor; we had the benefit of two small boys, the brothers Mehmet and Osman, who could not have been more than eight, barefoot, wearing only striped pyjama trousers, with catapults looped about their necks. In 1982 they lived in the tiny gathering of houses at the foot of the hill, with water running here and there, and a noisy clatter of ducks, turkeys and their silly chicks, goats, and a puppy, all running wild, and among the damp rocks of the spring they retrieved for our pleasure a tortoise and some indignant struggling toads. Toads make me feel guilty; in the summer of 1944, when London was troubled by Flying Bombs, I was despatched to an inn near Mentmore run by an amiable woman with five sons who advanced my sexual education apace, taught me the only really filthy songs I've ever known, and had a winning way with toads – this involved inserting a hollow straw into the anus, blowing until the wretched creature was inflated to twice its size, and then putting it in the nearest pond to fart its way to safety.

The boys scampered off up the hill, following the ramped road that corkscrews round it, steep, and now broken – in its heyday it could have been held by half-a-dozen men, and it must then have been (and is still) an impressive piece of architectural engineering at fifteen feet in width, and buttressed against the sheer side of the rock. Bean suggests that it may have been roofed to make it even less accessible to enemy intrusion. We trailed after the children, slowly, in the blazing shadeless heat; without them it would have been much less fun, and less instructive, for no cut or lettered stone, no cistern, stayed hidden in their company, and they ensured that we peered like ostriches, heads hidden, beneath fallen stones whose undersides were inscribed, even though they were impossible to read or photograph. Not that they were solemn budding archaeologists – too young for that, they played a telephone game with the handles of amphorae that may well have been two thousand years old or more, hallooing noisily in the pretence that one of them was in Istanbul or Ankara; a suggested call to New York was beyond the limits of their geography and for a moment damped their spirits. It struck me that they had exceptional strength and stamina for children of their age, and exceptional powers of exchange and communication both with each other and with us – at one point they went into a slow-motion wrestling match, always missing with their kicks and chops, striking interlocking attitudes without touching, assuming grimaces that would have done credit to antique theatrical masks – yet the skilled violence was there, for they effectively chopped with the edges of their tiny hands every dry stick and suitable sherd; they thought nothing of dropping ten or twelve feet from the ruined walls, over and over again, and venturing like goats to the perilous edge of the landslip that carried away the theatre in 1969 – the top six rows of seats remain, looking out over the plain towards the distant sea.

Water supplies to the top of the hill must always have been a problem; Bean records one cistern, but the boys showed us a string of them roughly following the long sides of the hill's oval shape, and on the northern tip there are too many to map – if this was a domestic area of the city, it suggests that most houses had access to stored water in large quantities. East of the landslip, on the slope at the foot of the hill, a narrow tunnel runs some thirty yards into the rock to three chambers whose purpose is thought to have been a waterworks, though how it can have benefited the city above I cannot conceive, unless there was some kind of lifting or pumping gear to supply the three large cisterns more or less directly overhead – the passage is barely wide enough for a man's shoulders, pitch dark, and a terrifying and beastly experience for anyone who suffers claustrophobia and the other, nameless, nightmare fears encouraged by recollection of the recent rock-fall. Some yards in from the landslip (it carried away the odeon as well as the theatre) is a group of public buildings that in this context are impressive – though it must be admitted that in Side, for instance, they might be worthy of less notice; their purpose is not known – two are Hellenistic, one a windowed hall 180 feet long with one wall still standing to the height of 20 feet, the other, much smaller, celebrated for an inscription rather than its architecture. The inscription is cut in the door-jamb, runs to thirty-seven lines that apart from odd words and phrases (including *Selyviios*, the name of the city as it appears on its earliest – third century BC – coins) have not yet been made to make sense, and is the most important document known in Pamphylian Greek dialect – suppose the literary fantasies of a lavatory wall were to be the only lengthy document in English to survive some atomic holocaust, it would give some future non-English-speaking remnant of the human race a curious idea of our language and social habits, though it might have some small documentary importance. The third building is a handsome Byzantine structure, square, with indications of a triple vault and a floor dividing it into two storeys.

In late Hellenistic times the city expanded on the lower ground to the west and south-west where the spring is still running; there is evidence of fortification, and it is in this area that the scanty remains of a stadium and a large building known for convenience sake as the Palace, lie. Further afield there are short stretches of paved road. Fellows identified Sillyum as a site on the side of a rocky hill in wooded country; continuing his journey, he found himself midway between Manavgat and Side, and this indicates that he had found Seleucia instead. He did not know it, but he had already found Sillyum, identifying it as Isinda (Isionda in his spelling), which is in fact near Korkuteli, seventy kilometres due west – his description of the stadium and the ramp are unmistakable:

> On approaching the city is seen a long line of wall, partly fallen, giving the appearance of strong fortifications having existed; but, on entering, it is found to be the support of a long range of seats, forming one side of a long stadium; the opposite seats being cut in the rock, which rises from this theatre, the end of which is circular, as at Perge. The whole side of the rock has been built upon, and it requires close examination to ascertain where the natural rock ends, and the colossal masonry begins. There are many strong walls and towers, and several buildings which may have been either palaces or temples, although but very few columns or ornamented friezes are visible [none at all now]. The summit of the hill, which perhaps may be two miles in circumference, was walled; but I had not time to examine this Acropolis. I was told that the whole surface was strewn with fragments of columns, but that none were standing; the tombs are numerous, and are scattered round the town for a mile in every direction [none survives now].

What is curious is that in his description of what he thought was Sillyum, he observed two towers, described first as in 'pure Greek taste' and then as 'in the same style as those seen in Italy, built during the middle ages'; he drew one, topping it with the pedimented portico that he believed had fallen from it; nothing like it survives in Seleucia, but a tower that conforms closely with Fellows' drawings is the best-preserved part of the rampart walls below the hill at Sillyum.

The last difficult site in the area is Termessos; it is not difficult in any serious sense for it is possible to drive with bumpy ease the five winding miles of the new unsurfaced road as it climbs steadily to some 3,500 feet above the Antalya–Korkuteli road, and park under a tree just below the city; the adventurous will take the footpath that roughly follows the old 'King's Road' and footslog it for two hours – this has the slight advantage of sharing the experience of Alexander's approach to the city through a gate in the outer fortification wall (on this are inscribed the idiotic verses of a dice oracle, for which you threw a number and then checked the list of numbered answers, whether or not they were relevant to your question). Within the upper city the authorities have marked narrow and now well-worn tracks up the over-grown hillside leading to the most accessible monuments, and though steep, these are no more hazardous than the approaches to many English beauty-spots – it is only when the visitor grows ambitious that he will experience difficulties.

It is a curiously enclosed site – a steep and quite narrow valley at the top, ending abruptly below a semi-circle of cliffs some hundreds of feet high and impossible to descend; it would have been possible for an enemy to surround the city on these cliff-tops, yet never breach its defences, though there must have been paths when the city was occupied, for high in the rock-face pigeon-hole tombs have been cut, and into these the corpses were lowered, not raised – but we could find no trace of any paths now. Looking down from this high bowl into the valley far below it is easy to see how the city was supplied with food, and how defensible it was, even on its one open flank – an approaching force of any size would have been in sight hours before it reached the city, and probably within sound too; to the untrained ear the direction of sound is confused, but the presence of others on the site is always identifiable, and a car can be heard from the main road. It is said of Crusader armies that they could be smelled seven miles off, stinking in their armour and chain-mail.

Termessos is heavily overgrown and green in high summer, but only one obvious source of water survives, and that not much more than a trickle – the earthquakes that tumbled the buildings must have changed the watercourses. As with Sillyum, it is so sensible a situation that it must have been occupied from a very early age, and certainly long before the colonizing Greeks from the north and west arrived in the area. The Greeks did not colonize Termessos. In the earliest records the people called themselves Solymians, from Solymus, the name of the mountain that shelters it, and even in Strabo's day spoke a language distinct from Pisidian, that survived very late in the names of its inhabitants. The first mention of Solymians is in Homer's tale of Bellerophon, who was sent to subdue them, and not expected to survive (see Olympus, p. 163, Tlos, p. 127). The city thus had some reputation as far away as Ionia in *c.* 750 BC, whether Homer was born in Izmir or Chios (or elsewhere); and if Homer were merely knocking into shape (as it were) an oral tradition of which all the embellishments were as old as the historical narrative of the Trojan War, then the Solymian reputation extends at least as far back as *c.* 1240 BC, though the five centuries between the Sack of Troy and the Homeric poems are far and away the worst documented in Greek history, and almost any corruption could have crept into the tales.

Alexander, in 333 BC, by this stage travelling light and fast, could not risk long sieges of cities that did not willingly decide to be his allies; he was obstructed by a large force of Termessians at a defile on the Korkuteli road, but instead of fighting them, pitched camp; at nightfall most of the Termessians returned to the comforts of home, and Alexander, after routing the small force of sentries, climbed the hill in the darkness and camped outside the city, where he was joined by a force from Selge, enemies of Termessos. No explanation of a Selgian presence in the area is offered by Arrian (AD 95–175), the Greek officer in the Roman army who narrates this tale; the two cities may have been constantly skirmishing, in which case no explanation is necessary, but if they were not, then communications and mobility in Alexander's day were remarkable, either by the long route through the river valleys to the coast, or by a now unknown short route across the mountains, if one ever existed. The Selgian support was not enough to make him attempt to break the city's defences, and he marched north to Sagalassus, just short of present-day Isparta.

One of Alexander's generals, Antigonus, was to return fourteen years later; in the Macedonian army's division of Alexander's world after his death in Babylon in 323 BC, Great Phrygia had been apportioned to him – he had in fact been given the satrapy of Phrygia by Alexander himself during the journey north from Termessos, and had held it for the remainder of Alexander's life, playing a vital role against the Persians fleeing *westward* across Cappadocia after their appalling defeat at the Battle of

Issus in the far north-eastern corner of the Mediterranean. One-eyed, and much older than Alexander, he long outlived him (he had indeed been a veteran officer under Alexander's father, Philip of Macedon). In the turmoil after Alexander's death he claimed first the whole of Asia Minor, and then the whole of the new empire, proclaiming himself King in 306 BC. But Ptolemy, Seleucus, Lysimachus and Cassander also claimed the royal title, and in the general dissolution of the Empire, Antigonus was defeated and killed at Ipsus in 301 BC, and his territories were divided between the victors Seleucus and Lysimachus. Ipsus was in Phrygia, but no-one now knows where – Şuhut, south of Afyon, has been suggested, but Afyon itself makes better sense since the confrontation was on the great road from Syria to the Bosphorus, and the forces involved were considerable – Antigonus had 70,000 foot, 10,000 horse, and 75 elephants, against 64,000 foot, 10,500 horse, 400 elephants and 120 armed chariots – in present-day Şuhut there is no room for such a battle, but in Afyon there is.

In Pisidia, immediately to the south of Phrygia, Antigonus had an opponent in Alcetas. Alcetas had been an infantry general with Alexander throughout his campaigns in the East; his brother, Perdiccas, as another of Alexander's generals and his brother-in-law, had as much claim as anyone to part of the dissolving Empire, but Antigonus and the others had united against him, and two years after Alexander's death had had him murdered in his tent. Alcetas thus had a powerful personal reason for opposing Antigonus on his own ground, but he lost a crucial battle in 319 BC and was forced to take refuge in Termessos, provoking a particularly nasty episode of treachery; while the younger Termessians were seduced into pursuing a pretended retreat by Antigonus, the elders of the city (who had arranged the pretence) betrayed Alcetas, who committed suicide. The elders smuggled the corpse out of the city and gave it to Antigonus, who cut off its nose and other projecting parts, and generally abused it until after three days it began to stink; he then marched off, leaving it unburied, but the young Termessians retrieved it and gave it a splendid burial within the city.

One tomb in Termessos is outstanding, and it may well be that of Alcetas; it is high up the valley on the north side under an overhanging rock, in a natural right-angled crevice that has been extended into an open cave. One wall seems to have been conceived as a bed – a two-poster; the bed itself is the hollow sarcophagus, with behind it, carved in the rock, two pilasters with trellis or netting slung between them, and the suggestion of a pediment above; other, much smaller, rectangular hollows in the rock may have been intended for water, or ashes, or food. It has been smashed, with all the evidence of recent vandalism (indeed, some of it very recent – post 1975), and it is now difficult to decipher, but the scheme includes the figures of Hermes and Aphrodite, an eagle in flight with a snake in his talons, and lion masks. High on the opposite wall, under the overhang, the makers of the tomb cut a high relief of a warrior on horseback that is usually identified as a portrait of Alcetas – the face has been smashed, the relief is cracked by a natural fissure, and the horse's hind legs have fallen away with a rock split, and lie below; Alcetas, though an infantryman, fought his last battle on horseback, and the trophy of armour carved low to the right of the equestrian figure has been identified as that of Alexander's infantry – the figure itself wears the same armour as Alexander at the Battle of Issus, if the mosaic at Naples is to be believed. One aspect of the relief remains without explanation – the horse appears to be winged; comparison with the attitude of both horse and rider with the relief in the Bellerophon tomb at Tlos (see p. 127) suggests strong kinship – the wings at Tlos spring from low on Pegasus' shoulders, obscuring Bellerophon's trunk, while those in Termessos are much smaller, have no feathered details (though these may have been lost through erosion), and rise from the spine just behind the rider so that no part of him is concealed, but in all other aspects the iconography is identical, and only the inadequate grasp of proportion distinguishes the Alcetas relief as the more primitive and provincial (it has an uncanny resemblance to the figures in the late paintings of Claude Lorraine). Bellerophon is the only recorded conqueror of Solymian Termessos, and if its young worthies wished to give the rotting corpse of Alcetas a splendid burial and make amends for the treachery of their elders, they could offer him no more heroic image than that of Bellerophon. If there is an iconographical connection, then it may confirm the identification with Bellerophon of the Tlos tomb (presumably another heroic allusion), but it also raises the interesting point of a cultural transmission between two very remote cities, and perhaps a little weight to the ancient tale of Bellerophon at Tlos. The date of the Termessos tomb, if indeed it was hacked out of the cliff for Alcetas, must be immediately after his death in 319 BC; the tomb at Tlos must be considerably earlier. The temple tomb near the so-called tomb of Alcetas is a neat but not splendid example of the Lycian type, and is certainly later.

Higher up the valley, where it becomes steep and inaccessible, is an extensive jumble of sarcophagus tombs, higgledy-piggledy and ankle-breaking among the dense undergrowth; earthquakes must have been first to disturb them, but a great number retain their lids, turned more or less neatly askew to give access to what treasure may have been left with the cadavers. Tomb-robbing was the habit of the day and should not be blamed entirely on more recent vandals – inscriptions naming the occupants include the penalties of a curse or heavy fine for their disturbance, sometimes with half the amount to be paid to the informer (for similar penalties at Cyaneae see p. 155). Most of the sarcophagi are carved and swagged, with pitched roofs; a few are like pedimented theatre boxes, and had a second sarcophagus slotted into the space above the first, though none survives complete as a double-decker. An indication of their number is that the inscriptions on 650 have been published, yet many more have no identifying letters.

After hours of exploration the site begins to make sense; the necropolis was in and immediately below the cliffs where land was so steep that little else could be done with it and the configuration ensured that thermals would disperse any graveyard stinks; the rest of the site must have been a system of platforms and linking flights of steps, much like Priene, though that city's grid-plan could never have been imposed on so long and irregular a valley. Of these 'terraces' the present parking area may be an unidentified example – the only other large space is the agora, paved over a row of five cisterns, an irregular rectangle flanked by the remains of porticoes and a natural outcrop of rock on which there is a tomb (whose we do not know, though burial in the market-place was a singular honour). The theatre stands to the east of the agora – of the Greek pattern, small (capable of holding only some 4,000 spectators, and suggesting that the population of Termessos was also small), and with enough of its stage-building still erect to indicate its function; this has five doors opening from its single long narrow room onto the narrow stage; below the stage are five more doors only three feet high, through which wild animals were admitted to the orchestra where they had little room to fight and must have been alarmingly close to the spectators. The *cavea* is Hellenistic but the stage-building Roman; after its rebuilding to accommodate wild animals, they were found to be at too close quarters for the comfort of the important visitors who would normally occupy the front seats, and the space on the right between the stage-building and the *cavea* was filled in with a few extra seats and a 'Royal Box' that would have given a poor view of plays, but was safe for watching animals in deadly contest. The seductive beauty of the theatre now is its position, for from its uppermost seats, or for those brave enough to clamber onto the stage-building, it is poised above a gorge that sweeps past Mount Solymus on the left, and on, down into the far distance, as though to the sea at Antalya.

Just below the theatre lies a building identified as a gymnasium; it is not easy to get to, even if the chosen route seems obvious enough, for the jumbled masonry requires seven-league boots, and the snagging undergrowth is almost impenetrable for anyone unlucky enough to have already dropped chest-deep in it. The building divides into at least three large sections, but its doors are blocked by fallen masonry and its standing walls are too high and in too immaculate condition to climb. With the odeon and two small and beautifully finished temples to Zeus and Artemis, the gymnasium gives the impression that Termessos was a city where wealth went hand-in-hand with a taste that combined the monumental with restraint; if the sculpture of the tomb of Alcetas suggests provincial ineptitude, the standing buildings that substantially post-date it suggest an engineering competence the equal of any full-blown Roman city. But it was not without its Metro-Goldwyn-Mayer effects; not a single column is to be found on the site, nor is there any sign of marble cladding (though the walls of the odeon, roughly dressed, must have been covered with it), but in the traces of a road on the west side of the site, running north from the spring, and possibly originally ending in a fountain or basin, is a street of shops that was once lined with perhaps fifty columns on each side, with statues between and in front of them, whose inscribed bases survive, though they themselves do not. The wealth of the Termessians, whose basic economy was self-supporting, probably came from charging tolls on the Antalya–Korkuteli road; Freya Stark observed that a well-built wall with towers that crosses the road does not extend far enough on either side of it to be an effective defence – but it would certainly deter a laden caravan from outflanking, and Bean suggests that it was in effect a toll-gate. Looking at the map today one might wonder if there could have been enough traffic to bring profit, for the road leads across northern Lycia with no town of any size before Fethiye on the coast, but two thousand years ago it served Toriaeum, Balbura, Oenanda, Araxa, Cadyanda, Tlos, Isinda, and the Termessian outstation of Termessos Minor more than twenty miles away to the west, over the mountains, and was an important trade route.

We found the guardian squatting by the car and shared our hot Coca-Cola with him. He told us that he had been appalled when first appointed to the site – 'Nothing but a heap of old stones – but now I live with people from two thousand years ago.' Then he asked for Petter's lighter.

— XIV —

Aspendos * Perge * Side

The problems with Perge and Aspendos are not inaccessibility, but other tourists; the heat, the steep climb and the undergrowth deter most of them from being a nuisance in Termessos, but in the major sites on the Pamphylian Plain their coaches bring them to the door of what they feel they ought to see, and when the best-known German map of western Turkey prints such legends as *Das grösste Stadion* above Perge and *Das besterhaltene Theater* above Aspendos, you may be sure that diligent Germans will turn up in droves. It was at Aspendos that I encountered an improbable vehicle called the Romotel, a swish semi-double-decker bus whose occupants sat in armchair comfort downstairs as they were whisked from Hamburg to Hakkari, and slept in coffin cubicles upstairs through what they were persuaded were nocturnal doldrums; they seemed to be of an age for confinement to the wheelchairs and whirling baths of Bad Oeynhausen, but in their mobile beehive they could cover 10,000 kilometres in two weeks, see everything from the Towers of Trebizond to the Mausoleum of Halicarnassus and Noah's Ark, and live on pumpernickel, bratwurst and bottled water. What astonished me most was that they emerged immaculate from their air-conditioned mobile tomb, made a beeline for the shaded seats, spread handkerchiefs on them with an air of disapproval and distaste, sat still and obediently listened to their guide as she clapped her hands and yoo-hood to demonstrate the acoustics, and left. And so it was with all the coachloads – they invariably yoo-hood as they came through the central door of the stage-building and thought themselves objects of attention, and those most heavily-laden with cameras invariably took to stumbling flight up the seats to the arcaded gallery at the very top. By diligently photographing details of the stage-building, and spending too long on our backs taking upward-raking shots, we caused some small annoyance to a group who had no wish to return to Stuttgart with our prone figures in their photographs.

Most of the architectural embellishments of the stage have been destroyed, but the double register of projecting entablatures, pediments and stumps still has grandeur enough to astonish the Philistine, even if he does not know what it signifies in the way of niches and *aediculae* and sculpture; in the afternoon sun the stone is richly golden, with odd passages of sooty black, and extensive traces of plaster; had this beautiful honey-coloured stone once been covered with stucco, gleaming brilliant white, and painted? It seems inconceivable that this should be so, but the traces cannot be denied. Bean dismisses them as a later addition indicating that use of the theatre continued into Byzantine times; well so it probably did, and the crude zigzags painted in red on the stucco are familiar enough to anyone who knows the Byzantine churches of Cappadocia, but in plastering and painting the stage-building they must have been continuing a Roman tradition, however degraded. There can have been little Byzantine life after the Arab invasions of the seventh century, and by then the marble quarries that had made Aspendos splendid were exhausted.

Externally the theatre is unpromising; I have always thought that it closely resembles the better factories of the English Industrial Revolution, and was amused to find that Fellows thought the same. In his book he expresses irritation that he could not find Aspendos:

> On reaching the noble river Eurymedon we fell again into the track by which we had come . . . The maps are all so extremely incorrect that I am unable to trace my situation upon them . . . I have no definite clue by which to discover the ruins of Aspendos. Arrowsmith's map places the modern village of

Starus upon the site of Aspendos; but no remains of antiquity are to be heard of in the neighbourhood.

As it is the River Eurymedon that links Aspendos to Selge, it is difficult to understand his confusion (his description makes it clear that the salt Lake Capria between Aspendos and Sillyum had long since dried up) – but he had already been to the city without realizing it, and had wrongly identified it as Pednelissus, which was in Pisidia, probably to be identified with the ruins near the village of Kozan, some twenty miles north of neighbouring Perge. Leaving Perge he travelled eastward, mistaking Sillyum for Isinda (which is near Kokuteli), and found Aspendos, spending the night at the village of Bolcascooe, by which he must mean present-day Belkis. The country through which he rode early in April 1838 is now so changed that it is worth quoting his description in full:

> . . . we journeyed south-east for twenty miles over a country capable of producing anything, but with scarcely an acre cultivated. For the greater part of the distance the way was through woods, where the trees grow, die, and fall unheeded. Nature in this beautiful climate has produced a wilderness of the richest trees, shrubs, and climbing plants; I noticed seven or eight different kinds of oak; the delicate-leaved Judas-tree, with its beautiful blossom; the ash and carob; and, more abundant than any, the Siberian crab, with a great variety of the clematis and rose acacia; all intertwined with vine and fig, so that it was difficult to distinguish the stem which supported the rich cluster. The last year's fruit hung ungathered on most of the trees, or lay decayed beneath them, the whole district being used only for the browsing of camels and goats. The myrtles were prodigious bushes; I measured several which covered a circle forty feet in diameter, the stem being as thick as my body. In no country have I ever seen or heard such multitudes of birds. The nightingales in the evening were almost an annoyance.

Of this profusion, nothing remains.

Of the theatre, Fellows has this to say:

> On the east side of the hill is a theatre, highly interesting from being in so excellent a state of preservation; but the architecture, particularly of the exterior, is in the worst taste. It

resembles a large factory . . . On the top of the exterior are still entire the stone sockets for holding the poles which supported a screen or covering over the upper seats, as is seen in the Coliseum at Rome. In the lobby are brackets with inscriptions, but the statues which stood upon them have been removed. The remains of the inside of this theatre are far the most perfect of the kind that I have seen; indeed the whole might now be used for its original purpose. The proscenium is very richly ornamented with niches, and a balcony or portico, all of the most elaborate designs in white marble; the ornaments are heads, masks, dolphins, flowers and various animals. The eagle, in attitude like the Roman eagle, is several times introduced. The seats remain almost perfect, as well as the lobbies and galleries leading to them. The walls of the proscenium and sides of the theatre have been coloured, and still retain a common red pattern upon the white plaster marked out by black lines in zig-zag form; the niches have remains of a beautiful light blue upon their walls; the masks also retain their colouring. Around the back of the top seats of the theatre is a series of arches, which spring from ornamental circular brick columns, plastered over. The whole of the seats and steps, the floor of the area, together with the side doorways, and the lobbies and apartments to which they lead, are quite perfect. The other buildings in the city are all of the same date and style.

From this detailed description it is clear that in comparatively recent times the stage-building was much more complete, with niches in white marble; when it was first erected in the second century AD, probably in the reign of Marcus Aurelius, the whole building, which is constructed of brick, rubble and pudding-stone conglomerate of pebbles, must have been clad in the same material, and indeed the seats, stairs and arcade at the top of the *cavea* are in the same stone; thin marble facings would be the first to fall in any earthquake, and it may be that the Byzantines with their painted plaster were merely making quick, inexpensive and unskilled repairs, in the only available material once the marble quarries were exhausted.

The early Byzantines used Roman theatres for mime, mummery and music-hall, with lewd, dissolute, suggestive performances that continued the Dionysiac traditions of which there is a hint in Aristotle's *Poetics* when he states that phallic performances were common in his day. Antheas of Lindos composed comedies of this kind for the *phallophoroi*; Herodas of Miletus, working *c*. 270–260 BC, composed mimes concerned with the seamy side of his contemporary life, with prostitutes, brothel-keepers, and a schoolboy beaten for playing truant – the sexual humour is crudely explicit, as, for example, two women discussing particularly fine leather dildos bought from Kerdon the shoe-maker:

He works at home, doing business stealthily, for every door now shudders at the taxman . . . the handicraft of Athena herself . . . Men cannot make theirs so erect. And not only that, they were as smooth as a dream, and the lacings were wool instead of thongs. You may search for a cobbler kinder to women, but you won't find one.

The Empress Theodora (*c*. AD 500–47) is the most notorious of Byzantine actresses in this tradition, experiencing a Pauline change from theatrical licence to moral reformer. It is curious that puritanical Christian restraint, on the visual arts so immediate and deadly, should have taken so long to strangle theatrical performances – and perhaps it never did, quite, for the medieval traditions of carnival involved some gross humour, and the phallic jokes of ancient Greece survived still in the seventeenth-century Commedia dell'Arte, if Jacques Callot's engravings of the *Balli di Sfessania*, with their clear references to sodomy, are to be believed as accurate records.

Outside the theatre a mad girl attacked us; attack is too strong a word, for it was no more than an aggressive and persistent demand that we did not understand and could not satisfy with money; she was in the bright bloomers and cardigan that most peasant Turkish women wear, but bare-headed (a rarity) with her hair shorn. Most Turks have an amused tolerance for the feeble-minded, but I once witnessed an episode on a ferry crossing the Sea of Marmara, ugly enough for intervention, when an old woman was being relentlessly teased by a group of young men – it was at the stage when I knew hardly a word of Turkish and was by no means as certain as I now am of the kindness and goodwill of the Turk, and did not know how to break the ring of boys without turning their mockery to aggression against me; I had just bought a glass of tea, and with a peremptory and very English 'Excuse me, please', I passed between them and gave it to her, and they drifted away. In the grounds of the little school in Side a gigantic teenage boy used to play with the infants; Osman, embarrassed by his presence, explained that he was mad, to which I replied 'Less mad than touched', and then had to explain 'touched' as touched by God and claimed as his own. I don't know how that piece of sentimental nonsense found its way into my rag-bag mind, but it pleased Osman well.

We fled the girl and climbed to the other major buildings on the site, pestered by a boy the pockets of whose ragged trousers bulged with fake coins and sculptured heads made yesterday, but he was no more nuisance than a large friendly puppy. So few visitors bother to look beyond the theatre that the hill in which the *cavea* is hollowed is heavily overgrown with scrub and herbs whose fragrance is numbing to the brain until sight of the first snake startles the Bisto Kid into commonsense awareness. At the top, a deep gully separates the shoulders of the theatre from the larger part of the hill on which the city's other public buildings stand, surrounding the agora. One of these was a great basilica, over a hundred yards long, of which only the foundations remain, but at its northern end an annexe is still standing, fifty feet high, with walls six feet thick, a single arched door in the outer wall and three in the inner, leading to the aisles of the basilica; it is a handsome structure, extensively repaired in Byzantine times with much smaller, harder stones that contrast unhappily with the large blocks of pudding-stone used by the Romans. The opposite, west, side of the agora was occupied by a row of two-storey shops with a raised pavement in front of them, stepping down into the agora through a colonnade. The north side is closed by the two-storey façade of a nymphaeum, embellished with niches and entablatures; nothing of the plumbing survives, but the extensive remains of the aqueduct lead towards it, and Bean records the finding of a dolphin's-head water-spout nearby. Again Fellows is a vital witness, for much more of the structure survived in his day:

> . . . an immensely high screen or square wall at the end, which has been ornamented in front with a rich projecting marble cornice, a colonnade with a balcony above, and niches, the plaster of which yet retains its colouring of beautiful light blue. The panels of the ceiling in this colonnade still remain, and are ornamented with various devices of dolphins and sea-shells

. . . There are very few columns remaining; indeed so
generally were they formed of brick and plaster that I
should doubt whether there have been at any age many of
marble.

His comments on painted plaster in the niches, and columns
made of brick and plaster, may perhaps throw some light on the
original decoration of the theatre.

Bean is enthusiastic about the aqueduct; it may or may not be,
as he claims, the best surviving example (I might put in a bid for
Thuburbo Majus in Tunisia), but as a piece of engineering to bring
water in a channel pierced through solid blocks of masonry,
building up such pressure in its fall that it could then rise in
towers some hundred feet high, again fall, and finally lift itself
into the city, it is astonishing; as the channel was covered, the
aqueduct doubled as a viaduct across the marshy ground to the
north of the city; substantial relics of the arched towers at the foot
of the mountain and immediately to the north of the city still
stand.

A handsome Seljuk bridge stands near the main Antalya road,
marking the line of the old road that served from dark antiquity to
Atatürk's day. In its shade we ate a *karpuz*, the red-fleshed
water-melon, hacking at it with a knife too short to make a clean
cut, suddenly desperate with thirst and exhaustion now that the
stimulus of search, identification and note-scribbling was done;
we ate it like pigs, hands, faces and shirts running with juice, the
pips spread all round us, an extraordinary sense of relief and
refreshment increasing with every mouthful, even though the
great fruit was far from cool. Suddenly three small girls appeared
like miniature Harpies, screeching 'Hello Poof-poof' – slightly
disconcerting, until they changed it in turn to 'Hello Bon-bon',
'Sigara', and 'Para' (money), and it became clear that they had
not meant what I had first thought – Byron, who was convinced
that the Turks preferred sodomy and smoking to all else (and expressed his approval – 'They are sensible people'), might have
suffered the same misapprehension. One of the girls produced a
soft, warm tomato from her bloomers, and offered it for ten lira –
disconcerted by its recent lodging I did not take it, though I gave
her the money, and they all shared the *karpuz*. The Seljuk bridge
is a long low graceful structure, peaking only slightly over the
main span, which is not central, but astride the deepest part of the
River Eurymedon (a delight to swim in). Nearby there is a much

more recent relic – an ugly reinforced-concrete bridge, single-track, flat from bank to bank, with parapets rising as high half-circles, their diameters more or less matching the span; it is a design of the 1920s executed for Atatürk and built in great numbers all over Turkey, of which very few now survive. This example is on the old road, now disused, and if the Turks are true to character, it will stay there, surviving, for they seem unable to dispose of anything discarded – and in this case, just as well, for it would be a pity if all these ugly bridges were destroyed and replaced, and there were left no reminders of how much Atatürk achieved for his country by such simple means.

This was Alexander's road to Aspendos; envoys from the city came to meet him, perhaps where the Seljuk bridge now stands, and agreed to surrender on condition that he left no garrison – he demanded a little money and fresh horses, the deal was done, and he moved on to Side without leaving the main road, but the wily Aspendians gathered their flocks and crops, strengthened their defences, and closed their gates. Side did not oppose Alexander; his interest had been to close that stretch of coast to the Persians (a strategy that served him well after the Battle of Issus, when the routed enemy had to retreat westward and could find no ships to save them), and, leaving a peaceful garrison there, he returned to besiege Sillyum, again bypassing Aspendos. When he discovered the treachery of the Aspendians, he withdrew from the pointless siege of Sillyum (it was not a coastal or riparian city, and therefore served no purpose against the Persians), and himself hammered on their gates, took their most distinguished worthies hostage, and dunned them for more money and horses. It was an episode much in line with the rest of the city's history – prosperity briefly upset by invasions – the Persians in 469 BC, the Athenians in 389, Alexander in 333, and then the Seleucids, the Ptolemies and the Romans, and a long slow after-life in Byzantine times, until the Arabs ended it. The city bore no famous sons, and was yet another of the Argive colonies attributed to the inevitable Mopsus and Calchas. For once there is some slight evidence to support this; the name of Aspendos on the earliest coins is Estwediiys, derived from Asitawandas, the supposed founder of Karatepe (now Kadirli) in eastern Cilicia, where inscriptions in hieroglyphic Hittite and Phoenician dating from 700 BC claim his descent from Mopsus after a time-lag of only five centuries – and if at this point the complications of cross-pollination between Hittite, Phoenician and Greek civilizations seem insuperable, let it be remembered that there could be no inscriptions in Greek, for that alphabet (a Semitic import) was not developed until the middle of the eighth century.

Statues of Mopsus and Calchas, their surviving bases describing them as founders, also stood at the main gates of Perge in Roman times. The city had by then led a quiet life for a thousand years, with only the arrival of Alexander in 333 BC to disturb its calm. He came with only a small force, having waded the coastal route from Phaselis, and the Pergeans at once sent guides to bring the rest of his army by the land route through the mountains. For the few weeks that Alexander was in Pamphylia, Perge served as his base. After his death the city came under Seleucid rule, and it was they who first fortified the flat and open site. When the Romans defeated the Seleucids and Pamphylians under Antiochus at the Battle of Magnesia (Magnesia ad Sipyllum, twenty miles north of Izmir, far away from Pamphylia) in 190 BC, they handed their joint territories to Eumenes, the King of Pergamon, but a roving Roman consul, Manlius Vulso, took the opportunity to reconnoitre the distant south, moving through Caria to Termessos, Isinda, Aspendos and other cities, levying cash penalties for no good reason other than personal greed. It took him two years to get to Perge, where through some oversight on the part of the defeated Antiochus, no instructions to surrender to the Romans or the Pergamenes had been received, and a Seleucid garrison was still in charge; the forces confronted each other for a month of uncomfortable truce until Antiochus sent word that the city should surrender. No traces of Pergamene occupation survive; when Attalus III died in 133 BC he bequeathed his Kingdom to the Romans, who were responsible for his having a large part of it, but they were little interested in the south-coast cities, and did not include Lycia, Pamphylia and Cilicia in their first organization of Asia Minor as a Roman Province – only when piracy interrupted the Aegean slave trade (10,000 a day sold on Delos alone) did they show interest and establish, confusingly, in Pamphylia, the Province of Cilicia, excluding from it the whole of Cilicia itself. The first Roman Governors were so vicious and corrupt that they were prosecuted for robbery, extortion, expropriation of produce, and the plunder of statues and votive offerings from temples; Mithridates attempted to drive them out in 88 BC, but he was defeated by Pompey, who twenty years later finally wiped out the pirates and at last incorporated Cilicia itself into the Roman province of that name. Then came Mark Antony, high-handed, tyrannical, impulsive, and so obsessed with Cleopatra that he gave her the contents of the Library of Pergamon to add to those of the Library of Alexandria, thus ensuring the destruction of the greater part of the literary remains of the ancient world. It was not until Rome became Imperial under Augustus in 27 BC that Perge and her neighbours again experienced the long centuries of peace and prosperity that Alexander's arrival had interrupted.

St Paul came twice to Perge; his first visit was immediately after the thoroughly unchristian and discreditable witch-doctory of blinding the pagan Elymas at Paphos, in Cyprus – it was nothing less than a good old-fashioned curse in the name of God, and demonstrated yet again how unfit the man was to assume the mantle of Christianity; the second visit was part of a long trek through Pisidia and Pamphylia that ended with his preaching in Perge before taking ship for Antioch. His preaching seems not to have been particularly effective, for no church, neither in the sense of the groups of Christian converts addressed in his letters, nor as an architectural foundation, was established until late in the third century; in Byzantine times Perge and Sillyum were combined under one metropolitan Bishop (Byzantine remains are prominent in the much more easily defensible Sillyum, perhaps suggesting that Perge experienced the earlier decline) until the Metropolitan of Antalya replaced him.

The earliest settlement must have been on the flat-topped acropolis hill at the northern end of the site, though no early remains have yet been found there; the hill was quite certainly occupied in Byzantine times, but never fortified – the large vaulted cistern reuses earlier materials and is Byzantine – long empty of water, early visitors assumed it to be a church of sorts. The town spread to the south, and its extent in the years immediately after Alexander's death is marked by the great round gate-towers built by the Seleucids, enclosing a semicircular court with the niches in which stood the statues of Mopsus and his ilk. This gate is one of the most astonishing monuments in southern Turkey, standing almost its original full height, the masonry rough-cut and tawny, seeming barbaric from the outside, yet suddenly civilized within where the niches give rhythm to the courtyard. It now opens onto a Roman colonnaded street that leads straight to the remains of a nymphaeum set against the side of the acropolis hill, and this presumably reflects the original plan of the city; a water channel runs down the centre of the street, blocked at frequent intervals by cross-walls that checked its flow and cleared it of rubbish. This channel is now dry, but the spring that fed it from the nymphaeum is still rising below the street – we found a girl drawing water in a plastic bucket for the goats and cows that she had brought into the ruins, in much the same way as cattle wandered in the Roman Forum when Claude and Poussin were in search of Arcadian authenticity; the animals gathered round her, patiently waiting as she watered each in turn – Fellows too saw cattle pasturing in the ruins. Colonnades flanked the street, with shops behind them; at the northern end their walls stand almost waist-high, and some of the white marble facings are still in place – the contrast between this wedding-cake felicity and the rough grandeur of the gate must in its day have astonished even St Paul (if after falling off his horse he could be astonished by anything), though the arrangement was common enough.

Within the walls the diligent visitor will find an agora, a palaestra, baths, a church and another colonnaded street running at right angles just short of the nymphaeum; he will explore at considerable risk to his limbs, torn by thorns, pricked by sharp seeds, often embraced so close by brambles that he resembles some mock-Gothic fantasy by Alfred Gilbert or the '*Sleep of Merlin*' by Burne-Jones. The rewards are too few for all but the obstinate, and the wise man will content himself with the theatre and the stadium to the south, outside the city walls.

The theatre sinks its shoulders into the hill called Koca Belen, now marred by pylons and cables. The Romans extended and embellished the original Greek theatre, adding an arcaded gallery to the *cavea* and a new stage building, onto the exterior of which, at some still later date, they tacked an impressive nymphaeum. The interior is now confused by fallen masonry, but enough clearing has been done to make access easy, and to reveal the frieze of white marble reliefs of Dionysiac scenes (of surprisingly uneven quality) that decorated its lowest register. Fellows made no observation on the theatre other than that it was 'immense and beautiful'; his sleep had been disturbed by cold, the barking of jackals and the howling of wolves, and the need to wake his servant early and send him off to shoot duck 'at their breakfast in a neighbouring stream' – surely a rich archaeologist should have done his own wild-fowling, and surely it was the servant's duty to do the early rousing? Immediately after Fellows' breakfast, a curious Turk, not understanding the purpose of two barrels to a shotgun, nearly put an end to him. He struck camp and moved on eastward. One of the problems with using Fellows as a source is that his value judgements vary so greatly; by no means, compared with Aspendos and Side, could the the theatre at Perge be described as 'immense and beautiful', and the stadium was for him 'quite perfect' – which now it is not, though the arena is complete, and enough seats are left over their arched foundation to give a good impression of its capacity (perhaps, like the theatre, some 14,000). The formal entrance at the southern end and its external walls have been destroyed, and it lies open to anyone capable of clambering a few feet – compared with the stadium at Aphrodisias it is far from 'quite perfect'. Fellows found it in use as a crèche for nursing camels.

The earlier part of Fellows' journey had reversed Alexander's route to the north from Antalya, but both went eastward as far as Side, and then turned back. Side, which was for centuries the chief port in the area until supplanted by the newly-founded Antalya in the second century BC, did not resist Alexander, but accepted his garrison against the Persians; as with Perge, it was the beginning of three centuries of confusion, complicated by a long-running dispute with Aspendos, until peace became the norm under the Roman Empire for the next three centuries. In the fourth century Side went into a decline under attack from the Isaurians, a wild people from Bozkir, seventy miles to the north-east, high in the Taurus Mountains, with a long-standing reputation for pillage and rape; their depredations were so severe that the size of the city was reduced, but in the fifth century it expanded again, only to be again reduced, and indeed the population wiped out, by the Arab invasions that began in the seventh century. One oddment of history was the appearance offshore of the elderly Hannibal, attempting to bring a Phoenician fleet from Tyre to Ephesus to assist the efforts of Antiochus to dominate the Aegean and prevent the Romans from crossing the Dardanelles into Asia Minor, shortly before the great defeat at Magnesia in 190 BC; as Hannibal's ships sailed into the Bay of Antalya, they met a fleet from Rhodes, allies of Rome, were engaged, defeated and forced to flee eastward; it was a crucial battle, for without the Phoenicians Antiochus had too few ships of his own, and with the decisive defeat of the Battle of Myonessus he lost control of the Dardanelles, and Asia Minor was opened to invasion from the west.

Fellows is crushing in his contempt for the ruins of Side, 'inferior in scale, date and age to any I have before seen'; he found no village nearby, only peasants in tents, yet curiously enough he observed several limekilns busily burning cornices and capitals; he had read Beaufort's account of Side, and again comments on the folly of making judgements when travelling by sea, complaining that if Beaufort had gone inland a few miles, he, Fellows, would not have been led to expect that Side would be the climax of his travels, instead of 'the least interesting' relic. I, in turn, might observe that Fellows is at his least diligent and perceptive after a disturbed night, and has a marked prejudice in favour of anything that he considers Greek. He found the Roman theatre so full of earth that he could not judge its capacity, and 'a wood of trees' was growing in it; this was cleared within living memory, but the fallen masonry and marble that it concealed were left in chaos in the orchestra until the winter of 1984–5, when this too was cleared; the jumble added interest – its superhuman scale challenged climbers, gave backgrounds to holiday snappers, and inducement and authority to spontaneous performers with guitar and flute; more important, it lent the imagination some strength when conjuring the sound and fury of the earthquakes that felled the city. Now sanitized and made fit for Oedipus and Aida, of the impulsive performers in the theatre only the swallows remain – they still gather in the evenings to dart and dip and swoop on the thermals within the great bowl, seeming determined to dash themselves against the stage-building only to be plucked by some hidden lift a split second from disaster, drawn upwards, and thrown back into the circuit of the *cavea*, proving, to me at least, that bird-brained creatures have a sense of fun.

The theatre at Side is unique among Pamphylian examples in that, like the Roman Colosseum, it is free-standing, for though the city is situated on a promontory that forms a natural harbour, it is not high above the water, and the neighbouring land is almost flat – the theatre is a landmark seen easily from Seleucia. Built in the second century AD, it is thoroughly Roman in feeling, with great buttressing arches in the outer walls of the *cavea*, giving onto a system of vaulted corridors and stairways that, unusually, brought the audience into the theatre above their seats. The stage-building stands almost to its full height, and was richly decorated with white marble with a frieze of mythological reliefs in the lower register – all the decoration has fallen away in earthquakes, but the reliefs were deliberately damaged, probably by Christians, and their subjects obliterated. Perhaps a century after the construction of the theatre, a wall some six feet high was erected round the orchestra to protect the audience from the wild beasts whose bloody and often grotesquely mismatched combat offended no-one; *bestiarii*, the professional slaughterers, fought lions and tigers, bears and bulls, but these as often fought each other, or alligators, or hippopotami (imagine the time that it would take for a great defenceless hippo to die, for no big cat could throttle it or break its neck, and only shock and exsanguination would bring it mercy as small parcels of flesh were torn from under the leather hide), or slew a host of such defenceless creatures as deer, giraffes and ostriches. Suetonius noted with seeming pleasure the death of five thousand animals in one day at the inauguration of the Roman Colosseum, and Trajan saw three thousand slaughtered in two days; even if these great numbers died only on Imperial occasions, and the ordinary *venatio* accounted for comparatively few, those smaller figures must be multiplied by the number of theatres spread across the Empire, and the frequency of the occasions; scale too must have had its effect, for there would be little point in filling the great circus of El Djem in Tunisia for the death of a single ostrich, though it might have made a flurry in Termessos. Five centuries of slaughter wiped out the Caspian tiger, the Assyrian lion, and the Numidian forest elephant – the tough pigmy that carried Hannibal over the Alps – and there can be no doubt that the theatre at Side played its part in these extinctions. Cruelty was demanded and enjoyed by even delicately nurtured souls whose natures, sensitive in other respects, were not in the least repelled by slaughter for the sake of entertainment; even the Emperors joined in – Commodus on one occasion despatching an elephant, a hippopotamus and a tiger before lunch, and fighting as a gladiator after; and on another, having had so many animals penned that he could quickly and easily spear them, exhausted himself with their slaughter. Only Cicero (106–43 BC) protested, but he was forgotten long before the filthy business reached its Imperial peak – 'What pleasure can it give . . . to see . . . a fine animal transfixed on a hunting spear?'; but he raised no objection to gladiatorial combat, and indeed saw it as a practical example of stoicism. The first wave of revulsion was against women gladiators – women, dwarfs and cripples fighting with wooden weapons were light relief between the serious bouts of the men, but, as is the way of women, they edged their way into the real business, grim Amazons. Nero, not surprisingly, enjoyed their grotesque performances, which continued until Septimius Severus prohibited them in AD 200. Male gladiators continued to fight each other until the abolition of the gladiatorial schools by Honorius in AD 399, and of the Games in 404 – but for another century or so criminals were thrown into the orchestra with wild beasts for the entertainment of Christians, who had themselves provided so much entertainment (St Augustine's tale of his friend Alypius is a salutary example of Christian principle undone by the bloodlust of the crowds, a lifetime of Christian law abandoned in a sudden madness for the Games). The boxers and wrestlers wore a little black leather apron called a *campestre* to conceal their privates – the origin, perhaps, of 'camp'; the Christians were tied to posts on little wheeled trolleys and pushed with poles into the arena from a distance so that lions and tigers could not grab the guards in error; *bestiarii* occasionally wore stilted sandals that gave better purchase in the gore.

From the topmost seats the view is both splendid and profitable; at evening, already starlit in the east, the dying sun in the west silhouettes the Lycian cliffs beyond Antalya, as often with the pale subtleties of the eighteenth-century watercolour as with the lurid brush of Turner's 'Temeraire' or 'Slave Ship'; in the day, as the one high place in the city, and in its centre, it is the perch from which to plot and map its exploration. Behind the stage-building is a vast agora, just like any other. 'Agora' is a word that guides fling at tourists, turning them into Pavlov dogs that nod assent and recognition, and take photographs – yet an agora without its shops and other surrounding buildings is the most boring of classical remains, an open space, useful only in establishing the geography of a city and the nature of nearby public buildings – as here, with a well-preserved lavatory in its north-west corner (another boon to the guided tour and to judge from the smell of it, still in use). Just across the road from it are the baths, a late building, probably of the fifth-century revival of the city, with its spacious frigidarium, tepidarium, caldarium and sudatorium now converted into an admirable museum that houses the sculpture and other treasures found on the site – I hesitate to make a general quality judgement that may seem niggling in the face of such an achievement, but much of the sculpture is weak and provincial, and desperately disappointing compared with, for example, the site collection in the museum at Aphrodisias. This has a small refreshment area in which the visitor squats low on Corinthian capitals – Michael in so doing split the rear seam of his shorts from belt to nether regions, and had to return to the Turtel in a taxi.

Much of the city wall thrown across the peninsula in Hellenistic times still stands, but the Roman city spread far beyond it. The most remarkable structure just outside the main gate (which was a towered semicircular court as at Perge) is the nymphaeum; it stands to roughly half its original height, which was three storeys, with wings embracing a large basin fed by the aqueduct; fragments of reliefs carved with dolphins and decorative architectural elements suggest that it was a building of great splendour. The aqueduct brought water from twenty miles away, from the same source as the river that provides the waterfalls at nearby Manavgat; it fell into disrepair within a century of its construction in the later second century AD, and although again in use in Diocletian's day, its remains now are fragmentary and little more than romantic. Water sources for the city before the aqueduct was built must have been as inadequate in antiquity as now; it seems probable that the city's greatest period of expansion was in the second century (the temples by the harbour are of this date) and that the aqueduct was built, perhaps in haste and not soundly, to cater for a sudden increase in demand.

Other remains beyond the city wall are difficult to identify not only because of their desuetudinous condition, but because they are buried in sand and scrub; Side is often a windy place, and the sand from the eastern beach is whipped into the ruins, burning in the sun like the Sahara, yet supporting tough brambles that rip the skin – even the most romantic Byzantinist begins to wonder if the miserable structure that may or may not be a Bishop's palace (far too grand a word for those who may conjure visions of Lambeth) is worth the pain and discomfort of clambering about in it, after burning his feet to reach it. Despair may overtake the non-specialist, induced by the vast, spreading incomprehensibility of the site, and he would do well to retreat within the walls and make for the harbour – which was always silting with the winds and tides, and so often in need of dredging that 'It's a Sidetan harbour' was the proverbial description in antiquity for work that could never be completed. Immediately to the east of the harbour are the handsome ruins of two temples, and it does not require too much imagination to experience again the impression made on mariners as they beat up the coast from the Levant – great white marble structures changing their colours with the time of day, standing proud against their smaller neighbours. They date from late in the second century AD, are Corinthian, and were dedicated to the city's principal deities, Athena and Apollo. Like the aqueduct, they did not last for long; during the fifth or sixth century a large basilica was erected just to the east of them, and its forecourt occupies the ground on which they stood – this thoroughly dull and conventional structure of three aisles and an apse is largely still standing.

The cult statues of Athena and Apollo were imported – a recognition perhaps of the low quality of the local sculpture now in the museum. Bean, in his book on *The Inscriptions of Side*, is persuasive in his hypothetical description of their delivery:

> We may well imagine that a public holiday would be proclaimed. It is easy to picture the ship, gaily decorated, with the statue in the prow, sailing into the port, the cheering crowds, the stately landing of the statue and its ceremonial installation in the temple. What better occasion for the institution of a festival and games?

That there were games is proved by coins, but the hippodrome (if there was one) and the stadium have yet to be discovered in the windy wastes beyond the city wall. Bean's study of Sidetan inscriptions is of enormous interest in the wide-ranging if fragmentary picture it creates of the city's life – of these the earliest are in Sidetan pre-Greek script, written from right to left; one is a statue base dating from circa 300 BC signed by an otherwise unknown sculptor, presumably local, called Mnaseas – it was later reused as the base for a statue of the Emperor Claudius by the Side branch of the ecumenical synod of Artists of Dionysus, the Guild, as it were, of sculptors. The Sidetan language was explained by Arrian as corporate amnesia on the part of the Greek colonists who founded the city, who promptly forgot their native Greek and took on the local barbarian; both language and script appear to be unique to Side, but there is very little material to work from. Bean argues that it must be the original Anatolian language of Pamphylia, and that a small invading force of Greeks was unable to substitute their own tongue until after the arrival of Alexander; the absence of Mopsus, Calchas and other 'ancestors' argues that, unlike many other cities in the area, Side was well established long before the Greek colonizations after the Trojan War – and this finds some confirmation in the *Chronicle* of Eusebius, (the Bishop of Caesarea in Palestine who sought to establish his local baptismal Creed as a compromise between Arianism and orthodoxy in recognizing the human nature of Christ as well as the divine, but was one of those who got his head banged at the Council of Nicaea in AD 325) which states quite precisely that Side was founded in 1405 BC. A Semitic alphabet firmly established in Side suggests a sizeable Semitic element in its population – indeed the very name, which means pomegranate, recurs not infrequently in the east.

A recent plan to demolish some seventy modern buildings within the village of Side in the hope of illuminating the palimpsest of ruins has been dropped – that kind of deliberate dereliction might be informative, but it would be no pleasant substitute for the cheek-by-jowl jumbling of antiquity and Byzantium that gentles the present ugly concrete blocks. Side is now much more (or less) than an archaeological site – a lively village of a thousand souls, multiplied tenfold in summer, traditional village life accommodating itself to modern demands without losing its identity. An hygienic ruin allied to an hygienic village would repel too many visitors of every kind. And visitors there are in plenty – it is the kind of place where in the evening *passeggio* up and down the village street one of Mrs Thatcher's economic gurus, the doyen of New York booksellers, a fading Italian film star, art dealers, auctioneers, and the familiar faces of fellow shoppers in Harrods' food hall, are instantly recognized; it is the kind of place where serendipitous encounters impose isolated images on memory, unimportant, yet far too strong ever to be forgotten. Sitting with mad Mama and her children in a windy shack that passes for a restaurant above the eastern bay, a young gipsy joined us, with a small girl bound to her shoulders like a papoose; with a handful of very dry and battered haricot beans and two glass beads thrown in random patterns on the table she foretold Ali's future; Mama's hand she read with elegant passing gestures, to the repeated cry that the promises were wild and extravagant, but the two women nevertheless continued to look intently into each other's eyes with the gipsy pinching Mama's right nipple, until the papoose awakened, and, craning over the girl's shoulder, bit Mama's finger; what might have broken up with wails of anger instead broke down into a scene of purest domesticity – the papoose had the snottiest wet nose that I have ever seen, and we all set about mopping it with the restaurant's paper napkins. I, who had not had my hand read or my nipple pinched, was told by Mama to give money to the girl – 'It will come true if someone else pays for it, and it is very romantic.' As the gipsy left, the boy who ran the restaurant put on a tape of Turkish music, and Ali and Bengisu began to dance – he with his hedgehog hair and bull-like buttocks suddenly as sinuous as a woman, and with a woman's nipples prominent through his sweaty vest, she wasp-waisted, trembling her soft flesh in dance movements that scarcely concealed their sexual thrust; the skinny waiter summoned his little brother and they joined in with the shoulder-thrusting dance that we had last seen in Cappadocia; then, face to face, with the small boy's arms hooked under his brother's armpits, the elder boy bent further and further back, until his crutch was thrusting at the younger's belly, never once losing eye contact. It was in Side that I saw fishermen bury their catch, still living, in the wet sand at their feet – I remonstrated once, but without my usual energy – a few minutes extra of life, however wretched, means a few minutes extra before the rot sets in (in the bus station at Egredir a man offered us a great carp from the lake, flapping and gasping its life away in the wheelbarrow that it almost filled, scorching in the sun – had I been in a car I would have bought it and rushed it back to the water, but as a passenger in a bus that was pausing only long enough for us to pee, I could do nothing but turn away, hating myself for my priorities; why I should be so concerned for the suffering of a creature that I would cheerfully eat, I cannot fathom – nor why the recollection of its misery should last so clearly and so long.) It was in Side that my constant note-taking aroused suspicion and hostility, allayed by Michael's explanation that it was all about archaeology – wholly improbable, so late at night, drinking tea in the village square. It was in Side that a motley bunch of men whom we did not know took us to an upper room for supper, where no women were allowed, and fed us on tripe soup, calves' brains, fish, chips and kebabs, and told us dirty Turkish jokes that were quite without humour, grotesque in their imagery, and remarkably anti-feminist; that evening ended with deep intense conversation about the perfidy of the Armenians whom they accused of bribing the French police (another Turkish diplomat had just been murdered in Paris), and the untrustworthy Greeks who deserved to be driven into the sea, and who will go Communist and join the Russians; they lamented the absence of a statue of Atatürk from any public place in the village, and thought it shamed them. I ventured the notion that the events of sixty and seventy years past should by now be blurring in the memory and not conditioning present political attitudes; emboldened by their silence I went on to suggest that it was time that they shed Atatürk as an ever-present political hero – that he had done his work well enough in his day, indeed brilliantly, and deserved his reputation as the father of modern Turkey, which quite certainly could not have survived and been reborn without his autocratic purpose, but that his influence is now out of date and indeed damaging to Turkish prospects with the West, his ghost used to justify apalling acts of political injustice, his image a talisman to support blind belief in the rightness of the State . . . and so on, until I became aware that the silence of my companions was disbelief constrained by the obligations of hospitality, and that I had offended enough.

Coda

B y the summer of 1986, at the cost of some £20,000, the
villagers of Side had their Atatürk. Life-size, black, enthroned amid a dusty draggle of heat-stunned flowers, he
turns his back on the harbour and gazes up the climbing street
and on towards the main coast road. Side is the logical end of
south-western Turkey – Alexander went no further along the
coast but turned back to go inland from Antalya, and in almost
every city between Ephesus and Side today's traveller must dog
his footsteps. Side is not the last of the great Greco-Roman sites,
but it marks the point beyond which other cultures begin to make
a stronger impression. Even before the next city, Alanya, less
than fifty miles eastward, a Seljuk *han* and a Crusader castle
herald the changes – the one a graceful and melancholy reminder
of the beautiful stonemasonry of the East, the other an impregnable fantasy of the Gothick imagination to out-Ludwig Ludwig
with curtain walls that run up the pinnacle as frills of lace once
climbed the steeps of a woman's bosom. In Alanya another castle
tops the 800 foot bluff that shadows the town, put there by the
Seljuk Sultan Keykubad of Konya; it is possible to drive to its gate,
but the outward slope of the hairpin road is more terrifying than
the Leaning Tower of Pisa, and the walk is preferable. Onward,
yet another, Anamur, a vast empty shell, drops disappointingly

into damp sand on the seaward side – as with so many ruins, the idea is better than the reality. Near Silifke, Üzuncarbuç is perched on a peak, and Kizkalesi lies on an offshore island, its bones bleached by salt and sun.

Interspersed with these, and beyond them, are the ruins of Antiocheia ad Cragum, Elaeussa, Seleucia ad Calycadnum, Mopsuestia, Tarsus, Seleucia Pieria, Issus and a host of others – some not much more than gap-toothed stumps, others extensive or with the lasting magic of a household name. Low in the armpit of the Mediterranean is Antakya, the Antioch of Biblical times, now swamped by the silt of the Orontes, but about to equip itself with 50,000 hotel beds to house the tourists whom it hopes to draw there.

And beyond? And in the hinterland? – Konya, whirling with brisk business rather than dervishes, the quiet valleys of Cappadocia a hide-and-seek of mysterious early churches carved from a landscape devised by Hieronymus Bosch, and Trebizond entirely lacking the towers by which Rose Macaulay drew it from its Byzantine slumber into its British Romantic present . . . The wooded and watered Alps of the far north-east hide churches of magical beauty that keep alive the recollection of Armenia's great Christian past (long before Constantine's Creed and Decree), that form an architectural link between Roman and Romanesque that may have been the springboard for the great western cathedrals of Angoulême and Speyer, Hildesheim and Poitiers; they make the much-vaunted churches of Ani, mysterious though they must appear, deserted, poised over the Russian border, seem the decadent offerings of a demented confectioner, and the church on the island of Aghtemar the work of a gingerbread man. I have seen nothing more beautiful, astonishing or wonderful among the works of man or God than Mount Ararat from the north – the sudden shock of a white peak free-floating in the sky, its lower slopes lost in the matching blue of a heat haze, slowly solidifying into the form of a woman's ribcage, the great nippled breast sagging downhill to the west. I have seen nothing more vile than the public lavatory in Başkale, the highest town in Turkey, spitting distance from Iran – it was in such a dark, stinking, subterranean chamber that John had young Arthur neutered and his eyes put out. Nothing has seemed more inviting than the white-capped mountains beyond Hakkari, in the corner tight between Iraq and Iran, and the fast-running River Zap that twenty years ago I might have been allowed to follow down through those mountains into Persian Kurdistan. Nothing has seemed more deserted and remote than Lake Çildir, Russia a hump-backed hill away, shivering cold in high summer. Towards all these the road from Ephesus was but the first step.

Bibliography

Akurgal, Ekram. *Ancient Civilisations and Ruins of Turkey* (Istanbul, 1969)

Bean, George E. *Aegean Turkey* (Ernest Benn, 1966)

Bean, George E. *Lycian Turkey* (Ernest Benn, 1978)

Bean, George E. *Side Kitabeleri* (Ankara, 1963)

Bean, George E. *Turkey Beyond the Maeander* (Ernest Benn, 1971)

Bean, George E. *Turkey's Southern Shore* (Ernest Benn, 1968)

Chandler, Richard. *Travels in Asia Minor 1764–1765* (British Museum, 1971)

Durham, Edith. *High Albania* (Virago, 1985)

Fellows, Charles. *A Journal Written During an Excursion in Asia Minor 1838* (John Murray, 1839)

Gibbon, Edward. *The Decline and Fall of the Roman Empire*

Hogarth, D. G. *Accidents of an Antiquary's Life* (1910)

Kinross, Patrick. *Within the Taurus* (John Murray, 1954)

Mayer, Luigi. *Views in Palestine from the Original Drawings of Luigi Mayer* (R. Bowyer, 1804)

Metzger, Henri. *Anatolia II, Archaeologia Mundi* (Nagel, 1969)

Stark, Freya. *Alexander's Path* (John Murray, 1958)

Stark, Freya. *Ionia, A Quest* (John Murray, 1954)

Stark, Freya. *The Lycian Shore* (John Murray, 1958)

Stillwell, Richard. *The Princeton Encyclopedia of Classical Sites* (Princeton University Press, 1976)

Glossary of Site Names,
Ancient and Modern

It should be borne in mind that c and k, o and u are often interchangeable – Caunus may be rendered Kaunos, and Halikarnassos as Halicarnassus; I and J in capital form are also interchangeable.

The ancient name or names are given in capitals, modern and Ottoman names in lower case, the modern name preceding the Ottoman.

ALABANDA	Araphisar
ALINDA	Karpuzlu, Demircideresi
ANTIPHELLUS	Kaş, Andifli
APHRODISIAS	Geyre
ASPENDUS	Belkis
ATTALEIA	Antalya, Adalia
CAUNUS	Dalyan
CHIMAERA	Çirali
CNIDUS (old)	Datça
CNIDUS (new)	Knidas
COMBA	Gömbe
CYANEAE, KYANEAI	Yavu
DIDYMA, BRANCHIDAI	Didim, Yoran
EPHESUS	Efes and Selçuk
ETENNA	Sirt
GERGA	Gerga

HALICARNASSUS	Bodrum
HERACLEIA UNDER LATMOS	Kapikirik
HIERAPOLIS	Pamukkale
IASOS, IASSUS, JASUS	Kiyi Kişlacik
LABRANDA, LABRAYNDA, LABRAUNDA	No modern occupation
LAODICEIA AD LYCUM	Goncali
MILETUS	Milet, Balat
MYLASA	Milas
MYRA	Demre, Kale, Cacamo
NYSA	Sultanhisar
OLYMPUS	Tekirova (near)
PATARA	Kelemiş
PEÇIN KALE	Peçin Kale
PERGE	Aksu
PHASELIS	Tekirova (near)
PHELLOS	Çukurbağ
PHYSKOS	Marmaris
PINARA	Minare Köyü
PRIENE	Prien, Turunclar
SELEUCIA	near Manavgat
SELGE	Zerk, Sirk, Serük
SIDE	Side, Sida, Selimiye, Eski Antalya
SILLYUM, SILLYON	Asar Köyü
STRATONICEIA	Eskihisar
TELMESSUS	Fethiye, Makri, Macri
TERMESSUS	Termessus
TLOS	Düver, Zeyve
XANTHUS	Kinik

* * *

Aksu	PERGE
Andifli	ANTIPHELLUS
Antalya	ATTALEIA
Araphisar	ALABANDA
Asar Köyü	SILLYUM
Balat	MILETUS
Belkis	ASPENDUS
Bodrum	HALICARNASSUS
Cacamo	MYRA
Çirali	CHIMAERA
Çukurbağ	PHELLOS
Fethiye	TELMESSUS

Dalyan	CAUNUS
Datça	CNIDUS (old)
Demre	MYRA
Didim	DIDYMA
Duver	TLOS
Efes	EPHESUS
Eski Antalya	SIDE
Eskihisar	STRATONICEIA
Fethiye	TELMESSUS
Gerga	GERGA
Geyre	APHRODISIAS
Gömbe	COMBA
Goncali	LAODICEIA AD LYCUM
Kale	MYRA
Kapikirik	HERACLEIA UNDER LATMOS
Karpuzlu	ALINDA
Kaş	ANTIPHELLUS
Kelemiş	PATARA
Kinik	XANTHUS
Kiyi Kişlacik	IASOS, IASSUS, JASUS
Knidas	CNIDUS (new)
Makri, Macri	TELMESSUS
Manavgat (near)	SELEUCIA
Marmaris	PHYSKOS
Milas	MYLASA
Milet	MILETUS
Minare Köyü	PINARA
Pamukkale	HIERAPOLIS
Peçin Kale	PEÇIN KALE
Prien	PRIENE
Selçuk	EPHESUS
Selimiye	SIDE
Serük	SELGE
Sida	SIDE
Side	SIDE
Sirk	SELGE
Sirt	ETENNA
Sultanhisar	NYSA
Tekirova (near)	OLYMPUS
Tekirova (near)	PHASELIS
Termessus	TERMESSUS
Turunclar	PRIENE
Yavu	CYANEAE, KYANEAI
Zeyve	TLOS

Brief Glossary of Architectural Terms

Agora	Market place
Apse	A semi-circular end to a building
Architrave	A lintel resting on columns
Atrium	The court of a Roman house, roofed at the sides, open in the centre
Basilica	A rectangular central hall with aisles lower in height: the term is occasionally used for a church
Capital	Topmost unit of a column, immediately supporting the architrave
Cavea	Auditorium of a theatre
Cella	Main chamber of a Greek Temple
Coffer	A sunken panel in a ceiling
Dipteros	Temple surrounded by two rows of columns
Drum	A cylindrical section from the shaft of a column
Forum	Roman market place
Odeon	A roofed building in which musical contests were held
Palaestra	School for wrestling and other physical exercises
Parodos	Side entrance to a theatre between auditorium and stage
Pediment	Triangular or semi-circular top to an arch or niche, supported on columns or corbels

Peripteros	A temple surrounded by a single row of columns
Peristasis	A row of columns surrounding a temple
Peristyle	A courtyard surrounded by a colonnade
Podium	The raised base of a building, tomb or statue
Portico	An entrance marked by columns, often with a pediment
Proscenium	The stage platform of a theatre
Socle	Projecting foot of a wall or pedestal base
Stoa	A roofed hall with columns on the entrance wall
Stylobate	The topmost step of a temple podium, forming a platform for its surrounding columns
Temenos	A sacred enclosure in which stand one or more temples

Index

Numbers in **bold** type refer to the main entry.